*How
Cormac Works*

How Cormac Works
McCarthy, Language, and Style

BILL HARDWIG

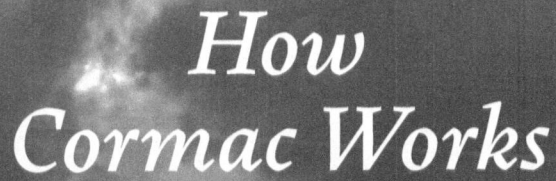

Louisiana State University Press
BATON ROUGE

Published by Louisiana State University Press
lsupress.org

Copyright © 2025 by Louisiana State University Press
All rights reserved. Except in the case of brief quotations used in articles or reviews, no part of this publication may be reproduced or transmitted in any format or by any means without written permission of Louisiana State University Press.

Designer: Kaelin Chappell Broaddus
Typefaces: Dolly Pro, text; Pliego, display

Cover photo: Adobe Stock/Las Huellas.

Library of Congress Cataloging-in-Publication Data

Names: Hardwig, Bill, author.
Title: How Cormac works : McCarthy, language, and style / Bill Hardwig.
Description: Baton Rouge : Louisiana State University Press, 2025. | Includes bibliographical references and index.
Identifiers: LCCN 2025018309 (print) | LCCN 2025018310 (ebook) | ISBN 978-0-8071-8549-0 (paperback) | ISBN 978-0-8071-8453-0 (cloth) | ISBN 978-0-8071-8547-6 (epub) | ISBN 978-0-8071-8548-3 (pdf)
Subjects: LCSH: McCarthy, Cormac, 1933–2023—Criticism and interpretation | LCGFT: Literary criticism
Classification: LCC PS3563.C337 Z685 2025 (print) | LCC PS3563.C337 (ebook) | DDC 813/.54—dc23/eng/20250509
LC record available at https://lccn.loc.gov/2025018309
LC ebook record available at https://lccn.loc.gov/20250183

in memory of Joe Mac,
who loved Cormac's stories
as much as anyone I know,
and who lived a few of 'em too

Contents

ACKNOWLEDGMENTS ix

LIST OF ABBREVIATIONS xi

INTRODUCTION 1

I. *Modes*

ONE Unexpected Registers:
McCarthy's Narrative Modes 27

TWO "Large Loose Baggy Monsters":
McCarthy's Epic Mode 67

II. *Moods*

THREE "Little More Than a Childhood Enthusiasm":
Thick Description and the Taxonomic Mood 109

FOUR The Precarious Mood:
The Passenger, Stella Maris,
and the Fragile Twentieth Century 149

EPILOGUE "Them Old Dreams" 189

NOTES 193   BIBLIOGRAPHY 207

INDEX 217

Acknowledgments

I would first like to thank the English Department at the University of Tennessee for support, both financial and personal, research leave, and resources. I would also like to thank my colleagues in this department. The conversations had in the mazes of McClung Tower motivated me and made this a better book. Mary Papke's precious insights about the gothic and naturalism and twentieth-century fiction helped me as this book came into focus. Brad Bannon provided rich conversations about McCarthy's work in a wider context of American literature. I would like to thank, too, the students and visitors in my graduate class on McCarthy and the Refuge of Language—Adel Alshammari, Jade Bowman, Dakota Collins, Emily Ellis, Bethany Gareis, Caoimhe Harlock, Cameron Hashmi, Giulia Koutsoyanopulos, Blake Reno, Dirk Weddington, and Sarah Yancey: Our conversations in class allowed this book to take shape. Thanks, too, to the community and friendship at the Cormac McCarthy Society, especially as offered by Stacey Peebles, Steven Frye, Lydia Cooper, Dianne Luce, Nell Sullivan, and Scott Yarborough, although I could name so many more. The kindness and support of the people in this society continues to amaze and inspire me.

Ray Smith, historian for the city of Oak Ridge, was so generous with his time, expertise, and stories about the nuclear age and the "secret city" of Oak Ridge. I did not understand the final two books in a nearly as accurate and meaningful way until we met. Thanks to Palmer Murphy, whose generous sharing of tales of his engagement with McCarthy and permission to reprint his splendid cartoon "Cormac Visits Oprah" helped bring this book to life. I would also like to thank Hideki Tokushige for permission to print an image from his wonderful artwork *Honebana*.

The University of Tennessee Special Collections aided my research with their Cormac McCarthy collection and other materials related to East Ten-

ACKNOWLEDGMENTS

nessee history. Pam Rhoades and Catholic High School in Knoxville helped with images and history related to McCarthy's time at the school. Thanks, too, to the *Cormac McCarthy Journal*, which published a different version of a section of chapter 4, "Making Bombs in the Hinterlands: The Manhattan Project and Regional Displacement in Cormac McCarthy's The Passenger and Stella Maris," which appeared in Volume 22.2 (2024) of this indispensable journal.

I would also like to thank Wes Morgan. Our conversations at the Golden Roast, Hodges Library, conferences, and wherever anyone was talking about McCarthy provided encouragement and motivation. No other scholar on the planet knows as much about McCarthy's time in and connection to East Tennessee. Wes's generosity and patience as I was learning a fraction of what he has known for decades inspired not only this book but my decision to become more deeply involved in McCarthy scholarship.

Finally, thanks to Peggy and Lily for working through the Spanish passages with me, to Ezra for thinking through McCarthy's style with me over coffee or pizza or eggs, and to all three for their encouragement.

Abbreviations

All the Pretty Horses	*AtPH*
Blood Meridian	*BM*
Child of God	*CofG*
Cities of the Plain	*CofP*
The Crossing	*TC*
"A Drowning Incident"	"DI"
"The Kekulé Problem"	"Kekulé"
No Country for Old Men	*NCfOM*
The Orchard Keeper	*OK*
Outer Dark	*OD*
The Passenger	*TP*
The Road	*TR*
Stella Maris	*SM*
The Stonemason	*Stone*
The Sunset Limited	*SL*
Suttree	*Sut*
"A Wake for Susan"	"WfS"

How Cormac Works

Introduction

As different as his novels are from one another, Cormac McCarthy's writing, which spanned a career of six decades and twelve novels, feels cohesive. When we pick up a novel by McCarthy, no matter the length or style or topic, we know we are reading McCarthy. There is something about his writing that feels unique and enduring and consistent. One aspect of his writing that links all his novels is his unswerving commitment to formal experimentation, motivated by a love of language and the possibilities therein. While it's McCarthy's grim depiction of violence and his texts' complex philosophical perspectives that receive the most attention by scholars of his work, readers who treasure McCarthy's novels are typically drawn to the work initially (as I was) at the level of language, the breathtakingly original way McCarthy strings together words and paints images in the reader's mind.

Readers are enthralled by McCarthy's ability to describe characters and scenes that spring to life in unexpected ways, such as the portrayal in *Blood Meridian* of his most legendary character, Judge Holden. The Judge is known for his violent acts and his perplexing philosophical utterances, but he is almost as famous for McCarthy's imaginative description of his physical appearance. He is, by all accounts, huge: nearly seven feet tall, twenty-four stone (336 pounds), very round, and without a hair on his head or his body. He frequently wanders the deserts naked or nearly so with a surprisingly delicate gait. McCarthy seems to encourage the reader to marvel at his existence, to interpret his life by reading his physicality, as when he delicately dips his toe in the water preparing for a rare bath: "He shone like the moon so pale he was and not a hair to be seen anywhere upon that vast corpus, not in any crevice nor in the great bores of his nose and not upon his chest nor in his ears nor any tuft at all above his eyes nor the lids thereof. The immense and gleaming dome of his naked skull looked like a cap for bathing pulled down to the otherwise darkened skin of his face and neck... he looked about with considerable pleasure, with eyes slightly crinkled, as if he were smiling under the water like some pale and bloated manatee surfaced in a bog" (BM, 167–68). The grammatic construction of this passage is strange with its old-fashioned series of "nor" phrases, but not as strange as the images McCarthy places in the reader's head. At other random moments in the book, the Judge is compared to a "great pale deity" and his bald head is described as shining "like an enormous phosphorescent egg." His hairless forehead becomes a "pleated brow not unlike a dolphin's" (BM, 92, 327, 93). The proliferation of unique and mischievous descriptions we get of Judge Holden resists our desire to envision what is being described. His appearance is as mysterious as his arcane speech. What exactly does a pleated dolphin brow look like on a human, especially one who is also bloated like a manatee? Does comparing the Judge to a "phosphorescent egg" help us see him or make it more difficult? The Judge reveals McCarthy's fearless commitment to an original and experimental method of character development, one that at times strains the reader's ability to envision the world he so playfully creates for us. These moments hover in what writers have identified as the centrality of "aesthetic bliss," "wonder," and "whim" in our worthwhile reading experiences.[1]

Let's turn to a second example from McCarthy's third novel, *Child of God*. Lester Ballard stands as another of McCarthy's perplexing central characters. As Lester becomes unhoused and wanders around the mountains, he lives much like an animal. Even so, McCarthy's startling descriptions complicate how we think about his animality. Lester is, at various times, a "gothic doll," a "crazed mountain troll," a "sympathetic ape," an "it" in drag, a "part-time ghoul," and a "weedshaped onearmed human" (*CofG*, 140, 152, 159, 173, 174, 192). Perhaps one of these characterizations on its own might bring Lester into focus for the reader; we can, for example, see a "weedshaped" man missing a limb as a down-and-out character at the end of his rope. But all of these descriptions in succession do as much to defamiliarize Lester, and the accretion of descriptors threatens to tumble in on itself.

As Lester's violence escalates and he shows an interest in necrophilia, the reader watches as he violates a recently deceased woman's body. Like *Blood Meridian*'s insistence that we see the Judge's physical body and his acts of transgression, *Child of God* makes us witnesses to Lester's violation. However, as is with the Judge, the more descriptive and detailed the scene becomes, the more difficult it becomes to envision the exact action taking place behind McCarthy's words. After Lester has carried the body back to an abandoned cabin, undressed it, and knelt between the legs, we get this phrase: "A crazed gymnast laboring over a cold corpse" (*CofG*, 88). The idea of "laboring" might produce some images of physical exertion, but a "crazed gymnast" doing this laboring? McCarthy's creative, and some might say excessive, play with language forces us to acknowledge this violation, but then distances us from its horrors through such strange language that obscures our ability to envision the scene clearly. The scene both relies on and withholds its violence. James Franco directed a film adaption of *Child of God* that was generally panned by the few who saw it and the movie was not distributed widely.[2] One problem with the adaptation is that in the filmic version we are forced to watch in excruciatingly exacting detail what McCarthy distances the reader from through his careful modulation of language. In the novel, we both see Lester's violation and don't see it. In the movie, we see it all too clearly. In the novel, the odd animal descriptions of Lester almost serve to humanize him (through his alienation from human community). In the movie, he is simply a disgusting and terrifying animal.

Readers are captivated by McCarthy's ability to apply language in unique and startling ways even in the most violent of scenes, such as in his accounting of a fight between hunting hounds and a wild boar: "[He] watched this ballet tilt and swirl and churn mud up through the snow and watched the lovely blood welter there in its holograph of battle, spray burst from a ruptured lung, the dark heart's blood, pinwheel and pirouette, until shots rang and all was done" (*CofG*, 69). And, again, the reader recalls with curiosity a similarly vivid description of a knife fight between humans:

"From the red boutonniere blossoming of the left pocket of his blue workshirt there spurted a thin fan of bright arterial blood. . . . Some of the men in the hall had already stood to leave. Like theatre patrons anxious to avoid the crush" (AtPH, 201).

While fans of McCarthy are transfixed by his poetic descriptions of gore and depravity, readers marvel, too, at McCarthy's ability to describe abstract concerns (such as the environmental devastation of the Anthropocene) in powerful, concrete, and unexpected images: "Once there were brook trout in the streams in the mountains. You could see them standing in the amber current where the white edges of their fins wimpled softly in the flow. They smelled of moss in your hand. Polished and muscular and torsional. On their backs were vermiculate patterns that were maps of the world in its becoming. Maps and mazes. Of a thing which could not be put back. Not be made right again. In the deep glens where they lived all things were older than man and they hummed of mystery" (TR, 286–87). This passage serves as the final lines of McCarthy's most famous novel, *The Road*, and appears in the text after two hundred pages of unrelenting gray and lifeless scenery. Mystery is a poignant word to end a novel that feels so often utterly hopeless. It can also be used to characterize McCarthy's appreciation of language and his literary style, expressing the potential for the magical, but also the terror of the unknown. Like McCarthy's language more generally, mystery is not contained by boundaries, but neither is it easy to discern the patterns within, or perhaps to even determine if such patterns exist.

In his role as associate art director for Knopf Publishing, Peter Mendelsund thinks a lot about beauty in books. In his book *What We See When We Read*, he writes about the relationship between the words on a page and the images that come into our head when we read these words: "*What do we see when we read?*" asks Mendelsund. "(Other than words on a page.) What do we picture in our minds?" This book calls attention to how our minds fill in the considerable gaps of actual description in fiction. We claim we can see *our* favorite literary characters in our mind, and we really feel like we can see them quite vividly, but the more we think about them or try to describe or imagine them specifically the farther away the faces of these characters recede. This is, according to Mendelsund, because we are generally provided very little concrete description of characters in our favorite novels, so the act of reading is, in many ways, the act of creating. "Literary characters," he contends, "are physically vague—they have only a few features, and these features hardly seem to matter—or, rather, these features matter only in that they help to refine a character's meaning. Character description is a kind of circumscription. A character's features help to delineate their boundaries—but these features don't help us truly picture a person." To illustrate the point, he draws on one of the most famous characters in American literature: Herman Melville's Ishmael, from the classic *Moby Dick*. "What color is your Ishmael's hair? Is it curly or straight? Is he taller than you?"[3] If seeing any character is ultimately an act of creation—of us filling in the gaps through our own engagements with the text—what do we do with McCarthy's attention to detail that often seems to obscure intentionally the characters and our ability to see them clearly? *How Cormac Works* explores this relationship between the innovative language McCarthy so clearly cherishes, his strikingly original characters, and the stories he wishes to tell at the intersection of these interests.

In *How Cormac Works*, I suggest that McCarthy's defining attribute as an author falls not in the realm of psychology or philosophy or theology or history but in language. Mentioning that a fiction writer's chief tool is language seems fairly obvious, and it is. As I have gestured to above, what is not so obvious is the ways in which McCarthy utilizes and manipulates language, how he uses it to create and withhold meaning, to draw clear images, and, at times, resist this clarity. In his book *Mere Reading: The Poetics of Wonder in Modern American Novels*, Lee Clark Mitchell speaks of the "medley of styles" in accomplished writers that leads to "heightened poetic status" of the language that removes the reader from the pressures of plot: "Narrative regularly pauses, often yielding to description, for reasons not always clear at first, though in every instance the effect is similar to that achieved in poetry—to inspire a keenly responsive sense of awe, mystery, wonder."[4] This book seeks out these pauses and digressions in order to consider the way they contribute to the reader's sense of wonder. McCarthy's distinctive style might also be defined by this "medley of styles." It resides in the push and pull of his explorations of the possibilities that exist within language and the ability to express a vision creatively through the unique combination of words.

There have been many excellent studies of McCarthy's fiction that have explored his philosophical commitments (and given superb readings of the Judge's utterances, for example).[5] There has also been much valuable attention given to McCarthy's choice of subject matter—his near obsession with violence and blood, his desire to stare into the darker crannies of existence and the corresponding darkness within human communities, as well as his steadfast commitment to an exploration of the metaphysical implications unearthed by such topics. This book seeks to do something different. *How Cormac Works* focuses less on the *what*—what McCarthy writes about or what the characters say—and more on the *how*—how McCarthy structures his fiction, how this structure contributes to his literary style, and how this style creates unique reading experiences for those who engage with his work carefully. It is telling that McCarthy's first editor, Albert Erskine (who was also William Faulkner's longtime editor), recognized long ago that McCarthy's value resided chiefly in his language and style. Malcolm Cowley, editor of *The Portable Faulkner*, congratulated Erskine for finding a young writer in McCarthy who "loved language" as much as Faulkner had.[6] *How Cormac Works* seeks to acknowledge and give some structure to McCarthy's love of the written word.

Almost by definition, style is concerned with the superficial, the surface of a text. Novelistic style more specifically is understood conventionally through surface features, such as the prosody, structure, and formal elements of a book. It turns our attention to the construction of a written text rather than to its content, story, or message. In this study of McCarthy's style, I lean on the theory of "surface reading," as defined by Stephen Best and Sharon Marcus. Best and Marcus explain this term as resisting the critical tendency to "plumb [the] depths" of literary texts at the expense of attention to their surfaces: "We take surface to mean what is evident, perceptible, apprehensible in texts; what is neither hidden nor hiding; what, in the geometrical sense, has length and breadth but no thickness, and therefore covers no depth. A surface is what insists on being looked *at* rather than what we must train ourself to see *through*." This attention to the surface can take any number of shapes: surface as materiality, surface as intricate verbal structure, surface as affective and ethical stance, surface as a text's "own truths," surface as a consideration of patterns within and across texts, and surface as literal meaning. For Best and Marcus, this mode of reading allows one to avoid "symptomatic reading," an analytical stance that searches for what the text has repressed, the "absences, gaps, and ellipses" that reveal the "hidden depths" of a work of literature. In short, symptomatic reading looks for the unstated in texts, while surface reading pays attention to and gives value to what is written on the page.[7] *How Cormac Works* shares in this belief of the value of attention to a text's surfaces rather than to its hidden depths.

This study is also energized by related work often described under the umbrella title of New Formalism, an expansive term that essentially signals a return to the form of a text, rather than its context. Timothy Aubry, in his 2018 *Guilty Aesthetic Pleasures*, gives a splendid account of the twenty-first-century return to formalism and its desire to "renew investment in the specificity of literary form." Leaning on Marjorie Levinson's earlier "What Is New Formalism?" (2008), Aubry attaches this interest in form to related notions of aesthetic theory in order to argue that "aesthetic pleasure" is often an unacknowledged motive behind political-minded literary scholarship.[8] However, whereas Aubry is interested in considering how aesthetic form and pleasure contribute to political/ideological arguments about literature, I am exploring here what happens when we try to frame or eliminate these arguments from our considerations of McCarthy's style. I wish to do so not because it is wrong (one could find, for example, any number of political and ideological commitments in McCarthy's writing) but because it is a well-worn and familiar path.

Even so, I do not wish to suggest that we abandon considerations of "hidden depths" or ideological commitments in McCarthy's work entirely. How could one consider his legacy without also considering, for example, the often unexpressed anxiety between sons and fathers that runs throughout his novels or the consistent attention to the pernicious impact of governmental authority and surveillance in his novels. However, this book is committed to the idea that McCarthy's power as a writer and his uniqueness as a novelist resides in his style, the surface language of his novels. Attention to the patterns on this surface reveals the complexity, inspiration, tendencies, and emotive power of McCarthy's maneuvering within the constraints of language. It allows us to see the affective, narratological, and ethical considerations in his fiction as they emerge on the surface of his texts.

Just as Best and Marcus resist the interpretive method of symptomatic reading and its attention to a novel's repressed ideas underneath its language, Rita Felski, in her book *The Limits of Critique*, takes aim at what she calls "suspicious reading." Sharing many of the problems of symptomatic reading, suspicious reading has, for Felski, become the dominant mode of literary "critique," a mode that her study questions, thus the title of her book. Her goal has a lot in common with that of Best and Marcus: "In short, the aim is to de-essentialize the practice of suspicious reading by disinvesting it of presumptions of inherent rigor or intrinsic radicalism—thereby freeing up literary studies to embrace a wider range of affective styles and modes of argument." Felski uses this approach to ask a couple of questions: "Why is it that critics are so quick off the mark to interrogate, unmask, expose, subvert, unravel, demystify, destabilize, take issue, and take umbrage?" and "Why... are we so sure that we know more than the texts that precede us?" Often, this type of critique that Felski questions can end up feeling like a "history of ideas, biography, psychology, ethics, or bad philosophy,"[9] rather than a consideration of the unique and powerful ways that literature works. For Felski and those she cites as like-minded scholars, an attention to types of literary study that fall outside of the traditional model of critique encourages the possibility of a "more affirmative or engaged aesthetic response" to literature.[10]

Of course, when it comes to aesthetic responses to art and in-depth discussions of style, commentary can feel too subjective. An evaluation of style can feel a lot like a discussion of one's favorite musical band—it is perhaps an interesting conversation but ultimately may not reveal much more than the fact that the conversant likes ska or has a nostalgic connection to old-school rap or an adoration of classic jazz. It is useful to make a distinction here between style, which suggests an artist's production, and taste, which suggests an audience's reception of the art. Both taste and style can have political and socioeconomic resonance, as we see with phrases such as "tacky style" and "cheap taste."[11] In *Elements of Taste*, Benjamin Errett explores these tensions between personal taste and the social expectation and meaning of taste: "By mapping physical tastes onto cultural taste, we can explore a new way of thinking about what we consume."[12]

Felski negotiates the potential for idiosyncratic randomness of taste and style by borrowing Bruno Latour's notion of actor-network theory. This theory about social relations allows her to place a literary text in a mesh of interactions that negotiate meaning and value within the exchanges between different actors and within different networks: "To do actor-network theory is not to soar like an eagle, gazing down critically or dispassionately at the distant multitudes below.... It is to slow down at each step, to forgo theoretical shortcuts and to attend to the words of our fellow actors rather than overriding them and overwriting them—with our own. The social, in other words, is not a performing being but a doing, not a hidden entity underlying the realm of appearance but the ongoing connections, disconnections, and reconnections between multiple actors."[13]

In her next book, *Hooked*, Felski turns attention away from the limits of previous modes of scholarship and toward her articulation of a new theory of attachment. For Felski, thinking about attachment becomes a way to explore how readers engage and become "hooked" on their favorite pieces of art:

> How does a novel entice or enlist us; how does a song surprise or seduce us? Why do we bridle when a friend belittles a book we love or fall into a funk when a favored TV show comes to an end? Attachment, I've suggested, has more than one meaning: to be attached is to be affected or moved and also to be linked or tied. It denotes passion and compassion—but also an array of ethical, political, intellectual, or other bonds. *Hooked* makes a case for "attachment" as a vital keyword for the humanities. Why do works of art matter? Because they create, or cocreate, enduring ties.[14]

How Cormac Works does not seek to "unmask" McCarthy's deeper truths or to demystify his hidden agendas. It, conversely, as Felski recommends, seeks to offer an affirmative exploration of his linguistic commitments and inclinations.

How Cormac Works takes inspiration from Felski's focus on attending carefully to how the words of the text call to us and generate ties with the reader. In this regard, it shares much with Mitchell's *Mere Reading*, which seeks to consider "the poetics of wonder" that emerge when we engage in a "slowed-down immersion in prose" that "alter(s) us."[15] What better subject to engage this approach, after all, than McCarthy's lavish writing, and it is not surprising that Mitchell dedicates an entire chapter of his study to dialogue in *The Road*. While Felski works to avoid the limitations of subjective tastes by focusing on the networks of meaning "between multiple" readers, *How Cormac Works* pays special attention to McCarthy's experimentation with language. I think by this point it goes without saying that I have chosen this topic because I am drawn to Cormac McCarthy's style. What feels excessive or showy or precious to some of his readers nearly always hits home and resonates for me. The title of this book plays on the idea of "working" as a means of production (Cormac *working* on his craft as a writer) and the idea of functioning or operating (how his literature *works* both as singular artistic pieces and across a literary career). For this reason, I have chosen to avoid organizing this book chronologically, as so many studies of McCarthy's fiction do. I will not start with his first novel, *The Orchard Keeper*, and march steadily ahead until we end with his last, *Stella Maris*. Instead, I have focused on the modes he adopts and the moods he creates in his books. Felski reminds us that "mood is not synonymous with method."[16] While I substitute the term "mode" for method in this formulation, I am committed to exploring the relationships between mode and mood, between McCarthy's technical and formal experimentation and the feelings such experimentation can evoke.

Exploring his novels at the level of language also allows me to ask a series of interconnected questions about McCarthy's fiction. How does McCarthy use or manipulate language to create very specific dynamics in his fiction? How do readers understand and feel the sensations being created? What are the aesthetic contexts in which McCarthy writes these stories into existence? What are the tools he uses to influence our reaction to these stories?[17] At the intersection of these concerns, this book asks how a text is constructed and how this construction affects our reaction to it—when we are moved, confused, excited, or grossed out and why.

INTRODUCTION

A portion of this project is indebted to narrative theory and its commitment to the meticulous exploration of narrative construction and method. Building on the ground-breaking research by Gérard Genette, Wayne Booth, and many others about the rhetorical implications within the language in fiction,[18] James Phelan has more specifically worked tirelessly to chart out the relationship between a novel's creation and the reader's consumption of it. He has developed what he calls "a rhetorical communication model" of thinking about texts that examines the complex and convoluted meaning-making that happens when a reader opens a text and begins to read.[19] For Phelan we should think about the "structure of meanings" that is created through the interaction of the author, the text the author creates, and the reader. While some narrative theory can feel cold and mathematical, thus losing the beauty of language and thought, Phelan's model attempts to explain the ineffable quality of the communication between text and reader, and he characterizes his project appropriately as "rhetorical poetics": "The goal of the rhetorical project," Phelan explains, "is a comprehensive understanding of how authors and audiences draw upon the resources of narrative for multilayered communicative exchanges. These layers include cognitive, affective, ethical, and aesthetic dimensions of author-audience relations."[20] This method has been especially helpful to my thinking in the first half of this book and its attentions to the modes of McCarthy's writing.

Phelan illustrates the complexity of his project by discussing William Faulkner's *The Sound and the Fury*. He explores the multiple forms of communication in the opening scene of this novel, wherein a golfer yells "Caddie," which the reader subsequently learns is a homonym for Benjy's sister's nickname Caddy. To understand this scene completely, Phelan suggests, we need to understand multiple levels of communication: between the golfer and his caddie, between Benjy and Caddy, between Luster (who is caring for Benjy) and Benjy, between Benjy's naïve reporting and the text's communication about this reporting. The depth of Faulkner's opening passage depends on the reader identifying and synthesizing a response to these multiple "channels."

Looking at style from a rhetorical standpoint allows us to consider that style is both constructed by the author in the writing of the text and by the reader who responds in unique ways to the written words on the page.[21]

Ultimately, Mendelsund, Felski, and Phelan are asking related questions. What tools or resources does an author use to communicate to the audience and what does the reader bring to the text that plays a part in creating that text? They see the text as an action, one that involves the author who is writing and the audience who is reading. My image of Melville's Ishmael is not the same as yours; my attachments are not necessarily the same as yours; Faulkner's story is completed by us.

Style, from this approach, involves a creation of a text, a striving for beauty, that is confirmed in the reader's reception of the style: "Literary styles offer themselves to the reader as genuine forms of life, engaging behaviors, methods, constructive powers, and existential values."[22] Attention to style can thus bring the author into clearer focus, as an agent seeking beauty and seeking to create meaningful art. There has been much desire for a biography of the mysterious Cormac McCarthy, but this desire has been up at least until his death proven difficult, in large part because of how private he preferred to keep his personal life. The most respected and knowledgeable McCarthy scholars still have major gaps in their basic knowledge of his life. The attention to his style provided here offers a different kind of biography, an aesthetic biography that can reveal, if not facts and dates, McCarthy's affective longing and aesthetic goals. As Dorothy Hale writes about one of McCarthy's literary heroes, William Faulkner, attention to the "beautiful style" of the writing "repersonalizes literary language": "The bid for beauty breaks the illusion of impersonal narration and calls attention to the person who might find such language to be beautiful" (in Hale's case, like Phelan's, Faulkner). Just as Hale sees the ability for Faulkner's *The Sound and the Fury* to contain the potential to "constitute the author" precisely "through its acts of style" for the reader,[23] it is my hope that *How Cormac Works* will help constitute McCarthy more clearly for its reader through his commitment to beauty and mystery.

A study of style, while focusing on the surface of literary texts, is anything but superficial. McCarthy's "bid for beauty" and his "eruption of lyrical style" (again echoing Hale) become precious means of understanding the author. They allow us to "read for the joy of it." Jacobs identifies this joy as the liberating idea of whim, which he suggests is often denied us, as we are

INTRODUCTION

told that instead of being a whimsical pleasure, "reading [should be] good for you."[24] This resistance to the idea of reading as some kind of straitlaced and rigorous act of self-improvement brings to mind the enchantment that Nabokov has in mind when he tells his class of aspiring writers to be wary of the "scientific coolness of judgment" and to instead "caress the details, the divine details.... Style and structure are the essence of a book; great ideas are hogwash."[25] He has style in mind when he describes to these same students the reader's response to a great work of art: "In order to bask in that magic a wise reader reads the book of genius not with his heart, not so much with his brain, but with his spine. It is there that occurs the telltale tingle even though we must keep a little aloof, a little detached when reading."[26]

Ever since reviews began pouring in for McCarthy's work, he has been defined by his lyrical style. At times this was intended as a compliment, as when a review commented on his "hard-wrought" style that "is not in the least precious" or when another commented on his "masterly subtle shifts in style." Other readers have found stylistic "flourishes" in his prose that lacked substance or meaning and anointed McCarthy as the leader of a "cult of the prose medium."[27] More recently, scholars have turned our attention to the relationship between McCarthy's style and his works' thematic and structural logics. David James asks whether the style in *The Road*, McCarthy's most popular book, compensates for the bleakness of plot in part by creating a narrative vitality at odds with the plot's despair: "What McCarthy's wretched tale suggests is that prosodic ingredients of description can reroute the negative affects we expect them to affirm. Refusing entirely to reinforce the turbulence it portrays, description jostles against the discomfiture that a text like *The Road* seems bent on imparting."[28] James identifies what he sees as the competition between content and form and asks whether the language or style (form) might offer a type of consolation or solace, even as the plot (content) offers none. Andrew Hoberek, too, has written about the formal structure and style of McCarthy's *The Road*, specifically the "aesthetic of exhaustion," a concept he uses to suggest that the novel's language at times "stylistically undermines its own assertions."[29]

In their different ways, both James and Hoberek call attention to the incommensurability of McCarthy's loving and fearless language and the dire subject matter in this apocalyptic novel. *How Cormac Works* explores such incommensurability, which I contend exists throughout McCarthy's entire career. Whereas consolation is one result of the cross-purposes between language and plot in *The Road*, when we look at other novels and other characters, we get different modes and methods of incommensurability. *Blood Meridian*'s description of Judge Holden that I used to begin this introduction hinges on the incommensurability of the playful, almost goofy physical descriptions of the Judge and his heinous and unforgiveable transgressions. The language McCarthy uses in his fiction, in other words, creates a feeling or a mood often at odds with the scenes and subject matter being described. One scholar sees this disparity as one of the principal challenges when reading McCarthy's novels: "How do you use language to represent an order of reality fundamentally alien to the reality in which and for which our shared language has been framed?"[30] There is oftentimes an understated tenderness folded with McCarthy's creation of his books' most disturbing moments, such as when the man in *The Road* is dropping burning paper down into an overturned trailer to see what was inside, only to discover human remains: "The small wad of burning paper drew down to a wisp of flame and then died out leaving a faint pattern for just a moment in the incandescence like the shape of a flower, a molten rose"(47). In other novels it is the incommensurability of the determination to make us watch scenes of devastation and the odd descriptors that seem to strain our ability to see them. We get tenderness where we expect horror, meaning where we expect none, and a lack of meaning when we most expect and need it. We get strange and unfamiliar descriptions where we expect clarity and precise and concise prose where we expect evasion or deferral.

In her book *No More Heroes*, Lydia Cooper points out that at first glance McCarthy's dire subject matter seems to produce a narrative style in which "an omniscient narrator alienates readers from fictional characters" through a narrative distance from these characters.[31] If James wonders whether language can provide solace for the dire subject matter, Cooper applies an ethics of empathetic reading and finds therein an "aesthetics of empathy" in McCarthy's novels. Focusing specifically on McCarthy's use of "syntactic style shifts" that introduces related shifts in perspective, Cooper suggests that these stylistic turns allow McCarthy to explore and reveal "many different levels of morality."[32]

Similarly focusing on what Cooper calls "style shifts," Andrew Bartlett describes McCarthy's narrative modes, specifically in the novel *Child of God*: "The aesthetic power of *Child of God* results from McCarthy's superb regulation of narrative distance and perspective, his command of four degrees of proximity to Ballard, four kinds of narrative position with differing visions: the voyeuristic, the oblivious, the blind (blinded by darkness), and—most inventive—the archeological."[33] Bartlett's focus on modes helps us think about how McCarthy's fiction works, and "modes" is one of the organizing principles of this book. Where Bartlett focuses on narrative distance, this book will focus on language; where Bartlett speaks of perspective, I want to speak of style, and at times of reader's taste. I want to allow for what Vladimir Nabokov has in mind about the value of wonder in literature: "For me a work of fiction exists only insofar as it affords me what I shall bluntly call aesthetic bliss, that is a sense of being somehow, somewhere, connected with other states of being where art (curiosity, tenderness, kindness, ecstasy) is the norm."[34] As much as Nabokov and McCarthy differ in terms of literary style, they seem to share this notion of the power of language to create a type of bliss and a frustration at having to defend their art against those who would reduce their novels with their violence and violation to nothing more than obscenity or pornography.

Modes and Moods

I am striving to tell a story in this book about how McCarthy's writing operates, relying on my decades-long commitment to the study of his writing but not being overdetermined by the academic debates surrounding it or the theories dominating English departments. I seek to document and explain relevant scholarly conversations, but to minimize my treatment of them in the body of the work. My notes and bibliography point the way for readers interested in such academic pursuits, but the main stakes in *How Cormac Works* and the vast amount of discussion herein are dedicated to

McCarthy's experimentation with language, not to a sustained navigation of and engagement with the academic world.

I am using the terms "mode" and "mood" to organize this book into two parts. I am also using them as a means of describing what I see as McCarthy's formal strategies and the emotional registers created through these strategies. His attention to language, both our current language and his obsession with the archaic and obsolete words and patterns—the power both to engage and to defamiliarize through language—directs us, I suggest, to useful ways to approach his work as a whole. While the terms "modes" and "moods" have multiple meanings, I am thinking of and borrowing from the terminology of music for the naming of these parts to emphasize that an important element of McCarthy works occurs at the level of sound, his commitment to the ineffable music of language. I keep in my conception of the term "modes" the notion of the technical construction of a piece of music. I keep in my use of the term "moods" the more slippery ways that art calls to us. Musical modes and musical moods can provide the soundtrack that organizes this book.

Part 1 of *How Cormac Works* is concerned with what I am calling modes and what we might also think of as narrative strategies. This part of the book shares much with Timothy Aubry's sense of the specific requirements needed to attend to the formal characteristics of fiction: "To consider the formal aspects of a literary work usually means to pay as much attention to the language, the sound and look of the words, the rhythm and the syntax, and so forth—as to what that language represents. It can of course also mean concentrating on patterns of images, motifs, actions, or other narrative structures that are not linguistic elements strictly speaking but can nevertheless be categorized alongside the linguistics elements as means of representations."[35] What Aubry calls the patterns of language, images, and structures in fiction I am lumping together under the idea of modes—a linguistic logic of telling a story, painting a picture, or creating an emotion. In a related way, modes are generally understood in musical theory as technical concepts that can give music structure and feeling. In music, modes relate to, among other things, the different effects and tonality that notes and scales can provide. Think of the difference between major and minor scales, the difference in feeling that exists between, for example, A major and A minor. The differences can be described mathematically (the dropping of the third note in a scale to a flatted third), but they create very notable tonal impacts transcending a narrow sense of mathematics even as they are defined by them—major scales and chords are "happy" while minor scales and chords are "sad." One can get increasingly technical and mathematical with musical modes; take, for example, the seven diatonic modes: Ionian, Dorian, Phrygian, Lydian, Mixolydian, Aeolian, Locrian. Each of these modes is defined mathematically and can be charted logically by counting interval sequences (whole and half notes).[36] The term "mode" can also be used to identify and discuss the difference between polyphony (multiple simultaneous melodies in a composition) and a singular melody. These charts and definitions do not give us the music behind these differences, but understanding *how modes work* can.

Once again, the idea of mode is one of theory and technical specs. It is something that can be classified and charted. However, as jazz musician and instructor James Melton reminds us, mode is also about "tonality." To return to the diatonic modes one more time, "Though the different modes are all made up of the same sequence of notes as the parent scale, the tonality of each mode is unique because the relationships to the root note depend on where you are in the sequence."[37] In order to use the different modes effectively, one must understand their tonality and how to get the most out of the structure of the mode. In short, one must convert the technical mode to a musical tool. The mathematical definitions give way, if the musician is talented enough, to the tonality and aesthetics of the music. Anyone who has struggled to learn how to implement the diatonic modes in music, rather than just learning them and rehearsing them by memory, can attest to the difficulty in this step.

It is this exchange, the movement between technical specifications and aesthetic beauty, that I seek to explore with McCarthy's work in part 1. His technical modes, his narrative strategies, are always part of but ultimately secondary to the feelings they evoke and the musicality of language they open. When critics write of McCarthy's "nomadic sentences" and syntax in his Western novels or his biblically infused "peculiar use of language" in *Outer Dark*, they are speaking in terms of what I am calling narrative modes, modes which create a tonality that becomes essential to the reader's experience of the novels.[38] The technical details fall away in service of the story being told.

Chapter 1, "Unexpected Registers: McCarthy's Narrative Modes," is the first in-depth examination of McCarthy's commitment to a fearless and consistent experimentation with language. This experimentation, chapter 1 and the book more generally argue, grows out of McCarthy's enduring faith in and love of language. Language is precious, if not infallible, to him precisely because of its ability to bring to life for the reader startling scenes, breathtaking visions, and riveting characters. This initial chapter engages McCarthy's love of language by arguing that one cannot understand the author's novels without thinking about his various narrative modes and his frequent switching between these modes.

Depending on the novel—and even passages within certain novels—McCarthy's writing can be characterized as minimalistic, meandering, esoteric, humorous, terrifying, pretentious, sentimental, or folksy. Some novels depend heavily on dense passages of narrative exposition and philosophizing, while others lean heavily on everyday dialogue. Some books celebrate regional stories and vernacular, and others adopt a neutral, removed, and clinical tone. This experimentation feels like more than simply an attempt to demonstrate his virtuosity as a writer; instead, it reflects his love of words and the endless possibilities of language.[39]

Chapter 1 contends more specifically that three identifiable modes—what I label the tender, the biblical, and the dramatic—can be traced by any number of means: the narrative proximity to fictional characters, the tone and mood of the prose, or the density and rhythm of the language unique to each mode. The tender mode uses delicate language in the most unexpected of places; the biblical mode invokes the language of the King James version of the Hebrew Bible to give an otherworldly feel to McCarthy's early fiction; the dramatic mode relies on the dialogue of drama to engage from multiple perspectives the enduring questions of faith and meaning. By tracing these illustrative modes, this chapter argues that McCarthy's ability to evoke such strong emotional responses from his readers is deeply rooted in his technical manipulation of narrative voice and perspective.

Chapter 2, "'Large Loose Baggy Monsters': McCarthy's Epic Mode," focuses on McCarthy's "epic mode," found most consistently in his mid-career novels—*Suttree*, *Blood Meridian*, and *The Crossing*—as well as in his penultimate novel, *The Passenger*. This mode is more allusive and more consciously cosmic and referential than others. We can see McCarthy intentionally placing himself in conversation with literary and philosophical heavyweights. References to James Joyce, Fyodor Dostoyevsky, William Faulkner, Flannery O'Connor, William James, and other masters abound in these novels. The title borrows the phrase "large loose baggy monsters" from Henry James, who used it to characterize long, detailed books. I argue that McCarthy's mid-career novels feel looser and can be seen as "baggy monsters" (for James this was not a disparaging quality). The prose in these books, too, feels intentionally reflective of the literary past, be it the dime store Western or more often the works of titans of the Western literary canon. As Steven Frye puts it, "Like many of our greatest innovators, [McCarthy] approaches literature with a creative mind and perceptive capacity not as an admirer, but with the active motivation of one who intends to break apart and rebuild, to absorb and re-envision."[40]

Chapter 2 explores the implications of Frye's comment by suggesting that *Suttree*, *Blood Meridian*, and *The Crossing* more consciously and intentionally invite comparison to other twentieth-century epic novels. These novels have moments that seem to consciously evoke the "high narrative voice" often associated with epics; they seem to place themselves in conversations with other writers dealing with "big issues," and they seem to be written for posterity in ways that some of his other novels do not. You might be able to keep McCarthy's earlier *The Orchard Keeper* in the box of U.S. southern regionalism or to discuss *No Country for Old Men* within the hyperfocalized framework of narco-wars of the late twentieth century, or even see *All the Pretty Horses* as updating but largely staying within the standard Western novel tradition. *Suttree*, on the other hand, is in no way containable within a regional context, even though the entire book is based in the Appalachian town of Knoxville, Tennessee. Nor would one suggest that *Blood Meridian* be considered a traditional Western, even though it superficially invites such comparisons. These books have a scope and style that feels cosmic and epic.

Part 2 of this book shifts from "modes" to "moods." If modes chart the technical and theoretical side of craft, musical moods are not so easily captured by the mathematical. Modes are related to the formal implements used to create works of art. We could say, then, that moods are often the effects of this creation—rather than offering a technical approach to understanding a work of art, moods are less traceable and more ephemeral. In music, moods are often simply labels that one can use to describe the emotion connected to the composition. There are happy songs and sad songs, but musical moods can be much more nuanced and refined than that. The All Music website identifies 305 distinct musical moods and invites listeners to explore their database through these moods.[41] In this list you can choose the mood "crunchy," where you will find selections from Black Sabbath and Bo Diddley; "feverish" will connect you to the music of the Velvet Underground and Leonard Bernstein; "kinetic" pairs Philip Glass with Soundgarden; "quirky" suggests Captain Beefheart and the Dead Milkman; "sparkling" gives you Oscar Peterson alongside ABBA. As these idiosyncratic lists suggest, moods are very subjective, as we don't all agree on which artistic expressions belong to which moods. Many listeners would resist placing the revered jazz pianist Oscar Peterson in a category that also includes the pop- and disco-inspired ABBA. How would one characterize McCarthy's fiction with these labels? Would one put McCarthy's *The Road* in the All Music category of "brooding" or "cathartic" or "anxious" or "unsettling" or some other mood entirely?

Recently, a group of Tufts computer engineering students sought to quantify and chart musical moods through a computer adaptation of Robert Thayer's model of moods, which attempts to chart moods on two axes; the energy axis moves from "calm" to "energetic," while the stress axis travels from "happy" to "anxious/sad." The Tufts authors also looked at definitions provided by the BNM Institute of Technology in Bangalore, India, to chart these moods alongside other musical considerations: intensity, timbre, pitch, rhythm. After running a variety of music through an algorithm designed to account for these measurables, the group concluded, "Breaking a song down into quantifiable musical components such as rhythm, harmony, and timbre can allow for the matching of songs to specific categories based upon expected data for each type of mood."[42] As fun as this project is to consider, one could argue that this classification is no more determinate than All Music's mood list, and the reason is revealed in the second line of the study's abstract: "The emotional reaction to music is different for every person, so analyzing it will not likely yield perfect results." We are talking here about enchantment, which, as the project from Tufts explores, is as difficult to categorize as it is to monetize.

How Cormac Works does not try to classify McCarthy's literary moods algorithmically, and I do not foresee an interest in my grouping from tech companies such as iTunes and Spotify, which the study above suggests might be possible landing spots for their work. Even so, I do believe that the moods being created through McCarthy's musical language are worth paying close attention to, perhaps through the rhythms of his language, rather than through their algorithms. How and when does McCarthy seek to create an anxious mood? When does he express the melancholy, the sentimental, the indulgent (to refer to the All Music list one last time)? How do these moods mesh with or butt up against the stories being told in the novels and how do they inform these stories and color the reader's reception of them? An early review of *Outer Dark* seemed to recognize McCarthy's attention to the musical aspects of language and the sounds within his writing, describing the book as having an "Irish singing voice imbued with southern biblical intonations."[43]

In chapter 3, "'Little More Than a Childhood Enthusiasm': Thick Description and the Taxonomic Mood," I examine McCarthy's counterintuitive engagements with the natural world. There have been several studies on notions of environmental damage and *The Road*, but this chapter will depart from such an ecocritical line of inquiry, focusing instead on McCarthy's painstaking reconstruction of plant life and geological processes found in unexpected places—the town dump, the urban parking lots, desert "wastelands," marble quarries. Rather than searching for some elusive and utopian natural purity, McCarthy uses these natural spaces to explore the vast changes in our industrial and postindustrial landscape. I chart McCarthy's interest in a taxonomic understanding of these environments that can be found as early as in his first short stories as an undergraduate student and that persists into the final words of his last novel. Drawing on the theories of vegetal politics,[44] this chapter also explores McCarthy's interest in "weeds" and vegetal/human interaction. His interest in down-and-out protagonists seems to be matched by his interest in the down-and-out natural world as well.

Chapter 4, "The Precarious Mood: *The Passenger, Stella Maris*, and the Fragile Twentieth Century," takes up McCarthy's two novels that were released in 2022, *The Passenger* and *Stella Maris*. This chapter explores the "duality" of these novels and their insistence on creating a mood of precarity. Drawing on McCarthy's newer interest in theoretical physics and abstract mathematics, both of these books use these scientific concepts to create new literary styles, but they also use them to explore from a different vantage point questions that one can find running throughout McCarthy's career. Tracing these connections and stylistic choices through his new work will provide an opportunity to consider McCarthy's entire oeuvre, its evolution and consistencies.

One aspect of *The Passenger* and *Stella Maris* that feels new and radical is that they not only engage the philosophical and scientific implications of theories of indeterminacy and chaos but they are formally determined by them. By this I mean the very ideas of radical indeterminacy and quantum entanglement that McCarthy's protagonists struggle to comprehend in the world of mathematics become part of the organizational structure of the twinned novels. The two novels cannot be separated, at least without losing their center. Nor can they be reduced to one novel. In many ways, they present two different yet interconnected versions of the world. They become like Schrödinger's cat, both alive and dead in a hypothetical and unobserved box. Indeed, in *The Passenger*, Alicia is dead in the first paragraph, and the novel follows her brother's attempt to come to terms with his loss. In *Stella Maris*, Alicia is very much alive, although boxed into a series of psychological interviews that spiral toward her suicide, which begins *The Passenger*. This organizational structure creates a mood of provisionality that calls attention to how interlinked these novels are. As they conclude, the reader is left, too, with a mood of subsidence, of a wonderful and energetic writing career winding down. Rather than resolution or denouement or even tension, these last two books feels like they expire or burn out.

This chapter explores these new elements of his last novels as well as the enduring commitments in McCarthy's literary career. By examining the books' interest in the dispossession of East Tennessee citizens in the atomic bomb project and the TVA hydroelectric initiatives, the chapter concludes by suggesting that McCarthy's career-long distrust of governmental fiat, his love of rural voices and patterns of life, and his sense of the precarity of twentieth- and twenty-first-century existence find a familiar home in these final novels.

The epilogue, "Them Old Dreams," concludes this book with a brief consideration of McCarthy's career-long commitment to and love of regional voices and stories. McCarthy kept a folder of sketches he had written, at times tailored from stories he heard in public and with friends. Many times he wrote these sketches without having a place for them within a specific novel. He would revisit and rearrange these stories, trying them out in different novels and contexts. This experimentation with the voices and tales shows McCarthy's enduring engagement with storytelling traditions, especially those rooted in southern Appalachian communities, an engagement that will endure as one of McCarthy's most precious legacies.

At one point in his book *What We See When We Read*, Mendelsund states that visualizing characters and scenes "seems to require *will* . . . though at times it may also seem as though an image of a sort appears to us unbidden. (It is tenuous, and withdraws shyly upon scrutiny)" (emphasis added).[45] It is precisely the exploration of this tenuous zone between the reader's will to understand and the unexpected feelings, ideas, and meanings that seem to emerge mysteriously in his texts that I argue characterizes McCarthy's matchless style. He calls attention to the very instability that Mendelsund argues operates in all fiction. McCarthy, I offer in what follows, brings this dynamic out of the shadows and places it at the center of his fiction.

I. *Modes*

> The task of the narrator is not an easy one.... He appears to be required to choose his tale from among the many that are possible. But of course that is not the case. The case is rather to make many of the one.... All is telling. Do not doubt it.
>
> —CORMAC MCCARTHY, *The Crossing*

> Literature occurs in a verbal woof of words, sounds, rhythms, patterns of syntax, figures of speech, even marginal asides and casual interruptions. Or from a different figurative angle, it emerges in the interstices, in odd formal patterns and disruptive sequences as words are invoked imaginatively, often fancifully and misshapenly, askew from their sometimes more obvious meanings and in constructions that draw our eyes away from straightforward plots to more disruptive cadences, our ears away from sense to sound.
>
> —LEE CLARK MITCHELL, *Mere Reading*

> Where all is known no narrative is possible.
>
> —CORMAC MCCARTHY, *Cities of the Plain*

ONE

Unexpected Registers
McCarthy's Narrative Modes

As anyone who is a fan of his work will recognize, McCarthy thought a lot about the role of the storyteller in fiction. The way the story is told is as defining as the plot of the information being conveyed. Not surprisingly, then, he was also highly attuned to the limitations of storytelling, especially the role that mystery and invention play in the stories we tell. "Where all is known no narrative is possible" the narrator announces in *Cities of the Plain* (277). In the conversations he painstakingly constructs in his novels, the love of gifted storytellers consistently emerges, such as the attention given to the Mexican wandering philosophers his protagonists so often encounter in his Border Trilogy and the community members of the East Tennessee mountain towns in his earlier novels. McCarthy, too, expresses a related love of language in his own narrative prose. He experiments consistently and fearlessly with perspective and technique, playing with the various means available for creating an atmosphere or developing a scene.

This chapter contends that we can understand this commitment to experimentation in a more fruitful way by thinking about McCarthy's use of multiple narrative modes and his frequent switching between these modes. After briefly exploring his commitment to the various formal and tonal possibilities within language more generally, I will explore what I identify as three specific narrative modes—the tender, the biblical, and the dramatic—that can be traced in his work by any number of means: the narrative proximity to fictional characters, the tone and mood of the prose, or the density and rhythm of the language unique to each mode. The tender mode uses delicate language in the most unexpected of places; the biblical mode invokes the language of the King James version of the Hebrew Bible to give an otherworldly feel to McCarthy's early fiction; the dramatic mode relies on the dialogue of drama to engage from multiple perspectives the enduring questions of faith and meaning.

Tonal Variation and Narrative Mischievousness in McCarthy's Language

Depending on the book—and even passages within certain books—McCarthy's writing can be characterized as minimalistic, meandering, esoteric, humorous, terrifying, pretentious, sentimental, or folksy. Some novels depend heavily on dense passages of narrative exposition and philosophizing, while others lean heavily on everyday dialogue. Some books celebrate regional voices and vernacular, and others adopt a neutral, removed, and clinical tone. This experimentation with narrative perspective feels more than simply an attempt to demonstrate his virtuosity as a writer; instead, it reflects his love of words and the endless possibilities of language.

One can see McCarthy's commitment to the multiple possibilities of narrative in his most famous book, *The Road*. In this novel, the reader encounters a variety of narrative approaches: bare and almost monotonous dialogue, naturalistic descriptions of the devastated environment, and strangely elegiac philosophical musings, typically with no transitions between them. What is perhaps most surprising formally is how many different modes of narration the book adopts, how many different styles it juxtaposes. Take, for example, the openings of five consecutive paragraphs that occur early in the novel:

> It was colder. Nothing moved in that night world. A rich smell of woodsmoke hung over the road. He pushed the cart on through the snow....
>
> In his dream she was sick and he cared for her. The dream bore the look of sacrifice but he thought differently....

On this road there are no godspoke men. They are gone and I am left and they have taken with them the world. Query: How does the never to be differ from what never was?

Dark of invisible moon. The nights now only slightly less black. . . .

People sitting on the sidewalk in the dawn half immolate and smoking in their clothes. Like failed sectarian suicides. (TR, 31–32)[1]

Each paragraph in this passage is different in tone, subject matter, place, and time from the previous and the following paragraph. The first quoted passage provides a stark description of the postapocalyptic landscape. As the paragraph continues, the narration emphasizes the disorientation that arises when crucial infrastructure has vanished and brings into focus the dependence we have on that infrastructure: "He pushed the cart on through the snow. A few miles each day. He'd no notion how far the summit might be. They ate sparely and were hungry all the time." The second paragraph describes the man's dream of his wife before her death by suicide. We are given in this paragraph very personal and introspective expressions of the man's guilt. The paragraph continues, "He did not take care for her and she died alone somewhere in the dark and there is no other dream nor other waking world and there is no other tale to tell." Unlike the rational attempts to understand the present world in the first paragraph, the second one is haunted by the past. It is fitting then that it begins with a dream. The third paragraph, only three sentences long, strikes a more philosophical tone, and the reader is given direct access to the man's thoughts: "They are gone and I am left and they have taken with them the world." While this paragraph shares with the previous paragraph some of the regrets of surviving the apocalypse, we get a shift in point of view, a personalizing move to first person (a very rare move in this book); the "he" is now, one paragraph later, an "I." Then, in the fourth paragraph, we are kicked out of these internal and personal moments to a more objective description of the "present" landscape and the night sky. We are also presented a poetic language that seems at odds with the man's pared-down mindset based around survival: "By day the banished sun circles the earth like a grieving mother with a lamp." The paragraph resonates with the pared-down naturalistic descriptions and figurative language often found in haiku.

The final paragraph in this quoted example is a flashback in heightened language. While the man has proven himself to be educated and introspective enough for such language, this paragraph doesn't sound like his voice or his perspective, at least as they are expressed after the apocalypse. Where is this description coming from? What prompted it? Finally, in this paragraph we are presented not with a dream but with the man's memory of the days immediately after the catastrophic event. Here the metaphorical language—people on fire after the event, like "failed sectarian suicides"—sounds closer to the perspective of the man, who is clearly traumatized and hardened by all that he has witnessed and survived. This type of linguistic movement on a single page of the novel of scene, dramatic register, narrative voice, and even vocabulary defines the novel. The combination of so many styles of prose without transition is unsettling. It feels as if the book floats along without a mooring, capturing at the level of language the disappearing foundation of the novel's postapocalyptic setting.

Early in the book, McCarthy writes of the father's "dull despair" at the loss of so much of the world: "The sacred idiom shorn of its referents and so of its reality" (TR, 89). Many readers, picking up on the word "sacred," tend to interpret this passage religiously, as either expressing the despair of a lack of belief or the absence of a sustaining engagement with the sacred.[2] While this interpretation is not incorrect, to me the passage is fundamentally about the loss of language, the "names of things slowly following those things into oblivion," as McCarthy puts it earlier in the passage. From this perspective, we might say the formal qualities of the book as a whole are committed to removing us from the usual novelistic references and expectations. There is no conventional plot or setting in the novel, and in some ways its most sustaining aspect is its commitment to language, even as it charts the obsolescence of beauty and much of our language in this world without human community, connection, or communication.

Since long before *The Road* was conceived, much less written, scholars have been commenting on McCarthy's disjunctive style. One of the earliest McCarthy scholars, Vareen Bell, characterized his lesser-known third novel, *Child of God*, in terms of its narrative fragmentation: "The strangeness of the story begins with the way the story is told.... An unusual degree of unassimilated raw material impedes—or seems to impede—the narrative flow. The narrative is so aimless and fragmented that an innocent reader might wonder if there is even to be a plot."[3]

Andrew Bartlett has similarly identified what he sees as distinctive and at times competing narrative modes in this novel. Bartlett understands the novel in terms of narrative perspective and argues that this perspective is its defining aspect: "The aesthetic power of *Child of God* results from McCarthy's superb regulation of narrative distance and perspective, his command of four degrees of proximity to Ballard, four kinds of narrative position with differing visions: the voyeuristic, the oblivious, the blind (blinded by darkness), and—most inventive—the archeological."[4] Other scholars have similarly identified narrative shifting as one of McCarthy's distinctive writing strategies that has endured throughout his career.[5]

We can see the shifting of tonal registers very clearly in the conclusion of *Child of God*. In these final pages, we see a worn-out Ballard turning himself into a mental hospital, and he is described in stark, depersonalized terms: "A weedshaped onearmed human swaddled up in outsized overall and covered all over with red mud" (*CofG*, 192). There is no action in this sentence and no predicate—just a phrase that removes him from his personality, his name, and his particularity. We can think of this stylistic move as the "deverbing of Ballard," a trope McCarthy uses increasingly as the novel's plot escalates and Ballard finds himself at the mercy of forces and urges beyond his control. Here he is reduced to a "weedshaped human." In the next section of the book, McCarthy further depersonalizes Ballard as we hear of his life in a mental institution and the fate of his body thereafter: "His body was shipped to the state medical school at Memphis. . . . He was laid out on a slab and flayed, eviscerated, dissected. His head was sawed open and his brains removed. His muscles were stripped from his bones. His heart was taken out. . . . At the end of three months when the class was closed Ballard was scraped from the table into a plastic bag and taken with others of his kind to a cemetery outside the city and there interred" (*CofG*, 194). I can think of no other novel that dispatches of its central character in this way. McCarthy first robs Ballard of his independence at the level of language by removing the predicates that are capable of ascribing agency and action, and then startlingly gives him back his named position *only* when he has been in the plot reduced to body parts and scraped into a bag.

These examples reveal McCarthy's narrative mischievousness and his embracing of unconventional and shifting narrative perspectives and stances. I will trace below how McCarthy's fiction can be understood through his precise control of narrative distance and narrative modes. By looking at moments of varying affective registers, we can understand this linguistic shifting, this play with registers and tone and perspective, which is perhaps the defining aspect of McCarthy's oeuvre. More specifically, this chapter will explore three specific narrative modes that McCarthy most consistently enters—the tender, the biblical, and the dramatic. While it is McCarthy's famous descriptions of violence and depravity that grab the headlines, I suggest here that it is his language's uneasiness with and decentering of these topics that propels the fiction.

Tenderness and the Refuge of Language

One of the most iconic moments in the rare public life of Cormac McCarthy is his 2007 interview with Oprah Winfrey on her talk show. Multimedia artist Palmer Murphy's 2007 illustration *Cormac Visits Oprah* (fig. 1) captures the common sentiment that many McCarthy enthusiasts had about the interview, that McCarthy's subject matter was a poor fit for Oprah's show and audience. One can see this impression in Murphy's depiction of Cormac's defiant arm-crossing, Oprah's surprised look, and the gestures of horror and shock in the foregrounded and shadowed audience. Stacey Peebles begins her book on McCarthy and performance with a newspaper headline about the interview that cheekily captures a similar mood: "Talk Show Goddess Meets Mr. End of the World."[6]

In addition to the sense of the ill-conceived booking of McCarthy on the popular daytime talk show, the illustration and newspaper headline also reflect many of the gendered assumptions about McCarthy's depictions of violence. Murphy plays up in his illustration Oprah's surprise/shock. Her civility, the illustration suggests, is no match for Cormac's unblinking ex-

FIGURE 1. *Cormac Visits Oprah* (2007).
Courtesy Palmer Murphy.

amination of violence and depravity. Needless to say, such assumptions ignore the fact that Oprah Winfrey had by this point already interviewed Toni Morrison, whose novel *Beloved* is every bit as violent and gruesome and unrelenting as is McCarthy's most graphic writing. Winfrey even played the starring role of Sethe in the movie adaptation of Morrison's most acclaimed novel. Nonetheless, the idea remains for many that Oprah is somehow too gentle, too polite, too tender for Cormac's disturbing subject matter.

Since McCarthy published his first novel, *The Orchard Keeper*, in 1965, and especially since the publication of his second novel, *Outer Dark*, three years later, it has become nearly mandatory for readers and scholars to characterize McCarthy's fiction as brutal, unflinching, and violent; the severed head, arrow-filled body, mangled skull, carrion birds, and ghostly figures in the background of Murphy's illustration perfectly capture this idea. These referents echo McCarthy's own famous comment in a 1992 interview: "There's no such thing as life without bloodshed."[7] Such descriptions, coupled with the common appearance of this bloodshed in his fiction, lead to what critics often label as his "aesthetic of violence."[8]

However, watching Winfrey interview McCarthy without reference to this preestablished context, I would argue that what stands out about the conversation is not McCarthy's brutality but rather *his* timidity, *his* gentleness, *his* tenderness. What some read as a defiance or arrogance or a reluctance to be on the national stage can also be understood as the behavior of a sweet older man with many mannerisms from his Appalachian childhood. McCarthy was uncomfortable in this interview, to be sure. But he was also soft-spoken with a gentle, high-pitched voice, a voice that seemed much more at odds with his subject matter than Winfrey's attempts to draw him out. Perhaps the interview met with such resistance from McCarthy devotees in part because it blurs the supposed lines between McCarthy's grit and Winfrey's polish, between his violent fictional worlds and her daytime gloss, thus complicating the image we have of the writer, and to a lesser extent, the talk-show host.

I am suggesting in this chapter that we can find this rupture of gentleness and the incommensurability of much of McCarthy's language and his fiction's content as defining tenets of what I am calling the *tender mode*. It is a distinctive element of McCarthy's style that can be used to characterize and understand his writing. As much as he seems to enjoy writing about dead babies hanging in trees and the spurting of arterial blood and heads split to the "thrapple," he loves equally the precious ability of language to paint images of tenderness where we least expect to find them.[9]

As is the case with most of McCarthy's novels, *Child of God* is not often discussed in terms of tenderness. Certainly this is the case when we consider its major plot points and its deteriorating central character. An early review similarly characterizes the diction in this novel as "cold, sour," adding, "Harsh words constitute the novel like bumps of dirty ice."[10] The novel tracks a man's descent into chaos, with ascending levels of criminality and violence marking his deterioration. The narrative perspective is also complicated by a seemingly omniscient third-person narrator who follows Lester Ballard's movements like a stalker but rarely gives us access to his inner thoughts. This narrator is accompanied in the first section by a series of first-person community voices that speak about and mythologize Lester's monstrous behavior after the fact.[11] So tenderness is perhaps not as obvious a narrative mode here as it is in *The Road*, but it is still one that appears unexpectedly and complicates the book's scenes of violence. One can ask a very similar question about these unexpected moments of tenderness in *Child of God*, one of his most brutal of books, as others have asked about *The Road*: What type of consolation does this linguistic tenderness play in a book about violation and destruction? Does the seemingly mismatched narration undermine or undergird this horrifying tale of murder, necrophilia, and depravity set in the hills of Tennessee?

Child of God offers a very different textual dynamic and expresses a very different literary style than *The Road*. The book is nearly devoid of love, except perhaps for a distorted love of the necrophiliac for his deceased victims, and the social interactions are not mournful or elegiac but gross and hard to watch. After the first several pages, the reader has already observed Lester Ballard spit, urinate, defecate, and ejaculate. McCarthy blurs the line between human, animal, and monster in his depiction of Ballard and the novel resists any initial desire to feel tenderness toward Ballard's isolation. McCarthy constructed an unusual disconnect between the determination to make us watch Lester's abominations and the odd descriptors that seem to strain our ability to see them.

The reader of *Child of God* is forced to oscillate between Lester Ballard's murderous necrophilia and McCarthy's tender descriptions that surround and contrast Ballard's violence. The oscillation of tone between chilling starkness and whispered tenderness begins as early as the novel's second page, when we are first introduced to Ballard. Sandwiched in the same paragraph between a characterization of Lester as "small, unclean, unshaven with a constrained truculence" and a description of him urinating on the ground is a tender description of the scene, one that doesn't appropriately fit the foreboding tone of the introduction of Lester: "Wasps pass through the laddered light from the barnslats in a succession of strobic moments, gold and trembling between black and black, like fireflies in the serried upper gloom" (*CofG*, 4). In this scene where Lester is about to be dispossessed of his family home, hit on the head with the dull side of an axe, and forced to wander the winter mountains in search of a new place to live, we have a brief but precious moment of quietude. Wasps passing through "*laddered light . . . gold and trembling*" (emphasis added). The effect here is not related to the plot or the rising scene (the stillness is not there to build tension, for example). Neither does the effect correspond with what is going on—we aren't to assume that Lester feels this tranquility or observes his setting with tenderness. The description doesn't bring sympathy toward the character either, and it is immediately undermined by an unpleasant description of Ballard urinating. But the reader is left with a moment of stillness that feels tender and dear.

The book is replete with moments of narrative tenderness that break through the action suddenly and unexpectedly. At one point, as Ballard wanders through the mountains, he comes across a group of robins hopping through the snow before scattering with his approach: "Ballard ran after them. They ducked and fluttered. He fell and rose and ran laughing. He caught and held one warm and feathered in his palm with the heart of it beating there just so" (*CofG*, 76). What interests me here is not the sentimental depiction of Ballard as playful and in some ways innocent. After all, this is immediately undermined as he gives the robin to an "idiot child," who promptly chews off its legs. Rather, it is the tenderness at the level of language. "Warm and feathered ... with the heart of it beating there *just so*" (emphasis added). There is preciousness here, a wonder at the fragility of the bird perhaps, but also the beauty of language, a beauty that doesn't align with the character or the scene or the setting.

This book follows Ballard as he commits crimes of sexual assault, necrophilia, and murder, and we watch his depravity in all its grotesquery and vividness. At one point, after Ballard escapes a vigilante lynch mob seeking vengeance for his murders, he flees to the nearby caves where he gets lost in the darkness. As he begins to believe he will die here, he hears mice and imagines them after his death nesting in the recesses of his skull, a dark scene to be sure. It is here where we get another moment of linguistic tenderness imagining Ballard's skeleton in the cave: "His bones polished clean as eggshells, centipedes sleeping in their marrowed flutes, his ribs curling slender and whitely like a bone flower in the dark stone bowl" (*CofG*, 189). We could examine from a different approach the idea of the fleeting nature of life here or Ballard's fear, but I'm struck once again by the language, "*polished clean as eggshells,*" "*ribs curling slender and whitely,*" "*a bone flower in the dark stone bowl*" (emphases added). This passage brings to mind David James's suggestion regarding *The Road* that we consider how description can "misbehave," "how it hatches rogue aesthetic plans, how indeed it becomes—through the sumptuous pressure it exerts on what it describes—a type of narration in its own right."[12]

There are a couple of ways we might think about the specific item of a bone flower in this passage. The first and common explanation is that the term is a synonym for the common daisy. The image in this light prefigures McCarthy's "misbehaving" images of the "molten rose" in *The Road* mentioned above and of *Blood Meridian*'s startling image of blood dropping in the water "like roseblooms" (*BM*, 291). These images reveal just how much McCarthy enjoys using tender descriptions in his unfolding of gruesome scenes. But in the passage the bones become a clipped flower in the bowl, its precious white pedals in stark contrast to the dark stone bowl. It is also very reminiscent of Ezra Pound's famous and sparse modernist poem "In a Station of the Metro" (1913):

> The apparition of these faces in the crowd:
> Petals on a wet, black bough.[13]

The surprise in Pound's poem comes from the erupting of the unexpected—a "flower" emerging ghostlike from the dark and dingy subway platform. In all of these examples, the image being connected to the flower is at odds with what a flower typically symbolizes (purity, innocence, beauty, delicacy). In the place of this expected symbolism, McCarthy aligns the images with blood, danger, and skeletons.

Another way to think about the idea of a bone flower has to do with the notion of memento mori, the long-standing artistic tradition designed to remind the viewer of the inevitability of death, an artistic genre that has for centuries combined bones/skeletons and flowers, suggesting the immutable cycle of life. There are traditions of carving flowers out of bones that can be found in early Egyptian, Mayan, and other ancient civilizations, as well as more recent combinations of skulls and flowers from artists such as Georgia O'Keeffe and from Mexican Día de Los Muertos celebrations. It is the holding together of the fragile beauty of a flower and the constant reminder of the temporary quality of worldly beauty. More recently, Japanese artist Hideki Tokushige has crafted *Honebana*, absolutely stunning flowers out of

FIGURE 2. *Chinese Lantern Plant #2.*
Courtesy Hideki Tokushige.

the cleaned bones of rodents (fig. 2).¹⁴ Tokushige was born in 1974, one year after the publication of *Child of God*, so I can't suggest that McCarthy was invoking his artwork (as much as I wish I could). Even so, I feel both artists are kindred spirits here, dedicated to the craft of connecting tenderness and violence, beauty and death, flowers and the bones of the deceased.

In his second novel, *Outer Dark*, McCarthy also connects the images of bones and flowers, this time with a tender treatment of a gruesome scene describing the rotting corpse of the tinker, who was left by marauders hanging in "his burial tree": "Black mandrake sprang beneath the tree as it will where the seed of the hanged falls and in spring a new branch pierced his breast and flowered in a green boutonniere perennial beneath his yellow grin. [The body remained this way through the seasons] until wind had tolled the tinker's bones and seasons loosed them one by one to the ground below and alone his bleached and weathered brisket hung in that lonesome wood like a bone birdcage." (*OD*, 238). As was the case with *Child of God*, the tender language clashes with the gruesome scene of a hanging victim decomposing in a tree. The mandrake (*Mandragora officinarum*) is a plant understood as far back at least as medieval times to have medicinal and magical powers, which provides a supernatural mood to the scene. Its unlikely growth up through the breast of the corpse to form a "green boutonniere perennial" mixes images of birth, death, and eternity, and the final image of the "bone birdcage" reminds us of Lester's bone flower and Tokushige's *Honebana*. Throughout the entire passage the prose is measured, whispered to the reader in a gentle tone that changes the way we see the body in the tree. Compare this to a later scene of human bodies in a tree in *Blood Meridian*, when Sproule and the kid come across a "bush that was hung with dead babies": "They stopped side by side, reeling in the heat. These small victims, seven, eight of them, had holes punched in their underjaws and were hung so by their throats from the broken stobs of mesquite to stare eyeless at the naked sky" (*BM*, 57). Here the language is meant to shock and horrify (as one might expect for such a scene). The act of hanging babies in the tree seems to be at odds with nature, as the "broken stobs of mesquite" abuse the bodies rather than serve as adorning boutonnieres to enhance their presentation.

McCarthy begins his final linked novels, *The Passenger* and *Stella Maris*, with yet another tender rendering of a body hanging in a tree, this time in a foretelling of the protagonist Alicia Western's suicide. *The Passenger* begins with a literary trope that McCarthy often turns to, the italicized preface:

> *It had snowed lightly in the night and her frozen hair was gold and crystalline and her eyes were frozen cold and hard as stones. . . . The shape of her coat lay dusted in the snow where she'd dropped it and she wore only a white dress and she hung among the bare gray poles of the winter trees with her head bowed and her hands turned slightly outward like those of certain ecumenical statues whose attitude asks that their history be considered. That the deep foundation of the world be considered where it has its being in the sorrow of her creatures.* (*TP*, 3)

FIGURE 3. Statue of the Virgin Mary.
Adobe Stock.

There is a beauty in the description that is not solely the more familiar sense of the beauty of the recently deceased. The quietness in the prose matches the solemnity of the scene. The hanging body has "her hands turned slightly outward like those of certain ecumenical statues." This depiction invokes the Catholic iconography with which McCarthy was so familiar, growing up as part of the community of the Church of the Immaculate Conception in Knoxville, Tennessee.[15] The frozen eyes that are as hard as stones and her white dress further suggest the figure of the Virgin Mary so prominent in marble statuary (see fig. 3 for an example of the "ecumenical pose"). Once again, the body is linked with nature in a tender description: "she hung among the bare gray poles of the winter trees."

Skilled Labor and the Tender Craft of Language

One of the earliest and consistent topics of interest in McCarthy studies has been McCarthy's admiration for and depiction of the intricacies of expertly performed manual labor. Scholars from Jay Ellis to Robert Brinkmeyer and Federico Bellini and most recently Lydia Cooper have explored in detail the attention that labor expertise commands in McCarthy's novels,[16] what Brinkmeyer defines as the combination of thinking and making that leads to "meaningful work." For Brinkmeyer, this work has the ability to sustain humans and to confront the hopelessness so often found in McCarthy's novels: "Small acts of valor, derived from and nurtured by a strict dedication to the rituals of work and craft, are the acts of McCarthy's heroes, those who keep their humanity alive and pass it along to others, holding back, at least for a while, the darkness of the coming days."[17] This kind of work in McCarthy's novels often constitutes a craftsmanship that is meant to be passed on, but that is, in Cooper's words, "vanishing." Representing this perspective particularly well are Ben Telfair's comments about stonemasonry in *The Stonemason*: "True masonry is not held together by cement but by gravity. That is to say, by the warp of the world. By the stuff of creation itself. The keystone that locks the arch is pressed in place by the thumb of God" (9–10). Or we can think of the blacksmith explaining his skill to Lester in *Child of God*: "You want to keep your fire high. . . . Three or four inches above the tuyer iron. You want to lay a clean fire with good coal that's not laid out in the sun. . . . Not too fast. . . . Slow. That's how ye heat. Watch ye colors. If she chance to get white she's ruint. There she comes now" (71–72). We can think also of the Judge's creation of gunpowder formed out of the materials around him in the hills of *Blood Meridian* and John Grady's expertise in all things related to the ranch and horse training in *All the Pretty Horses*.

While keeping this idea of craft and "meaningful work" in play, I'd like to shift the register a bit and talk about the term in a way that will be especially familiar to creative writers and those in English departments—the "craft" of language. Language serves for McCarthy a strikingly similar function as the expert craft of the skilled laborer. This vantage point gives the reader an understanding of the privileging of language that is being exhibited in many of McCarthy's passages. This language I suggest provides, again borrowing from Brinkmeyer's thoughts on craftsmanship, a "holding back at least for a while the darkness" so prevalent in McCarthy's fiction. In essence, I am arguing that McCarthy's language becomes a refuge, even in books where there is no physical or spiritual refuge to be found.

I'd like to once again return to the linguistic appreciation of craft in McCarthy's most famous novel, *The Road*. Toward the end of the novel, the father and the boy finally make it to the ocean, and devastatingly but also predictably, they encounter the same gray, dead world they have been traveling through. Looking for survival items—weapons, food, clothing—the man rummages through a boat wrecked on the coastline and stumbles on an object decidedly less useful at this moment, a marine sextant. He finds its box with leather straps and opens it: "Inside was a brass sextant, possibly a hundred years old. He lifted it from the fitted case and held it in his hands. Struck by the *beauty* of it. The brass was dull and there were patches of green on it that took the form of another hand that once had held it but otherwise it was *perfect*. He wiped the verdigris from the plate at the base. Hezzanith, London. He held it to his eye and turned the wheel. It was the first thing he'd seen in a long time that stirred him. He held it in his hand and then he fitted it back into the blue baize lining of its case and closed the lid and snapped the latches shut and set it back in the locker and closed the door" (TR, 227–28; emphases added). The "blue baize lining" perhaps reminds the reader of the interior lining of a coffin, and the man chooses to leave the sextant behind, almost as a sepulcher or memorial to the lost beauty of a vanished world.

Much like the passage with Ballard dying in the cave, the scene is described with preciousness, with care, with tenderness. McCarthy's use of the word "beauty" to describe the sextant is worth noting in this novel devoid of visual beauty. The word is only used four times in the entire novel, and the other three are connected in the father's eyes to the "strange" beauty of his sleeping boy, a fragile beauty that doesn't belong in the present world. So the sextant's beauty here is a recognition of the craftmanship that in this world is only equaled by his son's innocence. It is here a testament to the well-executed craft—McCarthy goes so far as to provide the name of an actual model and patent, "Hezzanith." The man recognizes and gives acknowledgment to its maker. The sextant in this moment seems incapable of "holding back the darkness," as Brinkmeyer sees in McCarthy's descriptions of craftmanship elsewhere, but McCarthy's description of it carries meaning nonetheless. In the novel's world, where everything is ruined, there is refuge in the craft of description, the tender evocation of an item that is irrelevant to the postapocalyptic story being told, but beautiful nonetheless. It is the beauty of creation, akin to the combination of carefully chosen words, that somehow buoys us up, to borrow from McCarthy's language elsewhere.[18]

At times, the importance of craft is emphasized through its desecration or lack of appreciation, such as when Lester Ballard in *Child of God* fails to acknowledge the skill involved in the blacksmith's sharpening of an axe blade. "Do what?" Lester hilariously replies after the blacksmith asks if he thinks he could now repair an axe after watching his example. It is emphasized again when Brown in *Blood Meridian* wants to saw off the barrels of an elegantly crafted gun. After Brown asks the farrier to saw off the barrels to make it better for close-range fighting, the farrier evaluates the construction of the weapon in great detail: "The man took the gun and held it in his hands. There was a raised center rib between the barrels and inlaid in gold the maker's name, London. There were two platinum bands in the patent breech and the locks and the hammers were chased with scrollwork cut deeply in the steel and there were partridges engraved at either end of the maker's name there. The purple barrels were welded up from triple skelps and the hammered iron and steel bore a watered figure like the markings of some alien and antique serpent, rare and beautiful and lethal." As with the sextant, McCarthy uses the idea of beauty as the guiding principle in the description of the gun and gives credit to its creator, mentioning twice the name of the maker. In what is McCarthy's most violent novel, the farrier refuses to desecrate this beauty, saying, "You can't pay me to butcher that there gun" (*BM*, 265–67). Brown is undeterred and the farrier has to flee the shop to save his life before Brown does the desecration himself.

The sense of the value in and appreciation for the craft in this example can be usefully compared to another description of a coveted gun in McCarthy's writing, that of sharpshooter Lester Ballard. Lester values his gun tremendously; he worked for a wage only long enough to purchase the gun and takes great pride in his ability to use it. However, in this pride, the gun is reduced to its function, its role as a tool. Lester is oblivious to the craftmanship of its making, only caring about its performance. As a result, McCarthy's description of Lester's interaction with his gun is markedly different from the description of the farrier in *Blood Meridian*: "He sits and dries the rifle and ejects the shells into his lap and dries them and wipes the action and oils it and oils the receiver and the barrel and the magazine and the level and reloads the rifle and levers a shell into the chamber and lets the hammer down and lays the rifle on the floor beside him" (*CofG*, 66–67). Lester cares *for* the gun, but seems to care very little *about* it, and McCarthy narrates accordingly, using a sentence structure that is repetitive, numbing, and without variation or creativity—subject-verb-object.

In *The Passenger*, McCarthy's interest in the expertise of craft takes on a more personal note and appears most notably when Bobby visits Wartburg and listens to his grandmother recount the family's history. We learn from Granellen that her grandfather and uncle built a house in Anderson County in 1872. Both Granellen's and Alicia's versions of this house construction are filled with McCarthy's attention to craft that runs throughout his career. Granellen states, "I don't know how they knew to do what they done, Bobby. I want to say that they could of done anything. . . . That house was the most beautiful house I ever saw. Ever floor in it was solid walnut and some of them boards was close to three foot wide. All of it hand planed. All of it at the bottom of a lake" (*TP*, 173–74).

Alicia in *Stella Maris* offers a similar version of the story: "I've seen photographs of [the house] and it was quite beautiful. They'd never built a house before. I'm not sure they'd ever even seen one built. What if they could have seen eighty years into the future? That's not very long. The simplest undertaking is predicated upon a future that has no warrant" (71). We can hear in Alicia's story echoes of Sheriff Bell in *No Country* and the father in *The Road* in this question about the role of craft and beauty in a world that has outlived a belief in its future. There is a preciousness in the language used to describe these crafted things:[19] the exquisite gun, the painstakingly erected house, the "perfect" sextant.

Before moving on to the next narrative mode I will discuss, the biblical mode, I would like to look at one last moment of tenderness briefly. Early in *The Road*, before the man and his son have reached the shore and the father has found the sextant, he remembers stumbling across the charred ruins of a library where blackened books lay in pools of water: "Some rage at the lies arranged in their thousands row on row. He picked up one of the books and thumbed through the heavy bloated pages. He'd not have thought the value of the smallest thing predicated on a world to come. It surprised him. That the space which these things occupied was itself an expectation. He let the book fall and took a last look around and made his way out into the cold gray light" (187). As we have seen with the sextant and the house, it is the belief in the "world to come" that surprises here, the dedication to the promise of the future. However, unlike the description of the sextant, we see no valuing of craft here, no attention to the beauty of the books or even the memorialized stories therein.

The difference here, I believe, is that tenderness is not reserved for showy libraries or books on display, just as craft is not evidenced only in the Sistine Chapel and royal forges. McCarthy's refuge of language is not literary in the stuffy sense of the notion of "high literature" and not about epic productions or aspirations of fame, although surely he has those as well. Instead, I have argued here that it is in the quiet and tender art of words in which McCarthy finds solace and hope, in the well-turned phrase, the pursuit of the "perfect" sentence that is simultaneously brazen and modest.

Language from on High: The Biblical Mode

If the reader discovers a surprising amount of tenderness in McCarthy's writing, there is in it so much Judeo-Christian iconography and language that we might place his work firmly within what Flannery O'Connor famously termed "the Christ-haunted South."[20] We see examples from *Child of God* with the line that first describes the protagonist Lester Ballard, "a child of God much like yourself perhaps" (4). There is the consistent and consistently submerged Catholic ritual and morality in *Suttree*, and the figures of the "ex-priest" Tobin and the devil-like Judge debating good and evil in *Blood Meridian*. We see the religious language of redemption in *The Road*, where the narrator characterizes a simple snowflake melting in the boy's hand as being "like the last host of christendom" (16) and the "ecumenical pose" of the hanged body in *The Passenger* discussed above (3). McCarthy describes nonreligious characters as "penitents" more than once as he invokes and defamiliarizes religious traditions, such as in *All the Pretty Horses*, when he describes John Grady leaving the town in which he was imprisoned "as if he were some newfound evangelical being" (217) or in *The Crossing*, where "a trinity" of bullet holes transform in a man's chest "in so perfect an isoscelian stigmata" (363).

Not surprisingly, then, there have been many superb studies that consider the proliferation of religious allusion and belief in McCarthy's work, with Lydia Cooper, Marcel DeCoste, Steven Frye, Alan Noble, and Richard Walsh serving as a few scholars who have explored fruitfully this complex concern in McCarthy's fiction. These conversations often consider whether we should understand McCarthy's work as essentially nihilistic or as sustained by a moral order and the possibilities of redemption or hope.[21] This line of inquiry enriches how we think about McCarthy's fiction, and these scholars have done an admirable job turning our attention to the ways in which he engages the Bible and religious/moral thought.

My notion of the *biblical mode* does something different. Rather than focusing on the religious implications of McCarthy's works, I am turning attention to his use of *biblical rhythms, language, and rhetoric* in his fiction, a stylistic tendency in which the use of a seemingly religious tone or register within the text often feels out of step with his barren landscapes and directionless characters. This mode also often appears in places that are seemingly removed from more immediate considerations of morality or belief that occur elsewhere in the novels. So it is a *mode*, I am suggesting, that is used to construct a feeling, rather than a *means* of orienting us to the metaphysical, or even the ethical.

Robert Alter has written convincingly of the echoes of the King James Version (KJV) of the Bible in *The Road*, seeing McCarthy's use of "paratactic terseness" and more specifically noun phrases in place of full sentences as creating a "hammering" effect that one can find modeled in the KJV.[22] For Alter, the accretion of noun phrases without conjunction or subordination and without hierarchical relationship characterizes McCarthy's language in *The Road*. Let me quote quickly a passage from that novel that Alter sees as particularly resonant of the KJV, so we can see what he is getting at: "In those first years the roads were peopled with refugees shrouded up in their clothing. Wearing masks and goggles, sitting in their rags by the side of the road like ruined aviators. Their barrows heaped with shoddy. Towing wagons or cars. Their eyes bright in their skulls. Creedless shells of men tottering down the causeways like migrants in a fever land. The frailty of everything revealed at last. Old and troubling issues resolved into nothingness and night" (TR, 28). For Alter, this passage, and McCarthy's borrowing of the tone of the Bible more generally, uses syntax in a way that "communicates a sense of truncation." And he sees this paratactic truncation as being crafted by McCarthy "to a purpose that is altogether antithetical to that of the Bible," in short to deny foundational meaning, rather than provide it.[23]

Alter's work is influential to my thinking here, and I share with him the belief that we should be thinking of the King James translation of the Hebrew Bible in this context, rather than what we might expect as the heightened language of apocalypse of the book of Revelation. Even so, instead of looking for strict biblical parallels or phrasing or meaning, I want to borrow from and adapt what Dawn Coleman has termed the "sermonic voice" in antebellum literature. For Coleman, the sermonic voice can be found in prominent sermons in the literature (such as Dimmesdale's Election Day sermon in *The Scarlet Letter* or the Jonah sermon in *Moby Dick*), but it can also, more interestingly for my purposes, be found in "novelistic speech that mimics *the sound* of the sermon."[24] It is this second option, a narrative voice that temporarily adopts a sermonic or biblical sound, that can help us understand stylistic elements of the biblical mode in McCarthy's fiction. Where Coleman locates the sermonic voice in moments in nineteenth-century literature that often come across by today's standards as "preachy," I am interested in the fact that the heightened language and sermonic rhythms in McCarthy often appear where we might least expect to find such stylistic attributes, at times precisely where he seems to be avoiding any preachy statements about meaning and the imperatives of living at all. This sermonic mode can be found in many of McCarthy's novels, most notably *Outer Dark*, *Child of God*, *Suttree*, *The Road*, and *The Passenger*. There is, in particular, an affective alignment in McCarthy's creative vision between the East Tennessee mountains/mountain folk (including his imaginative return to this region in *The Road* and *The Passenger*) and the King James Version of the Hebrew Bible. This tone creates a feeling of the region being premodern, as strange and apart from the rest of the developing nation.

To explore this concept more fully I will focus on one novel, *Outer Dark*, in depth, as this early novel most perfectly captures the biblical mode. The connection between a biblical tone and the subject matter of McCarthy's second book has been articulated since the novel first appeared in 1968. One early reviewer noted the novel's "sub-biblical rhetoric" that detracted from the "better things" of the book.[25] *Outer Dark* begins with the protagonist Culla dreaming about a prophet, and the scene is painted with an apocalyptic and religious linguistic brush: "The sun hung on the cusp of the *eclipse*," opines McCarthy's narrator, "and the prophet spoke to them. This hour the sun would darken and all the *souls* would be cured of their *afflictions* before it appeared again. And the dreamer himself was caught up among the *supplicants* and when they had been *blessed* and the sun begun to blacken *he did push forward* and hold up his hand and call out" (5; emphases added). While this passage feels pregnant with meaning and full of sermonic qualities, it is unclear what we are to make of it, especially when we subsequently learn that Culla isn't at all familiar with the Bible, doesn't seem especially religious-minded, at least as far as we can tell, and doesn't even know what "a Jew" is.[26] Nor does the moment seem to represent a preachy authorial moment that Coleman has in mind with her term "sermonic voice." This passage cannot be said to represent the insights of the character Culla or even a consistent narrator. One could argue that it reveals Culla's internalized guilt, but the language of the passage so distances us from Culla that such a reading becomes hard to maintain. Instead of these possibilities, I suggest McCarthy uses this mode to present a grim strangeness to the events of the story, a form of defamiliarization that unsettles the reader rather than offering clarifying details. As many scholars have commented, McCarthy establishes a gothic fable mood in this novel, and the biblical mode is a large part of what gives the novel its otherworldly tone. Toward the end of this dream, the prophet descries, "I think that perhaps you will be cured" (*OD*, 5). I love this line. Here McCarthy employs one of his favorite words—perhaps—that suggests an uncertainty of utterance that is completely at odds with the assuredness of prophecy. McCarthy's use of the hedging term "perhaps" appears in other moments of supposed religious revelation in McCarthy's work—in *Suttree*, for example, when Suttree is watching his son's funeral in despair and shame and the narrator comments, "Perhaps he addressed his God" (154), or when Suttree is later being treated in the emergency room after a bar fight: "Perhaps the wrath of God after all" (188).

In a scene very soon after this opening dream in *Outer Dark*, McCarthy writes of Culla's unintentional return (after he loses his direction) to the baby he has just abandoned: "As [Culla] lay there a far crack of lightning went bluely down the sky and bequeathed him in an embryonic bird's first fissured vision of the world (and transpiring instant and outrageous from dark to dark) a final view of the grotto and the shapeless white plasm struggling upon the rich and incunabular moss like a lank swamp hare." This mouthful is followed by an even more ponderous sentence centered around the baby's crying: "It howled execration upon the dim camarine world of its nativity wail on wail while he lay there gibbering with palsied jawhasps, his hands putting back the night like some witless paraclete beleaguered with all limbo's clamor" (*OD*, 17–18). This passage has the accretion of detail, the kind of paratactic building and imagistic hammering that Alter ties to the King James Bible. It is also replete with religious imagery (crack of lightning, nativity, paraclete, limbo's clamor, grotto, bequeathed vision). But this passage, with its hypereducated, archaic language and abstract metaphors, also feels particularly disconnected from Culla's mind and doesn't offer a whole lot of insight into his character. It feels quite a bit different from something like Faulkner's interior stream of consciousness of his less-educated characters, seen mostly clearly in a text like *As I Lay Dying*. These kinds of interior moments in Faulkner's texts rely on language that the characters do not possess and could not understand, but are meant to reflect a more complicated, conflicted, and interior sense of their perspectives and struggles, perhaps their pre- or sublinguistic consciousness.

McCarthy's disorienting imagery in this passage about Culla—lightning as "an embryonic bird's first vision" or the seemingly contradictory phrase "witless paraclete"—only distances us from his struggles and internalized guilt. Instead, this language in *Outer Dark* serves to set a mood. It serves to create an otherworldly (or perhaps earlier worldly) tone more than add to character development. The echoes of the King James Bible and its "old-fashioned" language resound,[27] and McCarthy's rural mountain scenes are imbued with this feeling of a strange pastness. At the novel's conclusion, Culla is left to wander the swamp alone and runs into a blind man. After his waving to the departing man "in inane farewell," we get this description of Culla and the swamp: "Before him stretched a spectral waste out of which reared only the naked trees in attitudes of agony and dimly hominoid like figures in a landscape of the damned. A faintly smoking garden of the dead that tended away to the earth's curve. He tried his foot in the mire before him and it rose in a vulvate welt claggy and sucking. . . . A stale wind blew from this desolation and the marsh reeds and black ferns among which he stood clashed softly like things chained" (*OD*, 242).

At the novel's end, the blind man tells the story of a "healin'" preacher who wanted to cure "everbody." "But," he concludes, "they's darksome ways afoot in this world and it may be he weren't no true preacher" (*OD*, 241). After we hear this speech, we might be reminded of another "prophet," the blind man Ely in *The Road*, whose message to the wandering father seems not dissimilar from that offered above to the "gracelorn" Culla.

Once again, one could enter in a metaphysical discussion of whether the book or this passage offers meaning or evacuates meaning, and this is a worthwhile discussion. However, I'm arguing here that the biblical mode and style of these passages is not where McCarthy makes his intervention in this discussion. Instead, he uses these moments to create a mood, dark and foreboding, and an Old Testament sense of covenant between person and region, between author and reader. As Thomas Lask wrote in his 1968 *New York Times* review of the novel, and which Random House uses as a blurb on the novel's cover, "Cormac McCarthy's second novel, *The Outer Dark*, combines the mythic and the actual in a perfectly executed work of the imagination. He has made the fabulous real, the ordinary mysterious." I would argue that the biblical mode plays as large of a part in establishing this mood as does following the Triune's murderous rampage, Culla's blind wandering, and Rinthy's tireless, if directionless, searching for her child. It is at the level of language where this mode crystalizes, rather than the horrific actions and scenes of the novel.

Even the book's title is a shortening of the King James Bible's translation of the place for those excluded from heaven as "outer darkness." The Gospel of Matthew tells the story of the Centurion's faith and Jesus's response as follows:

> For I am a man under authority, having soldiers under me: and I say to this man, Go, and he goeth; and to another, Come, and he cometh; and to my servant, Do this, and he doeth it. / When Jesus heard it, he marvelled, and said to them that followed, Verily I say unto you, I have not found so great faith, no, not in Israel. / And I say unto you, That many shall come from the east and west, and shall sit down with Abraham, and Isaac, and Jacob, in the kingdom of heaven. / But the children of the kingdom shall be cast out into *outer darkness*: there shall be weeping and gnashing of teeth.[28]

The incorporation of an older, biblical style of writing that echoes the King James Bible develops an atmosphere, a feeling of an ancient culture that is out of step with modern life, not just left behind but differently oriented. This fundamental disconnect, which can contain a moral and ethical component, more often feels stylistic, creating a feeling of an Appalachia that is at times mythic, at others cruelly insular, and most often living in an older time lost to the rest of the world. Lask writes in the same review I quoted above, "Mr. McCarthy has . . . not merely written a gothic tale. The shadows and dark corners are not only there for atmosphere. A stubborn, impenetrable society lives in this book, one we hoped had long since disappeared. And in it are acted out the old patterns of crime, punishment and sacrifice."[29] This atmosphere becomes a trope that McCarthy consistently uses to describe his settings and communities in his Tennessee period. Ironically, then, or perhaps predictably, when we see him move beyond this geography to the American West, his attention turns to the unrecoverable past and the endless seeking of it.

Spiritual Searching and the Dramatic Mode

I have argued above through an examination of McCarthy's tender language and biblical language that one of McCarthy's most defining attributes as an author is his tendency to write in different modes, and how his switching of tone, word choice, feeling, and proximity to his characters are some of the defining attributes of his literary style. This section will offer that when he explores concerns of faith and belief in extended and in-depth treatments, McCarthy often moves away from the traditional novel format and drifts toward the territory of drama. *The Stonemason* is McCarthy's only published play. *The Sunset Limited* is perhaps a play, but there seemed to be some doubts and this text was termed "a novel in dramatic form."[30] Both of these dramatic pieces are defined by what John Cant calls McCarthy's "grappling with the limitations of theatrical realism," and by some standards they barely feel like plays at all. Peter Josyph has labeled *The Stonemason* a "kind of anti-play" and others have deemed it unperformable. Similarly, many scholars have commented on the ways in which *The Sunset Limited* defies dramatic conventions and falls apart as a conventional play, especially considering the fact that the entire novel/play consists almost entirely of two characters speaking to one another in one room. Stacey Peebles mentions in her book on McCarthy and performance that McCarthy considered drama "the hardest to write." Add to that that McCarthy admitted to Oprah Winfrey that he found women "tough" to write.[31] One wonders, then, what McCarthy is up to with his final novel, *Stella Maris*, and his decision to write the entire book as a dramatic dialogue with a brilliant and complicated woman as the protagonist. Maybe he was looking for one last literary challenge in a career of challenging book topics and perspectives.

One reason McCarthy might have been drawn to drama is that he is simply great at writing dialogue. Think of the conversations between Lester and the townsfolk in *Child of God*, the humorous conversation of the drunken compatriots in *Suttree*, the back and forth between John Grady, Lacey, and Blevins in *All the Pretty Horses*, the unsettling interactions between the Judge and his gang in *Blood Meridian*, Chigurh's interaction with everyone else in *No Country for Old Men*, or the heartbreaking conversations between the father and the son in *The Road*. It is interesting that while dialogue seems to come somewhat naturally to McCarthy, he sees drama as being difficult. What I suggest here gives us a way to approach and perhaps even resolve this seeming contradiction. In short, McCarthy is drawn to the dramatic format because it allows him a unique if challenging medium through which to explore issues of belief/faith/morality. Dialogues by nature contain the ability to present multiple perspectives and opinions, and this fact fits well with McCarthy's approach to this subject matter. What I am calling the *dramatic mode* that we see in these plays and in *Stella Maris* resonates with contemporary discussions in postsecular studies; that is to say in ways that legitimize ambivalence, uncertainty, and doubt but still hold onto the mysterious and the spiritual. Rather than a true exchange of competing ideas or a coming to some sort of resolution or moral perspective that informs classical forms of drama, dialogue in McCarthy's dramatic texts often provides very little resolution or agreement, while remaining committed to the struggle. McCarthy uses the dramatic mode to explore the moral and ethical dimensions of a familiar dynamic in his work—the way modernity complicates the values of premodern existence.[32] It is premodern or, more fittingly, timeless values that McCarthy consistently returns to, and these values are often presented as being in conflict with or jeopardized by modern realities.

The Stonemason, The Sunset Limited, and the Unstageable Play

The Stonemason, McCarthy's first published foray into drama, is a five-act play known as much for its abstract and impossible stage directions as for its content or performance. These stage directions ask the performers to consider the play as an "artifact of history" and mention the central character's "agenda which centers upon his own exoneration, and his own salvation." They also mention mysteriously that "the audience may perhaps be also a jury" (*Stone*, 6). In a precursor to his mathematics-obsessed final two novels, McCarthy invokes in the opening stage directions the German mathematician and physicist Carl Friedrich Gauss, to whom McCarthy attributes the dictum: "Go forward and faith will come to you."[33] This attribution is troubled by the fact that no evidence of such a quote by Gauss exists. Perhaps McCarthy included a misattributed quote to shake the foundations of the text to come (a common goal for him). Or perhaps he had in mind Gauss's quote about the power of explanation and misremembered its details: "It is not knowledge, but the act of learning, not possession but the act of getting there, which grants the greatest enjoyment. When I have clarified and exhausted a subject, then I turn away from it, in order to go into darkness again; the never satisfied man is so strange if he has completed a structure, then it is not in order to dwell in it peacefully, but in order to begin another. I imagine the world conqueror must feel thus, who, after one kingdom is scarcely conquered, stretched out his arms for others."[34]

In line with this misattribution or misquoting, the opening directions in *The Stonemason* seem to obfuscate as much as bring into focus the play's center. McCarthy later calls bafflingly in the stage directions for a "partial wall made of *actual stone*" and includes instructions for a real dog to act on dramatic cues—"There is a small dog sleeping by the stove and it looks up." He also includes odd details in the directions that aren't commented on in the play and aren't noticeable to the audience, such as the fact that the character Big Ben "has on three or four very expensive rings that he wears when not working" (*Stone*, 9, 12, 24–25, 14).[35] All of these interruptive directions occur in the first two scenes of the play, when dramatists traditionally attempt to build a foundation of context and understanding before moving forward.

The play gains some constancy as the character of Ben speaks. Unlike traditional plays, the character of Ben is represented by two actors—one who speaks from the side of the stage and talks behind a lectern, while the other Ben interacts with the rest of the cast. In the first stage direction, McCarthy draws a strict line between these two portions of the play, explaining that the action and dialogue at the center is "the staged drama," whereas Ben's contribution is "the monologue—or chautauqua—which Ben delivers from the podium" (*Stone*, 6). The term chautauqua is telling here, as it harkens back to the pre-twentieth-century speaking and education circuit with nondenominational Christian foundations. The topics of chautauquas often centered around moral concerns and notions of spiritual or ethical improvement. In *The Stonemason*, the audience is initially encouraged to take Ben's monologues as offering such commentary. Take, for instance, his early commentary on the dying masonry trade:

> For true masonry is not held together by cement but by gravity. That is to say, by the warp of the world. By the stuff of creation itself. The keystone that locks the arch is pressed in place by the thumb of God.... [My grandfather] talks to me about stone in a different way from my father. ... He always watched my eyes to see if I understood. Or to see if I cared. I cared very much. I do now. According to the gospel of the true mason God has laid the stones in the earth for men to use and he has laid them in their bedding places to show the mason how his own work must go. (*Stone*, 9–10)

As the play unfolds, masonry becomes, for Ben, evidence not only of God's laws enacted on the planet but also of the ability to understand this connection that is lost in the modern world: "In form and design and scale and structure and proportion I've yet to see an example of the old work that was not perfectly executed.... The beauty of the stonework is simply a reflection of the purity of the mason's intention.... But that the craft of stonemasonry should be allowed to vanish from this world is just not negotiable for me" (*Stone*, 91). Throughout the entire play, the Ben who offers the chautauquas links masonry with a type of transcendent and eternal meaning and rightness. He opines toward the play's end that "in the concept of a day's work [in masonry] is rhythm and pace and wholeness. And truth and justice and peace of mind" (*Stone*, 96).

For most of the play, the audience trusts the Ben at the lectern and sees him as a figure functioning like a singular member of a Greek chorus, a character that moors the action and informs the audience how to understand the drama, how to negotiate the moral dilemmas offered therein. I have argued elsewhere that this is a trope McCarthy has used before in *Child of God*, where the community chapters that interrupt Lester's story function as a type of inside-out Greek chorus.[36] As the play escalates toward its final act, Ben begins to lose precisely these moorings. His monologues are suddenly riddled with doubt: "I lost my way. I'd thought by my labors to stand outside that true bend of gravity which is the world's pain" (*Stone*, 111). He dreams that he has been judged harshly by God "and I stood in the full folly of my own righteousness" (*Stone*, 112). The second Ben, the character that interacts with the rest of the cast, also begins to crack. He interacts with his father, Big Ben, in ways that contribute to his father's suicide. He hides his nephew Soldier's death by heroin overdose from both his partner, Maven, and his sister (and Soldier's mother) Carlotta. At the play's conclusion, Ben is consumed with doubt and eviscerated by his family for his immoral handling of Soldier's death. "I thought you were different, Ben," says Carlotta. "So did I," replies a broken Ben (*Stone*, 130).

The Stonemason concludes with the deceased Papaw, who has "materialized out of the fog upstage," and Ben sees him not as a mason in touch with the eternal. Rather, "he was just a man, naked and alone in the universe, and he was not afraid and I wept with a joy and a sadness I'd never known. . . . I prayed as men must have prayed ten thousand years ago to their dead kin for guidance and I knew that he would guide me all my days and that he would not fail me, not fail me, not ever fail me" (*Stone*, 132–33). McCarthy leans on the seeming constancy of the dramatic monologue and the moral certainty of the chautauqua to ground this play about spiritual belief and the transcendent links between the labor of masonry and what is good and true and beautiful in the world. By the end, however, this truth has eroded for Ben and the drama becomes about the uncertainty of life and the difficulties in finding stable meaning in the world at all. Ben's final monologue is saturated with an uncertainty that would be right at home in Hamlet's most famous soliloquy. Whereas classical drama often moves from chaos and uncertainty to order and certainty, *The Stonemason* reverses this order and leaves the audience by the end grasping for meaning in the drama or perhaps determined to find this meaning in the naked imperfections within humanity that have stretched back for "tens of thousands of years."

Like *The Stonemason*, *The Sunset Limited* uses the dramatic mode to probe deeply into concerns of spiritual worth and the meaning of life. This "novel in dramatic form" pits an academic atheist against a devout Christian in a battle between the justification for suicide embraced by the atheist named

White, who is also racially white, and the dissuasion offered by the Black evangelical Christian named Black. The positions of White and Black become very entrenched in this drama, even as they come to understand each other as humans. In his *New York Times* review of the film version of the play starring Samuel L. Jackson and Tommy Lee Jones, Mike Hale famously called the text "Mr. McCarthy's dorm-room argument masquerading as a drama."[37] While this comment may resonate for some readers, it misses the ways in which McCarthy seeks to undermine or undo the rigid positions that these two characters initially seem to represent. The claustrophobic setting, lack of movement, and plotless "action" become the drama's power.[38]

In a style that foreshadows McCarthy's final novel, *Stella Maris*, the exchanges between Black and White are notable for the brevity of each statement and the lack of interiority that these statements reveal. There are quick back-and-forth exchanges that demonstrate the characters' facility with language but little about their interior motivations. We see Black trying to draw out White and get him in linguistic and logical knots, what Black calls his "trick bag."

> BLACK: Are you hungry? I can come back to this. I aint goin to lose my place.
> WHITE: I'm all right. Go ahead.
> BLACK: If you was to hand a drunk a drink and tell him he really dont want it what do you reckon he'd say?
> WHITE: I think I know what he'd say.
> BLACK: Sure you do. But you'd still be right.
> WHITE: About him not really wanting it.
> BLACK: Yes. Because what he really wants he cant get. Or he thinks he cant get it. So what he really dont want he cant get enough of.
> WHITE: So what is it that he really wants.
> BLACK: You know what he really wants.
> WHITE: No I dont.
> BLACK: Yeah you do.
> WHITE: No I dont.
> BLACK: Hm.

WHITE: Hm what.
BLACK: You a hard case, Professor.
WHITE: You're not exactly a day at the beach yourself.
BLACK: You dont know what he wants.
WHITE: No. I do not.
BLACK: He wants what everbody wants.
WHITE: And this is?
BLACK: He wants to be loved by God.
WHITE: I dont want to be loved by God.
BLACK: I love that. (*SL*, 58–60)

In this exchange, Black functions as a therapist of sorts or a spiritual mentor, asking questions to keep White engaged, and like the actual psychologist in *Stella Maris*, he recognizes when White is getting exhausted and sees if he wants to pause the conversation. Black's comments "Are you hungry? I can come back to this" in this exchange mirror the frequent repetition of "Do you want to take a break?" in *Stella Maris*. In both texts, the sparseness and rapidity of the exchanges and the lack of interior or expository commentary build tension. At times, it is the audience, as much as the conversant, who might call for a break.

As the drama crawls toward its conclusion, White begins speaking in longer stretches and his comments begin to feel like sculpted and rehearsed speeches. The realistic and minimalist exchanges give way to Shakespearean soliloquys, and White, for the first time, gains the rhetorical advantage.

WHITE: (*Coldly*) I dont believe in God. Can you understand that? Look around you man. Cant you see? The clamor and din of those in torment has to be the sound most pleasing to his ear. And I loathe these discussions. The argument of the village atheist whose single passion is to revile endlessly that which he denies the existence of in the first place. Your fellowship is a fellowship of pain and nothing more. And if that pain were actually collective instead of simply reiterative then the sheer weight of it would drag the world from the walls of the universe and send it crashing and burning through whatever it might yet be capable of engendering until it was not even ash. And justice? Brotherhood? Eternal life? Good god, man. (SL, 137)

What began as a more-or-less friendly, or at least cordial, exchange between very different people devolves into what feels like a treatise. Perhaps this black-and-white (pun intended here and, I think, in McCarthy's naming of the characters) presentation of belief is what Hale was responding to when he likened the play to a dorm-room argument. But this comment feels condescending toward both McCarthy and college students. These college conversations are often vital and tense and formative, precisely because your dorm roommate is different than anyone you have ever met, and so the exchange of ideas is awkward yet crucial to growth. A lazy reading of this play would suggest White "wins," as he gets the last word and presumably goes on to commit suicide, as he originally intended to do right before the play's opening. Such a reading is informed by the critical tendency to align McCarthy and nihilism. In this interpretation, White becomes the voice for McCarthy.[39] But this feels too neat, too predictable. White's soliloquys do not convince anybody of anything and could be a sign of empty and showy academic rhetoric as much as the play's moral center. While White may leave Black speechless and is then free to go end his life, the reader is haunted not by his words but Black's final words to God: "He didn't mean them words. You know he didn't. You know he didn't. I don't understand what you sent me down there [to the subway station where White was about to jump before the action of the play] for. I don't understand it. If you wanted me to help him, how come you didn't give me the words" (SL, 141–42). In the end, it is White's manipulation of language that haunts Black, rather than any moral or ethical or rational position. It is the power of language from a different perspective.

Stella Maris and the Dialogic Novel

As mentioned above, the stage directions of *The Stonemason* confound directors and readers, suggesting the unperformability of the play. I think we might profitably think of the opening one-page hospital document that begins *Stella Maris* as a kind of similarly obtuse set of "stage directions" for the novel that establishes the scene for the reader but also calls into question the reliability of parts of the drama. The one paragraph intake report that serves as a prologue of sorts for the book reveals that the subject Alicia is "Jewish/Caucasian," possibly anorexic, a doctoral candidate, in possession of at least $40,000, and has previously been diagnosed as paranoid schizophrenic with a history of visual and auditory hallucinations. Most of this kind of information might plausibly be found on an intake report, but the detail about her having a plastic bag with hundred-dollar bills feels out of place, as does the first adjective used to describe Alicia in the report (apart from her ethnic background): She is described as "attractive" followed by the diagnosis of being possibly anorexic (*SM*, 3). The multiple instances of sexual assault and abuse of Alicia by psychiatric doctors at this very hospital we subsequently learn about further emphasize the tension this description establishes. During one exchange with her current psychological doctor, Alicia asks, "Are you trying to fuck me, Doctor?" This question may be somewhat mischievous, as it seeks to make Dr. Cohen uncomfortable and reverse the power dynamics of the conversation. But it is also important to remember that it is prompted by Cohen's asking if Alicia knows that she is "extremely good-looking." This comment brings us back to the description in the intake document of Alicia being "attractive," and she goes on to connect this question to the sexual assault committed by a previous clinician at the hospital (*SM*, 43). If this introductory document gives any actual direction, it suggests the mysterious aura of Alicia and the consistent ways she is sexualized, even by medical professionals during psychiatric treatment. It also creates a level of distrust between the narrator of this book (presumably Cohen after transcribing the conversation) and Alicia. The report and hospital staff seem intent on defining Alicia in ways that fail to capture her or even understand her basic motivations and values.

In many ways, the moments of interaction between Alicia and Cohen parallel stylistically the types of unresolved dialogue we encounter in McCarthy's earlier dramatic texts, *The Stonemason* and *Sunset Limited*. One way that McCarthy's dialogue enacts the feeling of ambiguity is that the conversations in *Stella* often feel misdirected or stunted. As was the case with White and Black in *The Sunset Limited*, neither Alicia or Cohen are exactly getting their way in the conversations; there is no magical synthesis or breakthrough.

> Good morning.
>> Good morning.
>> How are things going? You seem a bit somber.
>> Somber.
>> Do you have everything you need?
>> Could you be more specific?
>> Sorry. I guess I'm just asking if you're reasonably comfortable. If there's anything I can do for you.
>> Why don't we just get started.
>> I'm not just being polite.
>> All right. How about a pingpong net?
>> Do you play pingpong?
>> No.
>> The general rule is to try to minimize any possible opportunity for the patients to harm themselves. So you really have to be pretty scrupulous. No belts or ropes or anything like that. Glass, sharp objects.
>> Ergo stainless steel mirrors.
>> Yes.
>> Have you been finding a lot of patients dangling from pingpong nets?
>> No, but it's probably happened. Somewhere. How about something I might put a request for without making a lot of trouble.
>> No deal. It's nets or nothing.
>> Sorry. What should we talk about?
>> I don't know. (SM, 87–88)

This passage tells us a lot about the characters and their investments in the interaction. Alicia is at times bored and at other times mischievous, but generally polite. Cohen is, in this passage, somewhat considerate of Alicia's responses, but through the book he is often less so. Multiple times in the text he asks her if she needs a break (as Black does with White in *Sunset*), but at other times he pushes through her desire for a break, ignoring her wishes. At still other times, Cohen stops suddenly when *he* is upset or feels the discussion is off track.[40] It is important to remember that Cohen is not Alicia's therapist; rather, he is a clinician who is researching and writing about Alicia as a psychological study and is clearly working on a paper or book about her. As such, he needs some original material from their conversations, at times pursuing this material callously. Rather than seeing Alicia as a patient under Cohen's care, the reader must recall she is a research subject who has signed off on his recording of the interviews and publishing his findings. Given this complicated and complicating context, it is remarkable how much we can learn about the characters from these relatively stunted exchanges. I'm reminded of the attempts to stage *The Stonemason* and the actors saying that there isn't enough information or background for them to bring the characters to life: "I don't know how to turn this into a character with these words," claimed one exasperated actor. Looking at *Stella Maris*, it seems as if this is, rather than a failing (or perhaps alongside a failing), McCarthy's consistent approach to dramatic dialogue. The background and the real concerns are submerged beneath and revealed through the quotidian, as in Hemingway's iceberg theory of literary minimalism.[41]

Another aspect of dialogue that we can see being very attractive to McCarthy is its ability to contain ambiguity. When I was a graduate student in Chicago, I was in the same department as the rhetorician and composition scholar William Covino, who was at the time developing a theory of freshman composition that depended entirely on dialogue.[42] Students would begin by writing two-person dialogue, then three, and then four. What these students lost in the creation of formal essays, Covino contended, they gained in complexity of thought and argumentation. There is no uniform answer in these complex dialogic exchanges. Instead, the student wrestles with ambiguity and nuance. With *Stella Maris* we see a similar approach to the value of dialogue in the conversations about some of Alicia's most difficult feelings—her desire to take her own life, and, earlier, to marry and have sex with her brother. How is the reader supposed to feel about Alicia's conviction to take her life or her taboo attraction to her brother? Is Cohen compromised by studying her as a research subject, even as he feels a modicum of compassion for her?

Alicia begins a conversation about her attraction to her brother, Bobby, which for Cohen (and surely most readers) violates the incest taboo:

> I told him he should resign.
>
> >Resign?
> >Yes. Resign his brotherhood.
> >How would he do that?
>
> I don't know. Turn around three times and say I denounce this bond of blood.
>
> >And then marry you.
>
> And then marry me. Yes. Although you could say that the facts were a bit more raw than that.
>
> >Meaning you wanted to have sex with your brother?
>
> Meaning. (*SM*, 163)

As the conversation develops and Cohen becomes increasingly uncomfortable with the freedom with which Alicia discusses these feelings and her desire to transgress the taboo, she begins to dominate the exchange:

> I suppose I was shameless but then shame was not something I was really concerned with. . . . I hadn't known until that night [when Alicia made her feelings known to Bobby] that at its worst lust could be something close to anguish. . . . A friend once told me that those who choose a love that can never be fulfilled will be hounded by a rage that can never be extinguished.
>
> >Are you enraged?
>
> I don't know. I know that you can make a good case that all of human sorrow is grounded in injustice. And that sorrow is what is left when rage is expended and found to be impotent.
>
> >Why don't we have some tea? (*SM*, 164)

As with White and Black in *Sunset Limited*, where White gets the rhetorical advantage through extended soliloquys of despair toward the play's conclusion, Alicia's movement toward suicide is accompanied with an escalating rhetoric in her response to Cohen. As the reader is immersed in Alicia's isolation, desperation, and loneliness, the text almost makes the reader wish she and Bobby could have just run off together, as she desired, taboo be damned! Early in his career, McCarthy encouraged the reader's empathy for a necrophiliac in *Child of God*. Now, we are placed in a position to root for a passionate brother-sister love affair. While *Stella Maris* invites comparisons to the incestuous undertones of Quentin and Caddy in Faulkner's *Sound and the Fury*, the dynamic is actually quite different here. The incestuous tensions in *Sound and the Fury* are largely about masculine honor and the concept of aristocratic purity. In *Stella Maris* the incestuous longing seems about genuine human connection between two people who struggle to find meaning and connection in a world that makes such connection extraordinarily difficult. In perhaps the purest display of Alicia's raw confessions and true emotions, Cohen cuts off the conversation, asking abruptly about drinking tea, reminding the reader of Prufrock's famous line suggesting the banality behind "the taking of a toast and tea."[43]

As we also saw with his two previous dramatic works, McCarthy in this book of dialogue exhibits a remarkable ability to convey strong emotions through what feel like sterile and misdirected conversations. Take for example the final passage of the book, where Alicia reveals her fantasy to visit her family's ancestral Romania. Alicia begins:

> Mostly I didn't want anyone to know about it [her planned and imagined suicide in Romania].
> > That you died?
> > Yes.
> > But you didn't.
> > Die.
> > No. Go to Romania.
> > No. I didn't
> > All right. How serious was this plan?
> > Pretty serious. It was called Plan 2-A.
> > Why was it called Plan 2-A?
> > It just was. It was subtitled or not 2-B.
> > The trip was not?

> I was not. I thought that I would go to Romania and that when I got there I would go to some small town and buy secondhand clothes in the market.... Then I'd hike into the mountains. Stay off the road. Take no chances. Crossing the ancestral lands by foot.

Alicia continues this soliloquy with a fantasy of starving to death in a cave, only to have her bones carried away by an animal to be their "eucharist." She continues:

> And that would be my life. And I would be happy.
>   I think our time is up.
>   I know. Hold my hand.
>   Hold your hand?
>   Yes. I want you to.
>   All right. Why?
>   Because that's what people do when they're waiting for the end of something. (SM, 189–190)

This is a breathtaking end to this novel and to McCarthy's literary career. The ending feels open-ended in a way, but very closed too, when we pair it with the opening of *The Passenger*. We know Alicia is soon to commit suicide, just as White's departure in *The Sunset Limited* suggests the same conclusion.

This discussion with Cohen is technically referring to Alicia's desire to visit her ancestral homeland in Romania and remain there for her last days, but there are echoes in these final lines of McCarthy's childhood in the mountains of East Tennessee, of roaming the mountains south of Knoxville like John Wesley Rattner did in his first novel published nearly sixty years earlier. From this perspective, in a move only rivaled by The Beatles concluding their recording career with the song "The End," the final line of *Stella Maris*—"That's what people do when they're waiting for the end of something"—feel like a final statement for McCarthy's career as a whole, and a gesture toward the cyclical rhythms and concerns that came to define this career.

There are countless other places in McCarthy's sixteen published works where one could locate the tender, biblical, and dramatic modes, and there is certainly room for thinking about narrative modes in addition to those outlined here. In this chapter I have endeavored to explore McCarthy's commitment to a fearless and consistent experimentation with language. This experimentation grows out of McCarthy's enduring faith in and love of language. Language is precious, if not infallible, to him precisely because of its ability to bring to life for the reader startling scenes, breathtaking visions, and riveting characters. He is not concerned with directing the reader to a specific message or meaning so much as to engage them. For that reason, not every reader will digest the words in the exact same way, and this is especially true for passages with the unusual syntax and confusing allusion we often find in McCarthy's novels. No reader sees *Blood Meridian*'s Judge in the exact same way that their fellow reader will, nor what happened in "the jakes" at that novel's conclusion. Peter Mendelsund explains the power of words for the reader that resonates with how McCarthy works: "Words are effective not because of what they carry in them, but for their latent potential to unlock the accumulated experience of the reader. Words 'contain' meanings, but, more important, words potentiate meaning..." From this angle, the narrative modes I outline in this chapter say as much about my reading experience as they do about yours, but I hope that by calling attention to the experimental nature of McCarthy's language, this exploration can potentiate meaning in just such a way. What each reader sees in McCarthy's narrative remains their experience. To invoke Mendelsund once more, "Specificity and context add to the meaning and perhaps to the expressiveness of an image, but do not seem to add to the *vividness* of my experience of an image.... They help me to understand, but not to see."[44] And it is what we see and what we hear in McCarthy's language that draws us to and into his novels.

TWO

"Large Loose Baggy Monsters"
McCarthy's Epic Mode

Even from the very beginning of his writing career, as evidenced by his very distinctive first three books, McCarthy's writing was experimental and fearless. He played with a variety of the narrative modes outlined in chapter 1, and he blazed new paths in storytelling that gained him the reputation as a young writer to watch. In a blurb that was originally written for McCarthy's first novel, *The Orchard Keeper*, and that was reprinted on the cover of almost every one of McCarthy's early novels, Ralph Ellison wrote, "McCarthy is a writer to be read, to be admired, and quite honestly—envied." Even so, his early work felt as if it belonged firmly in the realm of regional fiction. It is not surprising that this time in his career is known as his "Tennessee period," and the books and writing style were often understood in relation to other southern writers, most often William Faulkner, with whom McCarthy shared an editor, Albert Erskine. The prose, while unique and at times breathtaking, was clearly recognizable in a regional vein. There were the frequent echoes of southern local color writing with its references to the oddness of the East Tennessee citizens, and descriptions of the uniqueness of the setting and language abound. When we get to McCarthy's fourth novel, *Suttree*, *bam!* Something has changed, and the difference jumps off the page from the very first sentences in the novel: "*Dear friend, now in the dusty clockless hours of the town when the streets lie black and steaming in the wake of the watertrucks and now when the drunk and the homeless have washed up in the lee of walls in alleys or abandoned lots and cats go forth high-*

shouldered and lean in the grim perimeters about, now in these sootblacked brick or cobbled corridors where lightwire shadows make a gothic harp of cellar doors no soul shall walk save you" (Sut, 3).

This chapter will consider this difference, the heightened language and cosmic scope that found its way into McCarthy's books beginning with *Suttree*. What I am calling the *epic mode* appears most often in his big middle-career novels—*Suttree*, *Blood Meridian*, and *The Crossing*—with a return to the mode in his penultimate novel, *The Passenger*. In these novels, McCarthy consciously invites comparison to other modern epic novels. These texts have moments that invoke the "high narrative voice" often associated with epics; they place themselves in conversations with other writers dealing with "big issues," and they are written for posterity in ways that some of McCarthy's other novels are not. You might be able to contain McCarthy's earlier *The Orchard Keeper* within the realm of American regionalism or discuss his later *No Country for Old Men* within the localized framework of narco-wars of the late twentieth century, or even see *All the Pretty Horses* as updating but largely staying within the Western novel tradition. *Suttree*, *Blood Meridian*, *The Crossing*, and *The Passenger*, on the other hand, are in no way containable within a regional context, even though the entire books are based in very specific regional spaces. One would not, for example, suggest that *Blood Meridian* be considered a standard Western alongside *All the Pretty Horses*, even though it superficially invites such comparisons. These big books feel different, and they have a scope and style that feels . . . well . . . epic.

Scholars who think about the epic frequently talk about the cosmic order and perspective of the subject matter; there is typically a larger scope that seeks to tell a story of nationalistic or communal unity. Virgil begins *The Aeneid*, "I sing of warfare and a man at war. / From the sea-coast of Troy in early days / He came to Italy by *destiny*"[1] (emphasis added). Epics have a historical bent, generally spanning large swathes of time or focusing on the most crucial of events (culture-defining wars, for example). Traditional epics tell the stories of a people, conventionally offering a "moral vision" through which to understand the history of that community.[2] The epic genre has typically been limited to epic poetry from the classical period to the post-Renaissance era. According to this narrow sense of the epic genre, one might argue, as David Quint does, that the epic died as poetry gave way to novels. Mikhail Bakhtin makes a similar demarcation in his earlier examination of genre, when he makes a distinction between the monologic discourse of the epic and the dialogic nature of the novel.[3] Novels, from these perspectives, fracture the very formal stability and ideological unity that epics come to represent.

From another vantage point, however, we can suggest that writers have always been aware of the restraints of genre and the limitations of generic conventions, so even in the most classic of epics the writers exhibit a desire to "use [these conventions], manipulate them, and play with them" in order to create something new.[4] With McCarthy, I am thinking of an epic mode that has to do with form and style as much as it does with ideology or communal consensus. The title of this chapter, "Large Loose Baggy Monsters," is, as mentioned in the introduction, a phrase taken from Henry James's account of the long novel, such as Tolstoy's *War and Peace* and Alexandre Dumas's *The Three Musketeers*.[5] For James, part of these novels' art is their messiness, their "accidental" and seemingly "arbitrary" elements.[6] This looseness and bagginess runs counter to the concept of a tightly organized work of fiction. It is also a descriptor which can be used to characterize all four of McCarthy's novels treated in this chapter. The books have a wandering quality to them, and details often appear arbitrary or accidental, to borrow from James again. What these big novels lose in tightness, however, is balanced by an encyclopedic engagement with history, literature, and culture from the classical period until the current era.

In his guide to McCarthy's literary influences, *Books Are Made Out of Books*, Michael Lynn Crews examines McCarthy's archived materials to find his "direct references" to other writers, often in the margins of early drafts of his own novels. This guide can give a sense of the altered aspirations of McCarthy in the middle of his career; his stance toward allusion and reference shifts when we get to the epic novels. Crews's guide finds three references to other writers connected to McCarthy's first novel, *The Orchard Keeper*, and only one each for his next two books, *Outer Dark* and *Child of God*. Then, when we get to what I'm calling McCarthy's epic period, Crews documents forty-seven references to writers in McCarthy's fourth novel, *Suttree*, and thirty-two in the next one, *Blood Meridian*.[7] People often envision Harold Bloom's "anxiety of influence" when talking about literary references, how authors feel anxiety about their relationship to their literary predecessors and heroes precisely because they desire to be an individual and unique artist. Even so, Bloom argues, their work would not exist without the influence.[8]

With McCarthy, as well as other modernist epic writers, allusion becomes more intentional and potentially less fraught with anxiety, as the connections to predecessors become a very conscious part of the artistic work, whether this connection be in the form of homage and inspiration or manipulation and play. The title of Crews's study comes from a rare interview with McCarthy, when he commented to Richard Woodward in 1992, "The ugly fact is books are made out of books.... The novel depends for its life on the novels that have been written."[9] In McCarthy's epic novels, this borrowing or engaging with past literary contributions is a huge part of the cosmic feel of the novels. If epics are traditionally based around a national community, as in the case of Virgil's *Aeneid*, or a religious community in Milton's *Paradise Lost*, McCarthy's cosmos is a distinctly literary one, with his community being those residing on his overflowing bookshelves. At the time of his death, McCarthy was estimated to have in his possession more than 35,000 books, most of them in excellent condition and spread out over two states, two homes, and three storage containers. We might amend his comment about books above to suggest that writers' lives, and especially McCarthy's life, are in many ways "made out of books."

Suttree, an Existential Epic

More than any other book in McCarthy's oeuvre, with the possible exception of his penultimate work, *The Passenger, Suttree* fits James's idea of the "baggy monster" of a novel. There are extended scenes that do not seem to advance the plot or character arc in predictable ways, such as when Suttree goes to the mountains for what feels like a retreat or escape or vision quest only to return to Knoxville seemingly unchanged. There is also the digression as we follow Suttree on his mussel-brailing trip up the French Broad River, a section of the novel that ends with an awkward scene in which his love interest, Wanda, dies under a cliff avalanche during a rainstorm. Once again, as with his trip to the mountains, Suttree returns to his regular activities in Knoxville after this tragedy, saddened but largely unchanged. There are conversations that seem unnecessary or "loose" and scenes that could be removed without altering the major trajectory of the novel. Indeed, McCarthy struggled with which scenes to include in the novel and which scenes to take out. There are many long passages that appeared in early drafts of the novel that did not make the published version and are now in his archival materials.[10] However, this bagginess is part of the novel's power. It leads to the encyclopedic feel of the novel and invites comparisons to Joyce's epic creation of Dublin from a half-century before. The tedium of the characters, which to those of us who love the novel does *not* amount to a tedious reading experience, gives weight to the existentialist mood, as the events feel cyclical and directionless, and the characters are largely adrift within an uncaring city (and universe). As Suttree muses at one point, "There are no absolutes in human misery and things can always get worse" (*Sut*, 372).

But behind the characters' despair and degradation hums a literary project that feels vital and energetic. The entire italicized prologue of the novel—from which the quote in the first paragraph of this chapter is taken—that begins the journey of *Suttree* provides a superb example of the epic mode. It begins, as I already quoted, with an invocation to the reader, "*Dear friend.*" What follows is an almost unrelenting catalog of crudeness and darkness and ugliness. This opening passage sounds a lot like the beginning of T. S. Eliot's famous poem "The Lovesong of J. Alfred Prufrock." Like Eliot's poem, the book's opening is filled with images of hell that make the reader think of Dante's *Inferno*. In fact, Eliot's epigraph from Dante about an encounter with the damned soul of Guido da Montafeltro would feel right in place at the beginning of *Suttree*.

On the second page of the novel, McCarthy uses the communal "we" as the reader joins the narrator, like Dante being led by his guide, Virgil. We are ushered this way into the dark, hellish recesses of Knoxville: "*We are come to a world within the world. In these alien reaches, these maugre sinks and interstitial wastes that the righteous see from carriage and car another life of dreams. Illshapen or black or deranged, fugitive of all order, strangers in everyland*" (*Sut*, 4; emphases added). This sense of the hidden underbelly of the city is the focus of the book, an exploration of the lives of the invisible and ignored residents living at the margins of the city. At the novel's outset, we, the readers, like

McCarthy, like Virgil and Dante, are situated as the "righteous" who see this world only from the safety and barrier of our cars. However, as we read on, McCarthy wants to give us an immersive and intense experience that breaks down this distance between the readers and the people who lived in this world with all their warts and filth and desperation and longing.

At one point in the *Inferno*, Dante sees a sign at the gates to hell that reads, "Lasciate ogni speranza, voi ch'entrate"—"Abandon all hope, ye who enter." There is something of this foreboding tone to the opening of McCarthy's novel as well. There is a reason we tend to glimpse these scenes from the distant comfort of our cars. We will be going through hell, or as McCarthy has characterized his subject on the opening page, "the encampment of the damned." The epic allusions continue as we meet a "latterday Charon skulling through the fog" (*Sut*, 107) of the Tennessee River, which the narrator at other times calls the Tarn of Acheron. Always, in 1950s Knoxville, it seems there is "a fog hanging over the city like a biblical curse" (*Sut*, 168). On dry land, barroom brawlers "stumbled on like the damned in off the plains of Gomorrah" (*Sut*, 187). Indeed, "Whole legions of the maimed and mute and crooked deployed over the streets in a limboid vapor of smoke and fog" (*Sut*, 168). In a particularly Dantean moment, the narrator claims, "The river slouched past like some drear drainage from the earth's bowels" (*Sut*, 164). Often the scenes feel less classical, but the heightened tone of damnation and apocalypse continues, whether it is the "specter of mechanical proliferation and universal blight" confronting the ragman or the "white concrete of the unfinished expressway . . . where the ramp curved out into empty air and hung truncate with iron rods bristling among the vectors to nowhere" (*Sut*, 256, 471) at the novel's end. In this epic mode, the world is one of portent and damnation, of a promise lost or a garden besmirched. In *Suttree*, the narrator's warnings reverberate from the page, and the language feels particularly ominous.

In many ways, the challenges of the urban spaces Suttree encounters bring to mind the stark American city novels from earlier decades, such as Theodore Dreiser's *Sister Carrie*, Stephen Crane's *Maggie: A Girl of the Streets*, Upton Sinclair's *The Jungle*, and Frank Norris's *McTeague*. These novels depict the oppressive quality of and alienation within industrial urban spaces. These novels also represent, according to Gavin Jones, the nation's turn-of-the-century fear of linguistic degeneration, as immigrant and nonrefined voices began to dominate the speech in the novels. In this "degeneration," anxious contemporary readers could also find a contamination of American language and morals.[11] As Jones points out, this "contamination" was also noted by James in his 1898 essay "The Novel of Dialect," such as when he discusses the "invasive part played by the element of dialect in the subject-matter of the American fiction of the day."[12] These themes of degeneration, contagion, and cultural contact all can also be used to characterize the fears of the upper-class townsfolk in *Suttree*. Jones writes about the proliferation of immigrant voices in turn-of-the-century city novels, which reflected the anxiety about urbanization of the white middle-class American population: "The Americanization of the immigrant altered the very notion of Americanness."[13] In a more localized way, *Suttree*, too, is committed to using the margins of an increasingly urban Knoxville, the unassimilated and largely unassimilable unhoused and uneducated and nonwhite populations that alter our notion of what a city means. Finally, all of the naturalist novels listed above, except perhaps Crane's *Maggie*, would fit into James's notion of the loose, baggy monsters category, as the novels' epic designs are revealed in the sprawling chaos of the modern American city.

Some of the epic allusions within *Suttree* feel more playful and almost excessive or at the very least misleading, such as the opening of a section that reads, "In just spring, the goatman came over the bridge" (*Sut*, 195). This quote is an obvious allusion to e. e. cummings's "[In Just-]," which follows a balloon man who whistles to get the attention of children. There is very little discernable connection between cummings's balloon man and the goatman in *Suttree*, except that the Pan-esque balloon man is described as "goat-footed" and McCarthy's scene follows a man tending to a herd of goats, and the fact that cummings's poem, like the novel's scene, is set in springtime.[14] At other moments, the intertextual allusions feel more resonant and purposeful, reflective of the kind of textual manipulation that Steinberg argues is central to epic creation. The dense passage examined above ends with a clear reference to Shakespeare's *Hamlet* in the opening line of the final paragraph of the prologue: "*The rest indeed is silence*" (*Sut*, 5).[15] This sentence echoes almost exactly Hamlet's dying words in the play, "The rest is silence."[16] While there are numerous and substantial differences between the characters of Hamlet and Suttree, the allusion poignantly introduces the specter of death and the meaning of a fleeting life—constant themes in *Suttree* and *Hamlet*. McCarthy underlines the connection by returning in the paragraph to the image of the theater stage, a very common trope for Shakespeare. Think of Macbeth's famous "tomorrow, and tomorrow, and tomorrow" soliloquy in which he compares life to an actor's fleeting experience in a play: "Out, out, brief candle! / Life's but a walking shadow, a poor player, / That struts and frets his hour upon the stage, / And then is heard no more."[17] In a similar tone and metaphor, McCarthy ends his prologue: "*A curtain is rising on the western world. A fine rain of soot, dead beetles, anonymous small bones. The audience sits webbed in dust. Within the gutted sockets of the interlocutor's skull a spider sleeps and the jointed ruins of the hanged fool dangle from the flies, bone pendulum in motley. Fourfooted shapes go to and fro over the boards. Ruder forms survive*" (*Sut*, 5). In the allusions above, McCarthy refigures Shakespeare's concerns, removing them from the bard's Elizabethan language and sensibilities, and places them in a gritty, midcentury American, textile mill town. McCarthy's epic designs are apparent early and often throughout this "loose" novel.

The Medieval Hunt in *Suttree*

Throughout *Suttree*, McCarthy engages with literary traditions more generally, such as when he merges allusions to medieval sagas with the Southern gothic as Suttree wanders through a beat-up, old, pillared mansion outside of Knoxville. The scene begins with a description of a house that could be at home in a Southern Lit 101 course as an illustration of the theme of Southern loss and degeneration. Indeed, it is difficult to deny the connection to the fallen South mythology when we are first presented with the old mansion on a bluff above the Tennessee River. McCarthy describes the home as "a great empire relic that sat shelled and stripped and rotting in its copse of trees above the river," a "stark façade" that seemed to recoil before Suttree's footsteps. The mansion is described as having "cracked urns bedight with concrete flora, broad steps, tall fluted columns with their shattered paint" (*Sut*, 134–35). One need not take many leaps to imagine this abode in the world of Faulkner's Compson family or that of Emily Grierson. Scholars John Grammer, Wes Morgan, Georg Guillemin, and others have done a superb job of demonstrating precisely this theme, charting how this mansion signals McCarthy's sense of the failure of the pastoral dream, and his antipastoral bent more generally.[18]

However, McCarthy's epic intentions suggest we look beyond the typical Southern alliances for our inspiration. As Suttree wanders around the exterior of the mansion, McCarthy writes, "Across the river, the rainy hodden landscape, he could see traffic going along the boulevard, locked in another age of which some dread vision had afforded him this lonely cognizance." Even as these thoughts could evoke the past glory of this mansion in comparison to modernity, Suttree's "dread vision" and "lonely cognizance" here steer us away from the Southern pastoral. When Suttree enters the house's destroyed interior, which is filled with garbage, graffiti, and "small mounds of human stool," he calls out, "Gods and fathers what has happened here, good friends where is there clemency?" This plea calls to mind Suttree's personal guilt, sardonic humor, and Catholic past more than it does the symbol of fallen Southern aristocracy. The house triggers a memory of a scene at a racetrack with a boy (presumably Suttree himself) and an "aging magistrate." This memory contains thoughts not of a faded Southern empire but a meditation on individual and ultimately universal aging and death: The boy, McCarthy writes, "could see the shape of the skull through the old man's flesh. Hear sand in the glass. Lives running out like something foul, night-soil from a cesspipe, a measured dripping in the dark" (*Sut*, 135–36).

What reveals the epic mode particularly well in this passage are Suttree's next thoughts about this dilapidated mansion, or more properly his next flight of imagination. Thinking that "something more than time has passed here. In this banquet hall," Suttree curiously imagines not a Southern ball or dinner but a decidedly medieval one, a "scene of old heraldic feasts." His reverie continues, "A fat marcassin to adorn the board. The male bonecoupling rearing white and steaming up from the broken meat. Eyes watch... Mad trenchermen in armed sorties above the platters, the clang of steel, the stained and dripping chops, the eyes sidling. Yard dogs and starving palliards contest the scraps among the straw." Suddenly we are in the world not of the antebellum South but *the antemodern mead hall*, the world of thanes instead of colonels. As the master of the table looks up, McCarthy reintroduces perhaps the most important image of the novel, one that both opens and concludes the book, that of a hunter with his hounds: "Down murrey fields another hunt has cried the stag. A shield crashes to the floor and three white birds ascend to the rafters and roost uncertainly." The sequence ends as the hounds' baying fades into the distance and the hunters wait for the "waterbearer to come but he does not come, and does not come" (*Sut*, 136).

What, the reader wonders, is this medieval scene doing in the heart of 1950s Knoxville? Why does this scene speak to this disillusioned intellectual Suttree, and what does it have to say to him? The passage reveals what Steven Frye has called McCarthy's interest in "the remote past, the age before history."[19] Some have seen in McCarthy's interest in the premodern eras a more specific connection to Irish or Anglo-Saxon ancestry. And there is certainly evidence to support such a reading. In the novel published directly before *Suttree*, *Child of God*, McCarthy describes his main character, Lester Ballard, as having "Saxon and Celtic blood," as being a "child of God, much like yourself perhaps" (4). However, in *Suttree*, the lineage is less certain. After the imagined hunting scene in the mansion, Suttree is called a "reprobate scion of doomed Saxon clans," and later as having "old distaff Celt's blood" (*Sut*, 136, 286). In the prologue, hunters and woodcutters are identified as *"lean aryans"* and as being tied to their *"teutonic forebears"* (*Sut*, 4). We are talking about Indo-European bloodlines here, no doubt, but anything much more specific becomes difficult to pin down, and that seems to be McCarthy's point.

Rather than seeing a specific ethnic heritage being invoked here, I prefer the suggestions of Frye's remote past angle, as well as what Matthew Guinn has called McCarthy's "atavistic vision." Paying attention to McCarthy's fascination with "ruder forms" of existence, of animal and specifically primate imagery in the novel, Guinn writes that as opposed to the modernist attempt of a cultural reclamation of the past (Eliot's Fisher King, for example), "McCarthy moves farther back in time" to the "remnants of the evolutionary past." While this characterization of McCarthy's interest in evolutionary language, a language that is perhaps even more evident in *Child of God*, is compelling, I would like to suggest that McCarthy's imaginative engagement of the Middle Ages has as much to do with what I will call here the "contingency of meaning." This is why I find Frye's phrase "age before history" so apt. Scenes that evoke for McCarthy eras before events were systematically recorded and documented *as* history underscore the lack of fixed meaning in the world. Indeed, McCarthy seems to be suggesting that the illusion of permanency and dependable meaning is one that is rooted firmly in the recording of history, and the hubris of stability offered in such recording. McCarthy emphasizes this idea in the mansion scene by calling Suttree as he wanders through the rooms "a vain figure in the ruins."

This idea of vanity seems out of place in the scene, or at the very least perplexing. What, after all, is so vain about wandering through an abandoned mansion on the way back home from a trip to see relatives? Wandering around ruins is, in fact, a lot of fun and not particularly ego driven. McCarthy's answer comes in pieces throughout the book and is stated most clearly in a dialogue the hallucinatory Suttree has with a lightbulb toward the end of the book:

> [The lightbulb starts the conversation] *Supposing there be any soul to listen and you died tonight.*
>
> *They'd listen to my death.*
>
> *No final word?*
>
> *Last words are only words.*
>
> *Of what would you repent?* (asks the lightbulb)
>
> *Nothing.*
>
> *Nothing?*
>
> *One thing. I spoke with bitterness about my life and I said that I would take my own part against the slander of oblivion and against the monstrous facelessness of it and that I would stand a stone in the very void where all would read my name. Of that vanity I recant all.* (Sut, 414)

Suttree's vanity, it turns out, is that he believed he would make a lasting impression on history, that he would leave a mark on the world that would continue after his death. Here is the imaginative weight of the medieval images in *Suttree* and McCarthy's interest in the epic mode. Almost without exception, the lives, dreams, struggles, and hopes of the Middle Ages are forever gone; they have been erased from history, or more fittingly, to echo Frye one more time, they take place in "an age before history." As such, they call attention to the contingency of meaning for their lives, for Suttree's, and, the book suggests, ours as well.

McCarthy is, of course, not suggesting we do not record such history—after all, *Suttree* is a meticulous historical rendering of early 1950s Knoxville. However, he offers his history with a keen sense of its impermanence and imperfection. It is as illusory in many ways as Suttree's dream about the medieval feast. McCarthy's history is one that constantly reminds the reader of the impossibility of permanence. We see this theme as early as the prologue, when McCarthy describes another premodern scene—this time "*lean aryans*" with their "*abrogate semitic chapbook*" who are "*reenacting the dramas and parables therein and mindless and pale with a longing that nothing save dark's total restitution could appease*" (Sut, 4). We see it suggested more subtly at the book's conclusion, as the very city given life to in the book is being torn down to make room for an expressway.

McCarthy's novels more generally are rife with examples of erased history, from the previous civilizations blown away in the deserts of *Blood Meridian* and the Border Trilogy to the rock cairns left by who knows whom that appear in *The Road* and *Blood Meridian* and *Suttree*. From the fossils of ancient life forms found in the rocks in several of his novels to cave paintings and pottery shards, any sense of permanence, McCarthy suggests, is misguided and vain. Indeed, the prologue of *Suttree* concludes with the image of the "*gutted sockets of the interlocutor's skull in which a spider now sleeps ... Fourfooted shapes go to and fro over the boards. Ruder forms survive*" (Sut, 5). By the book's end, any attempts at transcending this bare reality do not survive. This concern for McCarthy becomes the epic scope of the novel.

The mansion scene in *Suttree* emphasizes such a point further by serving as a framing device for a multiscene sequence that underscores the all-encompassing claim of death. Suttree first approaches the mansion as he walks away from the river that he has rowed down to visit his aunt and uncle. After seeing the mansion, he encounters a Bible camp where believers are being saved via full-immersion baptism in the river. After dismissing this ritual and the believers' desire for eternal salvation, for permanence, Suttree arrives at his aunt and uncle's house, where he reluctantly views a family photo album. Suttree is both terrified and disgusted by the images of deceased family members, of his ancestral past. Staring at the faces in the photographs which are recoiling at the idea of "celluloid immortality," Suttree thinks, "Old distaff kin coughed up out of the vortex, thin and cracked and macled and a bit redundant. The landscapes, old backdrops, redundant too, recurring unchanged as if they inhabited another medium than the dry pilgrims shored up on them. Blind moil in the earth's nap cast up in an eyeblink between becoming and done. I am, I am. An artifact of prior races" (*Sut*, 129). Fleeing from the close intimacy of his aunt and uncle's house, Suttree returns, once again, to the mansion, where he imagines the medieval feast discussed above. This plot sequence does not feel accidental to me. All three scenes in this short passage, the mansion, the Bible camp, and the family photograph book, reveal various attempts at positing some permanency to life. Photographs, religion, and even monumental architecture, in this novel, seek to resist time's erasure and the contingency of meaning. McCarthy's epic allusions suggest just the opposite—a fracturing of coherence and permanence.

The mansion scene is important, too, for its place in the logical and symbolic order of the novel. The hunters and the waterboy mentioned in this scene reappear in the final pages of the novel. In Suttree's medieval dream, when he vainly attempts to assert some sort of permanence, the waterboy would not come. At the novel's end, a waterboy from a construction crew with "pale gold hair" offers Suttree a drink of water. Is the running from death, then, over? Has the obsession been quelled? Of course not. The book ends with the return of the medieval hunter and his hounds: "Somewhere in the gray wood by the river is the huntsman and in the brooming corn and the castellated press of cities. His work lies all wheres and his hounds tire not. I have seen them in a dream, slaverous and wild and their eyes crazed with ravening for souls in this world. Fly them" (*Sut*, 470–71).

This ending invokes the medieval fantasy at the rundown mansion once again, but it also echoes the imagery offered in the prologue. At the end of the intense and dense prologue, McCarthy brings up what will be for this chapter one final medieval image, that of the closing of the town walls to protect the townspeople from ambushes and night raids. In this scene, the pillager, reminiscent of Beowulf's archenemy, the beastly and evil

Grendel, is none other than death personified. "*Murengers* [the townspeople in charge of the outside wall] *have walled the pale, the gates are shut, but lo the thing's inside and can you guess his shape? ... Dear friend he is not to be dwelt upon for it is by just suchwise that he's invited in*" (*Sut*, 4–5). After his medieval fantasy, as Suttree leaves the destroyed mansion to return to his houseboat, he realizes what half feels like resignation and half like a knowing acceptance of the very contingency of meaning, the impermanence of life, that McCarthy's epic allusions evoke. "Old paint on an old sign said dimly to keep out. Someone must have turned it around because it posted the outer world. He went on anyway. He said that he was only passing through" (*Sut*, 136).

A Knoxville Anxiety of Influence

Okay, so here's the easy story. James Agee wrote a beautiful and tender and nostalgic ode to Knoxville, Tennessee, and used it as the prologue to his posthumously published novel *A Death in the Family* (1957).[20] Agee's prologue presented an elegiac picture of the quiet world of a middle-class Knoxville neighborhood at dusk, with families reclining on their small front lawns in peace and comfort: "*They are not talking much, and the talk is quiet, of nothing in particular, of nothing at all in particular, of nothing at all. The stars are wide and alive, they seem each like a smile of great sweetness, and they seem very near.*"[21] The piece, written from the perspective of a young boy before his father's death, captures the recalled innocence and tranquility before the tragedy. As such, the passage, and the book as a whole, contains both the childhood innocence of the time and setting of the novel and the awareness of the loss of this innocence, through an older, reflective narrator.

According to this easy version of the story, years later Cormac McCarthy, writing about the same era in which Agee wrote his novel (the early 1950s), penned an inside-out version of Agee's prologue, focusing on the dark and ugly underbelly of Knoxville, and created in his prologue to *Suttree* an antinostalgic reflection of the ignored aspects of the city—the unhoused, the corrupt, the desperately poor, the diseased. In this easy story, *Suttree* stands as a sort of naturalist corrective to Agee's romantic lyricism. Instead of quiet summer evenings, we are confronted with an "*encampment of the damned. Precincts perhaps where dripping lepers prowl unbelled."* Instead of finding comfort in stars, trees, fathers, and daily routines, McCarthy's narrator tells of *"dread waste"* in the river and its surroundings: used condoms, discarded fruit rinds, tins and jars that *"rear from the fecal mire of the flats"* (*Sut*, 3–4). Like most easy stories, there is an element of truth to this one, and like most easy stories, it ends up being essentially misleading and fundamentally problematic.

First, let me present the evidence supporting this easy story: Both Agee's and McCarthy's prefaces are set off from the novel proper and presented in italics; both are written in a heightened and stylized register that feels apart from the tone of the rest of the novel. Both novels painstakingly recreate a mappable world within downtown Knoxville, with historically accurate street names, people, and businesses from past eras.[22] This is all true. We also know that Cormac McCarthy saw Agee as a type of literary predecessor, as a previous documenter of the sleepy southern town that became his own obsession for more than a decade as he wrote *Suttree*. There is a rumor, almost certainly untrue, that accompanies this story that claims McCarthy collected/stole bricks from the razed pile of rubble of Agee's former house that was memorialized in *Death* (see fig. 4). He then used these bricks, the story goes, to construct a fireplace in his own home, a converted barn in Louisville, Tennessee, on the outskirts of Knoxville.

Whether we buy the evidence of the story in its entirety or not, it is a lovely tale of literary influence and homage, and we can safely say that McCarthy did have Agee in mind as he wrote his own Knoxville epic, *Suttree*. Both authors cared deeply for the city, and their books serve in different ways as tributes to and condemnation of this town. This attention to the minutiae of lived experience within Knoxville led both authors to a profound sense of ambivalence toward the city, an ambivalence that manifests itself in a recognition that the city fails to live up to their romanticized glorification of it. Is this still the easy story, or have we perhaps moved toward a more difficult one that blurs the lines of distinction between Agee's romanticism and McCarthy's modernist naturalism?

The complicated story is decidedly more . . . well . . . complicated. The relationship between prologues certainly gets murkier when we consider the publishing history of the relevant documents, especially Agee's posthu-

FIGURE 4. A photo from the early 1970s of McCarthy building a room, supposedly using bricks from the rubble of Agee's childhood home.
Reproduced from *Snapshots of Blount County History*, ed. Dean Stone, vol. 4 (2008).

mous novel. As several scholars have noted, including most thoroughly and convincingly Michael Lofaro in the scholarly materials within his "restored" *A Death in the Family*, Agee never intended to use what we now know as the prologue to the novel, the essay "Knoxville: Summer of 1915," in the book.[23] Agee first published this essay in the *Partisan Review* in 1938, and showed no intentions of recycling it within the novel. David McDowell's editorial note at the front of the 1957 edition does little to convince the reader that this inclusion was part of Agee's conception of the novel: "The short section *Knoxville Summer of 1915*, which serves as a sort of prologue, has been added. It was not a part of the manuscript which Agee left, but the editors would certainly have urged him to include it in the final draft."[24]

Lofaro and others see the essay "Dream Sequence," which was unpublished at the time of Agee's death in 1955, as his intended prologue to the novel. While we do not know whether McCarthy actually knew of "Dream Sequence," which was first published in the *Texas Quarterly* in 1968, he was a voracious reader, especially of materials related to literature and Knoxville, and he was at work on *Suttree* during the time it was published. It is not difficult to think that given his interest in Agee he would have been alerted to the publication of this essay. If so, he surely would have read it with keen interest. Either way, its representation of Knoxville—its citizenry and its urban spaces—resonates in intriguing ways with *Suttree*. It presents a bleaker image of Knoxville and a more challenging sense of the weight of his father's loss on the boy, who has now become the man, that complicates our sense of McCarthy's rewriting of Agee's nostalgic prologue.[25]

Bracketing this alternative introduction and relying on the traditional and well-known "Knoxville: Summer of 1915" allows us to explore McCarthy's epic use of allusion. Looking at specific intersections between Agee's lyrical essay and McCarthy's ominous prologue to *Suttree*, what follows will pinpoint the relationship between texts, the influence of Agee on McCarthy, and explore both authors' commitment to notions of contingency that undermine attempts to stabilize through history one's contemporary moment. Perhaps for no more complicated reasons than author biography and setting, these two novels have been intimately linked in scholarship since the publication of *Suttree*. Rich Wallach, longtime McCarthy scholar, makes the most detailed case for the connection: "We might justifiably regard *A Death in the Family* as the literary Old Testament of Knoxville, *Suttree* as its revisionary New. They are also, respectively, the books of the city's northern bourgeois high ground and its southern riverside wastes; of its heyday and of its decline. Agee's masterpiece haunts McCarthy's like a ghostly forebear."[26] Wallach perhaps mischaracterizes Agee's novel as representing "northern bourgeois high ground," as this description misses the book's focus on the tension between bourgeois culture (represented through Rufus's mother's family) and mountain country culture (represented through his father's family and, in some respects, the town more generally), as well as its setting in a working-class neighborhood. From the perspective of author biography Agee is no more "bourgeois" than is McCarthy, and neither is his book. Even so, Wallach's suggestion that Agee haunts McCarthy as a "ghostly forebear" is instructive. It would be easy to see in this relationship

Harold Bloom's "anxiety of influence" at work, as one could read McCarthy's prologue as revealing both McCarthy's reverence for Agee and his need to distance himself from his predecessor.

Both "Knoxville: Summer of 1915" and *Suttree*'s prologue begin with an invocation to the reader. Agee's essay begins with a lyrical and collective "we": "*We are talking now of summer evenings in Knoxville, Tennessee, in the time that I lived there so successfully disguised to myself as a child.*"[27] McCarthy's prologue similarly invites the reader into the world of downtown Knoxville: "*Dear friend now in the dusty clockless hours of the town when the streets lie black and steaming in the wake of the watertrucks and now when the drunk and the homeless have washed up in the lee of walls in alleys . . . no soul shall walk save you*" (*Sut*, 3). McCarthy's use of the antiquated "dear reader" invocation, so popular in novels of manners of the eighteenth and nineteenth centuries, feels odd in this gritty text, as a stylized vestige of a vanished notion of decorum. If Agee's opening develops a communal "we" and McCarthy's emphasizes the isolation of the singular "you," both openings nonetheless invite the readers as subjects, as actors, into the world they are about to experience.

Both short prologues also conclude with meditations on death. In Agee's "Knoxville: Summer of 1915," the reader does not yet know of the impending death of Rufus's father, but it haunts the conclusion of the prologue nonetheless through the final image of the speaker's crisis of identity: "*After a little while I am taken in and put to bed. Sleep, soft smiling, draws me unto her: and those receive me, who quietly treat me, as one familiar and well-beloved in that home: but will not, oh, will not, not now, not ever; but will not ever tell me who I am.*"[28] McCarthy's prologue emphasizes the topic of death at its conclusion as well, as previously mentioned, with multiple allusions to Shakespeare: Prince Hamlet, reflections on mortality and anonymity, and the conceit of life being a play. Both novels end up being concerned fundamentally with just these topics—absent fathers and the specter of death, as well as the meaning of life that such a specter brings into focus.

For Louis Palmer III, such thematic and textual parallels demonstrate that McCarthy consciously "rewrites, inverts, and parodies Agee's 'Knoxville: Summer of 1915,'" where Agee's prologue serves as a model or "pretext" for *Suttree*. To be sure, Palmer is also quick to point out that there are substantial differences between prologues. He notes, for instance, the dramatic difference in mood, as well as the focal intensity of Agee's prologue that moves from Knoxville to a specific block to the idea of fathers to the narrator's specific family. Conversely, he sees McCarthy's prologue consistently taking the "wide view,"[29] which surveys the speaker's surroundings but does not engage it specifically. Such a wide view involves more than just a notion of perspective; it reveals, as we have discussed, McCarthy's epic sense of scope. In his epic vision, Irish novelist James Joyce seeks in *Ulysses*, and to a smaller extent in *A Portrait of the Artist as a Young Man*, to bring an epic perspective to his humble city of Dublin. Similarly, McCarthy, partially through his reinterpretation of Agee's text, has the same goal for his depiction of the alleyways of Knoxville, Tennessee, which was famously labeled a "scruffy little city" by the *Wall Street Journal* in 1980.[30] For McCarthy, as well as for Joyce and Agee, to give such scruffiness an epic treatment is a large part of what it means to reconfigure the epic genre for modernity. Once again, we might think of Dreiser's, Sinclair's, and Wright's naturalistic depictions of Chicago or Crane's gritty portrayal of life in the Bowery District of New York.

A large part of the existential weight of *Suttree* comes from the characters' repetitive and redundant actions. They are either caught in a trap or unable to pull themselves out of the mire in which they find themselves. The book feels very circular, as the characters and the plot spiral toward the ending, when Suttree finally leaves Knoxville in what feels like a permanent move. With the focus on filth and "fecal mire" and floating condoms oozing through the Tennessee River,[31] the book's circular motion feels not unlike the movement of a toilet bowl with all this unpleasantness swirling toward the conclusion. McCarthy's archives suggest a more noble image for this infernal filth, one that I have explored above with reference to Dante's *Divine Comedy* and McCarthy's evocation of "medieval images of hell."[32] From this vantage point, the circular plot begins to look like Dante and Virgil's exit from Hell in *The Inferno*, which involves our heroes swirling around Satan's nether regions until they are discharged through a hole in the back into the night sky:

> My guide and I entered that hidden road
> > to make our way back up to the bright world.
> > We never thought of resting while we climbed.

> We climbed, he first and I behind, until,
>> through a small round opening ahead of us
>> I saw the lovely things the heavens hold,
>
> and we came out to see once more the stars.[33]

Unspooling the Epic in *Blood Meridian*

While *Suttree* recalls the spiraling descent of Dante's first volume, McCarthy's next novel, *Blood Meridian*, still retains an infernal mood, but the hellishness unfolds in a very different manner. The book does not circle around a central locale so much as unfolds itself through a series of "restless, incessant horizontal movements."[34] The novel spools out into the seemingly endless and indecipherable Sonoran Desert, following first a military group on a filibustering mission and later a mercenary group of U.S. scalp hunters working with Mexican authorities to fight the Indigenous and "renegade" communities in the borderlands. As the novel unfolds, the various sojourns and skirmishes begin to feel to the reader at times to be indistinguishable. In actuality, McCarthy painstakingly charts the marauding groups' travels. This charting was so detailed and accurate that several scholars have mapped the journey.[35]

But for the reader not focusing on the mappable details, the book seems to progress linearly from nowhere to nowhere. The refrain for the middle portion of the book is the ubiquitous and generic "They rode on." It appears dozens of times in the narrative, usually following an intense description of an individual scene: a pile of bones from an ancient slaughter, an account of the "blue coulees" with remnants of melting snow, an old stone wall the angle of which dwarfed the men on horseback, a bull attack on a mounted horse (BM, 90, 136, 147, 224). For an author known for his luxurious (or excessive) literary flair, an amazing number of sentences in this novel begins with "They rode" or "He rode" or the like. The oppressive repetitiveness of their activities and their numbed minds are replicated in the style of the novel and become part of its epic mode. There is a redundancy to the sentences that is only counteracted by the breathtaking descriptions within the typical subject-verb-object constructions.

While the tag line "They rode on" at times follows a scene of ancient or recent violence, it just as often follows a hyperspecific description of the landscape in which the riders find themselves:

> They rode on into the mountains and their way took them through high pine forests, wind in the trees, lonely bird calls.... They rode up switchbacks through a lonely aspen wood where the fallen leaves lay like golden disclets in the damp black trail. The leaves shifted in a million spangles down the pale corridors.... They rode through a narrow draw where the leaves were shingled up in ice and they crossed a high saddle at sunset where wild doves were rocketing down the wind and passing through the gap a few feet off the ground.... They rode on into dark fir forests, the little Spanish ponies sucking at the thin air. (BM, 136)

There is an epic splendor to many of these descriptions. In a way, the epic commitment to detail reveals the novel's huge scope. But, unlike traditional epics, it isn't a scope that relies on the valor of battle or the accomplishment of men. If anything, the men become less important, fading away in the sublime landscape like the shadows on the old stone wall in the passage above. Their missions are renegade, outside the confines of traditional morality or law. There is also a leveling of the human, the animal, the vegetal, and the geological subjects of the novel. Indeed, this leveling seems central to McCarthy's imaginative engagement with the Western desert landscapes: "In the neuter austerity of that terrain," he writes toward the novel's conclusion, "all phenomena were bequeathed a strange equality and no one thing nor spider nor stone nor blade of grass could put for claim to precedence.... In the optical democracy of such landscapes all preference is made whimsical and a man and a rock become endowed with unguessed kinships" (BM, 247).

While these descriptions level our traditional epic hierarchies, McCarthy's point isn't to suggest humanity is just as pointless and devoid of value as rocks or dirt, as we might imagine other modern writers suggesting. Rather, the "democracy" of the desert works to create a potential for beauty in the most unexpected places. As the novel decenters traditional human accomplishment, its language of epic grandeur remains ever-present. In *Blood Meridian*, McCarthy's prose is dense and works by way of accretion as the details pile up one after another. Take, for example, the famous scene where Captain White's gang of U.S. military filibusters encounters a band of Comanche warriors:

> A legion of horribles, hundreds in number, half naked or clad in costumes attic or biblical or wardrobed out of a fevered dream with the skins of animals and silk finery and pieces of uniform still tracked with the blood of prior owners, coats of slain dragoons, frogged and braided cavalry jackets, one in a stovepipe hat and one with an umbrella and one in white stockings and a bloodstained wedding veil and some in headgear or cranefeathers or rawhide helmets that bore the horns of bull or buffalo and one in a pigeontailed coat worn backwards and otherwise naked and one in the armor of a Spanish conquistador, the breastplate and pauldrons deeply dented with old blows of mace or sabre done in another country by men whose very bones were dust. (BM, 52)

I have quoted here barely more than a half of this extended sentence that rolls out in detail after detail, almost straining the reader's ability to picture such a scene. The reader simultaneously revels in such rich description and struggles with the ability to make sense of it all. The scene stitches together large swathes of history (conquistador attacks, nineteenth-century fashion, precontact Indigenous customs, and traditional Western weddings, just to name a few).

Walt Whitman wrote his epic poem "Song of Myself" in 1855, within the time span of *Blood Meridian*. In this revolutionary poem, Whitman famously juxtaposes contrasting images within long catalogs of description. In a very similar manner, McCarthy unveils his epic world by association more than explanation. Whitman places the bride's rumpled wedding dress alongside the opium user's "just-opened eyes" without commentary or explanation.[36] The combination throws traditional moral judgement (purity vs. depravity) into question. In the passage above, McCarthy follows the white stockings and "blood-stained" wedding veil with ancient and pagan battle helmets. At the novel's beginning, McCarthy includes an epigraph from a 1982 article in the *Yuma Daily Sun* that discusses a recent discovery of a 300,000-year-old fossil that "shows evidence of having been scalped." Part of the epic engagement with history considers this long trajectory, the way that violence rears up continuously throughout history. What we see as pivotal moments seem from a wider perspective to be a continuation rather than a departure. The leveling out of description attaches itself to our historical narratives as well, suggesting an "endless movement" rather than huge moments of rupture. The contingency of meaning from a wide vantage point begins to, all of a sudden, cohere.

As I have suggested above, part of what makes an epic feel epic is a sense of cosmic grandeur and what one critic identifies as epic's "huge scope."[37] However, what makes McCarthy's epics atypical is the subject matter to which he applies these sublime traits—the drunkards in the alleys of *Suttree* and the pointless travels and violence in *Blood Meridian*. At one point in *Blood Meridian*, the traveling mercenaries encounter a conducta of mules carrying flasks of quicksilver to be used in the mines. The gang callously forces the Mexican mule train and their handlers off a narrow path, and they topple down into the canyon. What one might expect to find here is a testament to the barbarity of the actions and the senseless loss of human and animal life. Instead, McCarthy provides a description so full of glorious detail that the epic grandeur announces itself at the level of language:

> The riders pushed between them and the rock and methodically rode them from the escarpment, the animals dropping silently as martyrs, turning sedately in the empty air and exploding on the rocks below in startling bursts of blood and silver as the flasks broke open and the mercury loomed wobbling in the air in great sheets and lobes and small trembling satellites and all its forms grouping below and racing in the stone arroyos like the imbreachment of some ultimate alchemic work decocted from out of the secret dark of the earth's heart, the fleeting stag of the ancients fugitive on the mountainside and bright and quick in the dry path of the storm channels and shaping out the sockets in the rock and hurrying from ledge to ledge down the slope shimmering and deft as eels. (*BM*, 195)

The scene is breathtaking not so much for the loss of life but for the surprising description: the wobbling mercury, the imbreachment of alchemic rites, the falling horses shimmering and deft as eels. As he did in the earlier passage with the battle of White's filibusters and the Comanche, this description is barely contained within one run-on sentence. Instead of periods or pauses, McCarthy provides a proliferation of "and" clauses so that the detail feels accretive and unrefined. But at the same moment the language is luxurious and deliberate. The lack of a moral voice to guide the reader through moments such as this one leads some readers to label McCarthy as nihilistic or at least amoral. I would suggest alternately that the epic grandeur and linguistic power provide a different type of meaning and beauty, one that is not contained within the contingent moral expectations and social mores that McCarthy sees as stultifying, misleading, and often false.

The Missing Epic Hero

Some scholars see conventional epics as presenting a "moral vision of a righteous nation," mentioning that epics customarily exalt the idea of the "heroic quest."[38] Others see the critique of such articulable communal values built into the epic genre, and that epics "tend to look critically at the heroic code" or at least build into their stories the ability to question this code.[39] To return again to the revolutionary American poem of the mid-nineteenth century "Song of Myself," Whitman revises the notion of the epic quest and heroic code by creating a "loafing" speaker who smashes together a bride and a drug addict in his catalogs of American life.

McCarthy also questions the expected ideas of an American heroic code, but at the beginning of *Blood Meridian* he introduces the protagonist, known only as the kid, in ways that suggest to the reader such a valiant code. "See the child," the novel begins, and the reader is asked to imagine the character arising from the first page of the novel. "He is pale and thin, he wears a thin and ragged shirt.... His folk are known for hewers of wood and drawers of water, but in truth his father has been a schoolmaster.... He can neither read nor write and in him broods already a taste for mindless violence. All history present in that visage, the child the father of the man"

(*BM*, 3). In many ways, this novel begins in ways the reader will find familiar: We are presented a mysterious man/child, and the attention given to him suggests the reader see him as a potential hero, even if he would be a hero who is defined by his "taste for mindless violence." See him, the narrator implores. Pay attention to this child. The genealogy that opens the book also feels prophetic, like that from a leader in the Bible, a military leader, or Ben Franklin mythologizing himself in his autobiography.

In his book *What We See When We Read*, Peter Mendelsund asks the question of what we are able to picture when we read, other than the words provided to us. "What do we picture in our minds?" he asks his reader. For Mendelsund, our experience of reading creates the impression that we really know the characters and can see them, but readers actually have a very hard time picturing characters in their minds. "Nothing so fixed—nothing so choate." He explains this dynamic posing in what he calls a thought experiment: "Picture your mother. Now picture your favorite literary character. ... The difference between your mother's afterimage and that of a literary character you love is that the more you concentrate, the more your mother might come into focus. A character will not reveal herself so easily. (The closer you look, the farther away she gets.)"[40]

Perhaps Mendelsund's sense of the elusiveness of our favorite characters and our inability to see these characters is one way to think about the unraveling of McCarthy's hero. He asks us to imagine the character, provides a decent amount of backstory, but apart from the details of his thinness, we get very little detail with which we can actually imagine this character. The narrator commands us to "see" him in the opening line but denies us the details that would make that possible. This dynamic, Mendelsund argues, is a fundamental characteristic of the reading of fiction to begin with. "Characters are ciphers. And narratives are made richer by omission."[41]

A couple of pages after the first introduction, we learn that this protagonist has left his family home in Tennessee and headed West, and, as part of this move, has reinvented himself. "His origins are become remote," McCarthy tells us, "as is his destiny" (*BM*, 4). This sets the reader up for a heroic story of self-fashioning, of the kid's discovering possibilities within himself, his shedding of the skin of everyman and perhaps his "taste for mindless violence" to reveal his epic potential. What this means to this character or the book, however, remains rather elusive, much like our ability to envision the physical aspects of characters that Mendelsund mentions. He is not enigmatic or hard to figure out as much as he is undeveloped, an inchoate character with motivations to which the reader is not privy.

In chapter 1, I mention how McCarthy regulates narrative distance, and that his treatment of central characters often remains at a voyeuristic distance. *Blood Meridian* keeps its distance but does not particularly relish the voyeurism. As the novel progresses, the "kid" disappears for large sections, perhaps not unlike Odysseus on his journey as told from Penelope's perspective. We know he remains with the gang, and perhaps our impressions are limited through his experiences of them in a vague way, but he is not mentioned or described for long stretches of the novel, and we do not learn what he is saying or even thinking. Our heroic protagonist falls into the background of the story, as his actions become indistinguishable from those of the other members of his group. Other characters in *Blood Meridian* rise to the level of attention, especially the leader Glanton and the mysterious Judge Holden, but they are not our epic heroes. Scholars often talk about the epic hero instantiating the moral vision of a community, but we see no candidates in this novel, even as it explores some of the most crucial and contentious moments in U.S. development—westward expansion, the gold rush, wars with Indigenous tribes. At one point, McCarthy memorably and unfavorably describes the packs of folks moving to California as part of the gold rush as "itinerant degenerates bleeding westward like some heliotropic plague" (BM, 78). The oft-mythologized explorers of the American West are here reduced to nothing more than degenerate biological imperatives.

One explanation of the decentering of the hero would be to characterize the novel as an anti-epic that seeks to demythologize these moments of American history and to emphasize the brutal violence that undergirds it. While McCarthy does an admirable job documenting this barbarity, it does not feel as if the novel's purpose is to critique the mythology that supported it. Rather, he wants to document it in all its gory detail and remove narratorial commentary. Some of his characters might be later mythologized as heroes by the U.S. community and government but won't be by the novel's narrator. McCarthy acknowledges the mythologizing rhetoric with the long-winded recruitment speech given by Captain White, who tells the kid, "We are instruments of liberation in a dark and troubled land." The book undercuts this logic as the reader quickly learns that the military outfit is a group of filibusters operating outside of martial law. Captain White's potential heroism is literarily bottled, when we later encounter his dismembered head displayed in a carboy of mescal (BM, 34, 69–70).

One effect of the kid's disappearance from what initially feels like his story is to emphasize how personal and individual morals or senses of justice get lost in the mob mentality of the filibusters and mercenary gangs populating this novel. It also provides a sense of numbness to all the murder and bloodshed that undergirds U.S. westward expansion. The reader isn't afforded the kid's displeasure or horror at what he witnesses or does, just as none of the other gang members are. We see civilians' trauma and outrage, but almost none of the members of the outfit, and the reader suspects that as the story develops, they register very little. As the book moves toward its violent climaxes, the kid reappears and even shows occasional moments of regret or confession.

Toward the end of the novel, the kid does not explicitly resist the mercenary gang's violence, but he does resist the Judge's murderous logic and taunting gestures of temptation toward the gang. In this regard, the kid represents a muted version of good in the epic battle of good vs. evil. The Judge even confirms this when he meets the kid after the kid leaves his compatriots, many of whom have been slaughtered, and chooses to wander alone through the Mexican desert: "There's a flawed place in the fabric of your heart.... You alone were mutinous. You alone reserved in your soul some corner of clemency for the heathen" (BM, 299). In yet another moment of potential moral growth that follows the Judge's evaluation of the kid, the narrator informs the reader that the latter is carrying a Bible that he'd found. Such a detail suggests remorse or perhaps the desire for redemption, but the passage is amended with the doubt-creating detail "no word of which could he read" (BM, 312). Perhaps the Bible has totemic value for him, but he is incapable of engaging its specific messages. Immediately after this scene, the kid encounters the bodies of a slaughtered family and beyond that an old woman kneeling with her "eyes cast down." Here is the only moment we get a true confession from the kid:

> He spoke to her in a low voice. He told her that he was an American and that he was a long way from the country of his birth and that he had no family and that he had traveled much and seen many things and had been at war and endured hardships. He told her that he would convey her to a safe place, some party of her countrypeople who would welcome her and that she should join them for he could not leave her in this place or she would surely die. (BM, 315)

Here is a moment of compassion and an expressed sense of the nurturing potential of community, two central components of the epic heroic quest. Once again, as with the inaccessible Bible, the novel eliminates this possibility as the kid discovers the woman was dead: "She was just a dried shell and she had been dead in that place for years" (BM, 315).

The novel's "endless horizontal movement" dominates until the italicized epilogue that concludes the story. In this epilogue, set nearly forty years after the present of the rest of the novel proper, McCarthy describes another set of wanderers who are moving "like mechanisms whose movements are monitored with escapement and pallet so that they appear restrained by a prudence or reflectiveness which has no inner reality" (BM, 337). If we see these wanderers and their "striking fire" in holes as surveyors or fence builders, the horizontal movement shifts from the narrative of westward expansion to the fencing in and cartographic domination of the Wild West. In the place of marauding soldiers, murderous outlaws, and the plague of gold seekers, McCarthy leaves us with the taming of the West through property rights, borders, and the mapping of wild spaces to incorporate them in a monitored national landscape. One can read the novel's complete title along these lines as well. *Blood Meridian <u>or the Evening Redness in the West</u>* (emphasis added). If one considers the idea of the meridian representing the apex or highest point of a national trajectory in this novel, one might reasonably think of Manifest Destiny and the glorified version of westward expansion. But it is marked by blood, and by the novel's end we have reached the setting sun, moving on to another chapter of the nation's complicated history.

"LARGE LOOSE BAGGY MONSTERS"

The Crossing, the Slightly Less Loose and Baggy Monster

It is tempting to consider the Border Trilogy, McCarthy's three-part story of the relationship between Mexico and the southwestern United States written in the 1990s and early 2000s, as an epic in its totality. Thematically this makes a lot of sense. It even makes sense in terms of plot, as McCarthy's three stabs at presenting this dynamic grow together, as John Grady Cole from *All the Pretty Horses* and Billy Parham from *The Crossing* come together in the final novel of the trilogy, *Cities of the Plains*. As he does in *Blood Meridian*, in all three novels of the trilogy, McCarthy expresses an intense interest in the mythology and history of the American/Mexican West. However, accounting for the trilogy as a stylistic whole presents a much bigger challenge. *All the Pretty Horses* reads as a sophisticated revision of the classic cowboy adventure novel, and *Cities of the Plains* also largely steers clear of the epic visions of *Blood Meridian*. I will suggest in the remainder of this chapter that *The Crossing* represents something of an epic hybrid somewhere between *Blood Meridian* and the other two border novels.

For the third time in four books, McCarthy explores the long-form novel, and *The Crossing* comes in over 132,000 words in length. Of all McCarthy's novels, only *Suttree* is longer, at 149,307 words. *Blood Meridian* and *The Passenger* are the only other novels in McCarthy's oeuvre that are longer than 100,000 words (at 110,214 and 112,801 respectively). So there is a depth of consideration and storytelling in *The Crossing* that is notable, and the book exhibits a commitment to patient revelations as Billy Parham wanders across the U.S.-Mexican border six times in less than a decade. The book has the scope of his other epic novels, considering the long history of the North American continent, Indigenous cultures, preindustrial agrarian economies, the clash between newer industry and older life rhythms, and the list goes on. Stylistically, *The Crossing* feels different from *Suttree* and *Blood Meridian*. James's sense of the messiness and arbitrariness of the "baggy monsters" of long novels is not as pronounced. The book has less stylistic flourish and less linguistic innovation. The infusion of the Spanish language in the text is pronounced, but if the reader is sent running to Spanish/English dictionaries, they are less likely to look to etymological dictionaries and classical encyclopedias to find the archaic English words and mythological references that seem to crop up in *Suttree* and *Blood Meridian* so frequently. Most scholarship on *The Crossing* has to do with ecological concerns or philosophical ones, but there is very little exploration of the novel's form or style.[42]

Certainly, one of the unique formal qualities of the book, at times breathtaking and at others almost too detailed, is the extended scene of Billy's trapping of the she-wolf and his attempt to bring her back to her homeland in the Mexican mountains. This series of extended scenes takes up the opening hundred-plus pages, nearly the first quarter of the entire novel. Compared to the exciting and confounding scenes in the opening of *Blood Meridian*, which include the murder of an innocent preacher, the burning of an outpost hotel, and the startling encounter with the Comanche, this staid opening of *The Crossing* creates an introspective and curious mood. As we watch Billy experiment with scents to bait the trap and learn from the older ranchers with experience in the art of trapping, we simultaneously follow the wolf and her thoughts, a decentering shift in perspective that makes the reader wonder what an epic hero would even mean in this context—is the hero Billy for attempting to catch and release the wolf in a safe space or the wolf for being cagey and determined enough to survive the mass slaughter of wolves at the hands of angry ranchers?

When the narrative mentions that the wolf would not engage in previous routine, as it would be too dangerous with the bounty put on wolves, the commentary on this behavior seems to come from the wolf as much as the human witness: "She would not return to a kill. She would not cross under a wire fence twice in the same place. These were the new protocols. Strictures that had not existed before. Now they did" (*TC*, 25). Just as the wolf seems to comprehend the new human threats, Billy seeks to understand the wolf's actions. His interest is not primarily to accumulate knowledge that could be used for trapping the wolf but expresses his desire for a deeper understanding, a connection to a past way of life quickly disappearing behind rancher fences and borders: "He closed his eyes and tried to see her. Her and others of her kind, wolves and ghosts of wolves running in the whiteness of that high world as perfect to their use as if their counsel had been sought in the divising of it" (*TC*, 31). As Billy "trie[s] to see the world the wolf saw"

(*TC*, 51), the reader gets the sense that it is the wolf's symbolic connection to a simpler past that Billy craves, and his journey to Mexico is provoked by the same craving.

The wolf finally becomes incapacitated due to the abuse of Mexican townspeople who see her as a spectacle and agent of horror, and Billy shoots her in the head as an act of mercy. When the wolf is mentioned for the last time, McCarthy's narrative once again gives her agency and a value that few of the characters in the novel recognized:

> He took up her stiff head out of the leaves and held it or he reached to hold what cannot be held, what already ran among the mountains at once terrible and of a great beauty, like flowers that feed on flesh. What blood and bone are made of but can themselves not make on any altar nor by any wound of war. What *we* may well believe has power to cut and shape and hollow out the dark form of the world surely if wind can, if rain can. But which cannot be held never be held and is no flower but is swift and a huntress and the wind itself is in terror of it and the world cannot lose it. (*TC*, 127; emphasis added)

This description exceeds the thoughts and language of the characters in the novel, and it expresses a sense of magnitude not even registered by Billy, who showed compassion for the wolf throughout his time in her life. McCarthy's use of the royal "we" in this passage extends the wolf's worth beyond the plot of the book and she becomes a symbol of the world, its beauty and cruelty and how, for McCarthy, these two aspects are almost always tangled.[43]

The Epic Language *y el Lenguaje Épico*

Another epic consideration with regard to *The Crossing* is the book's commitment to exploring the cross-cultural exchange that happens between the various groups in the United States and in Mexico. While the reader sees this exchange in nearly every interaction in the novel, as Billy meets U.S. Native Americans, various Indigenous peoples in Mexico, Mennonites,

Mormon settlers south of the border, and Mexican ranchers, townsfolks, hacienda owners, law enforcement, cooks and carnival barkers, salvage workers, and "primadonna" actors.

This attention to the effects of cultural exchange is not far away from Gloria Anzaldúa's project in *Borderlands/La Frontera*. In this multimodal gem from 1987, Anzaldúa writes poetry, history, memoir, feminist and political declarations, documenting what she calls the *herida abierta*, the open wound, of the U.S.-Mexican border, "where the Third World grates against the first and bleeds. And before a scab forms it hemorrhages again, the lifeblood of two worlds merging to form a third country—a border culture. . . . A borderland is a vague and undetermined place created by the emotional residue of an unnatural boundary. It is in a constant state of transition."[44] Anzaldúa's *herida abierta* of the borderlands resonates with McCarthy's vision as he, too, is interested in the vague and undetermined spaces on the maps of North America, especially the places that are feeling the strain of transitions. McCarthy's Border Trilogy is set in the same locations as Anzaldúa's book. In *The Crossing*, this contested space becomes a means of exploring these borders and this border culture, both the moments of true exchange and the grating that threatens to leave a scab. Billy spends a lot of the novel listening to and learning from the perspective and stories of various people at the fringes of Mexican culture, who are perhaps alienated in ways that are not so different than the way that Billy and the wolf are.

By no means is McCarthy writing the same story about the border as Anzaldúa is. She is much more interested in the harmful effects of white settler colonialism, especially its erasure of precontact Aztlan cultures. Anzaldúa is especially attuned to the ways that the Conquest, as she calls, it has "vanquished the feminine and matriarchal order," replacing it with patriarchal order. She traces the way these transitions have led to a homophobic Mexican culture that denies her life: "Not me sold out my people but they me."[45] Much like the epigraph from *Blood Meridian* that mentions evidence of scalping from a 300,000-year-old fossil, Anzaldúa is committed to a reconsideration of the long history of the region, as she, too, cites archeological evidence that discovered permanent Indigenous populations of the Southwest, which she calls Aztlán, from at least twenty thousand years ago.[46] McCarthy's narrator never places itself in the role of the Indigenous and

Mexican characters, and he seems very attuned to the potential problems of cultural appropriation, yet the mood of this novel, and the Border Trilogy more generally, is one that encourages cultural exchange and understanding, both with the past and present.

Perhaps McCarthy's most radical expression of the commitment to these exchanges is the book's reliance on extensive passages in the Spanish language that are offered without translation. If the reader does not speak Spanish, then they are not getting the entire story. In many ways, this move is reminiscent of other twentieth-century border texts, such as Anzaldúa's *Borderlands/La Frontera* and Tomás Rivera's *. . . y no se lo tragó la tierra*, where the authors implement a mixture of Spanish and English to signal to the reader the hybridity of the cultures on the U.S.-Mexican border and to suggest to the reader that without the ability to move between languages and to code switch, they are not able to fully access and understand the stories being told. The inclusion of Spanish is so prominent that a Cormac McCarthy website associated with McCarthy scholarship has made available a translation of all Spanish passages in the novel to help the reader who is unfamiliar with the language.[47]

At times the reader is completely at the mercy of their knowledge of Spanish, such as when Billy speaks to an old man about trapping scents and the area's master of those scents, Mr. Echols:

> Dónde está el señor Echols?
> > No sé. Se fué.
> Él murió?
> > No sir. Not that I've heard. (TC, 44)

The conversants understand both English and Spanish, but the reader is not privy to the conversation if they do not have at least a rudimentary knowledge of the language. At other times, McCarthy paraphrases the Spanish, often with the use of interior monologue, in order to give the reader a sense of the meaning behind the Spanish words, such as when Billy has an earlier conversation about the same trapping scents: "Concocemos por lo largo de las sombras que tardío es el día, he said. He said that men took this to mean that the omens of such an hour were thereby greatly exaggerated but that this was in no way so." The paraphrase does not translate the Spanish, which here means "We know how late in the day it is through the length of the shadows." But the explanation of the words helps the reader track the conversation. As the conversation continues to a specific bottle of scent labeled Number Seven Matrix ("la matríz" in the language of the old man), the narrator replaces the Spanish with a deeper level of conversation that, while spoken in Spanish, is rendered in the text in English: "He said that the matrix was not so easily defined. Each hunter must have his own formula. He said that things were rightly named its attributes which could in no way be counted back into its substance" (*TC*, 44–45). We know the man could not speak these words in English, and the language feels philosophical and poetic in ways that feel out of place in the ranchers' practical lexicon relayed elsewhere. In moments like this, McCarthy enters into a deep, almost preconscious language that seems to transcend actual language boundaries. Much as the narrator in McCarthy's early novels often speaks in a register and philosophical mode that his characters would be mystified by, here the ability to transcend language differences registers not only important plot components but deeper philosophical musings in the novel. We see this oscillation time and time again in *The Crossing*, from moments when Spanish creates a barrier for readers without knowledge of the language, while in other places McCarthy removes this barrier to entertain what the book suggests are more profound points of intersection and interaction for people communicating across cultural and linguistic borders.

McCarthy's attention to the deep language of the region also engages with the Mexican tradition of corridos, folk ballads that provide epic accounts of the precise history of contact that McCarthy and Anzaldúa explore. Indeed, one writer refers to the corridos as Mexico's "epic ballads."[48] Corridos were especially popular during the Mexican Revolution (1910–1921) and can be traced back a century earlier to the beginnings of the nineteenth century (see fig. 5). Before modern forms of media, they became a way for working and rural Mexicans to record and honor their own history, as opposed to the "official" national histories. These ballads often focused on inequities, injustices, revolutionaries, and, more recently, the lives and exploits of *narcotraficantes* and other "heroes" who are deemed criminals from other perspectives.

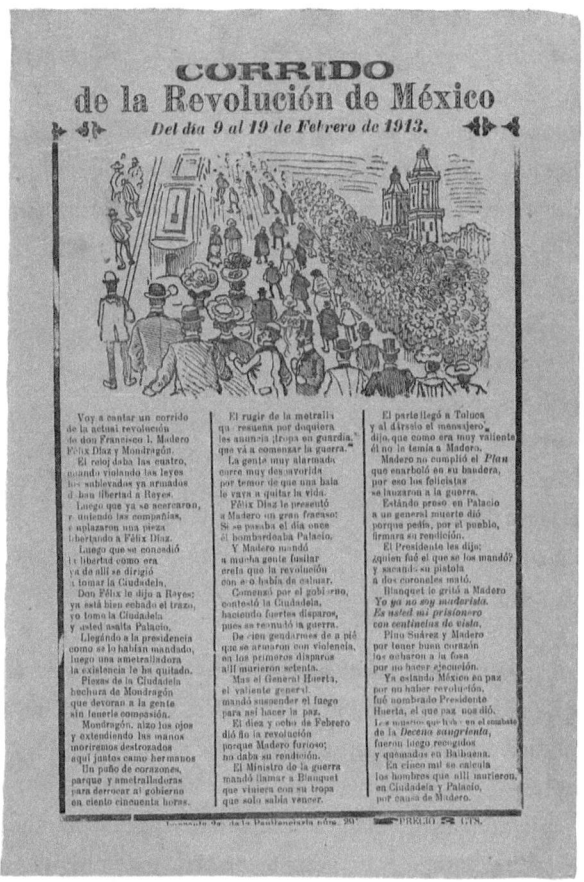

FIGURE 5. A 1913 broadsheet related to the Mexican Revolution.
Metropolitan Museum, The Elisha Whittelsey Collection,
The Elisha Whittelsey Fund, 1946.

The idea of the corrido first shows up in *The Crossing* with a former custodian for a Mormon church in the mountains and current "heretic" reeling from the devastation of an earthquake that impacted his family and the community around the church. For this man, a corrido connotes the truth of a history and is synonymous with a tale. The man opines, "Rightly heard all tales are one." Storytelling becomes a cohesive force in this man's version, the "joinery" that creates the world in the telling.[49] The novel invokes the more traditional notion of a corrido, as a ballad of the people, toward the end of the novel, as Billy's brother Boyd becomes the hero of recent corridos about his life, the "young güero down from the north. Pelo tan rubio. Pistola en mano. Qué buscas joven? Que te lavantas tan temprano" (*TC*, 375).⁵⁰

As Billy wanders the Mexican open spaces, he continues to hear the corrido that he believes has been written for his brother. At one point, he passes a girl working in a garden who is singing the ballad. McCarthy prints the words in lyric form, much like the corrido broadsheet in figure 5.

> Pueblo de Bachinava
> Abril era el mes
> Jinetes armados
> Llegaron los seis
> Si tenía miedo
> No se le veía en su cara
> Cauntos vayan llegando
> El güerito les espera. (*TC*, 381)

As Billy tries to figure out what happened to his brother, the corridos become a source of information. In this case, he learns that the "güerito" in this ballad died with his lover in each other's arms after they ran out of ammunition.⁵¹

Later, Billy runs into a man named Quijada, with whom he has traded before and with whom he is on good terms. The man provides an account of Boyd's death that feels more accurate and less distorted by the romantic notions of the corrido hero. He was gunned down and his lover was able to leave, perhaps returning to her family. He tells Billy that Boyd is buried in the town of Buenaventura and that he was "very popular with the people." This man's account both diverges from the corrido—Boyd was shot, but did not die in his lover's arms—and seems to share some of the ballad's valorization of the light-skinned traveler from the North—he was popular with the people of rural Mexico.

As Billy tries to discern the truths in the corrido from Quijada, it becomes an opportunity for McCarthy to ruminate on the power of storytelling and how storytelling constructs the reality in which we live. "Yes, it tells about [Boyd]," Quijada answers Billy's query, but adds, "The corrido tells all and it tells nothing. I heard the tale of the güerito years ago. Before your brother was even born.... It tells the tale of that solitary man who is all men.... Even if the güerito in the song is your brother he is no longer your brother. He cannot be reclaimed" (*TC*, 386). In this way, the epics of Mexico are much like the epic poem of Whitman that embraces the contradictions of life and the multiple realities that stories, epic and otherwise, tell. This conversation brings McCarthy back to the idea of the liminal spaces of the borderlands, as Billy expresses the desire to bring Boyd's body back to the United States: "I think the dead have no nationality," opines Quijada philosophically. "Your brother is in that place which the world has chosen for him. He is where he is supposed to be. And yet the place he has found is also of his own choosing. That is a piece of luck not to be despised" (*TC*, 387–88).

The book invites metaphysical speculation such as that offered by Quijada, as do McCarthy's other epics, but in so doing, *The Crossing* exhibits a stylistic restraint that feels very different from the earlier novels. We can see that restraint most easily by comparing passages between *Blood Meridian* and *The Crossing* that share philosophical commitments but create very different moods in the description of similar topics. Probably the most obvious departure in mood in the descriptions between these two texts is a description in *The Crossing* that is reminiscent of the "legion of horribles" passage from *Blood Meridian* I discuss earlier in the chapter. In that passage from the earlier text, McCarthy uses a conflict between Comanche warriors and U.S. filibustering soldiers to suggest the broad and bloody history of the region. The warriors were dressed in the armor and clothing of previous cultural exchanges and the scene is rabid and almost overwhelming.

McCarthy returns to the same subject in *The Crossing*, when he writes of Billy and Boyd encountering a group of Tarahumara, an Indigenous Chihauhaun tribe also known as the Rarámuri. There is a similar attempt to collapse large swathes of history into one chance meeting, and, like the *Blood Meridian* passage, this scene suggests that violence is one of the uniting elements of this long history, but the descriptions feel more detached and measured: "The Tarahumara had watered here a thousand years and a good deal of what could be seen in the world had passed this way. Armored Spaniards and hunters and trappers and grandees and their women and slaves and fugitives and armies and revolutions and the dead and the dying. And all that was seen and told and all that was told remembered" (*TC*, 192). Once again, the idea of Spanish armor and the conquistadors captures McCarthy's imagination. Compared to the passage from *Blood Meridian*, this passage feels removed and almost academic. By choosing a peaceful and minor exchange, the passage can introduce the history to construct a different mood; the intensity and spectacle are gone, and in their place an opportunity to think once again about storytelling and memory.[52]

The reader can notice a similar dynamic in *The Crossing*'s invocation of McCarthy's idea of "optical democracy." In *Blood Meridian*, this term invokes a cosmic leveling out that suggests a decentering of the anthropocentric perspective. When placed within the terrible, unprovoked, and often pointless violence within that novel more generally, the idea of an optical democracy also suggests that one part of the "unguessed kinships" between all things is a rudderless universe that will give no more heed to a suffering human than to a thirsty cactus or a dusty stone. In *The Crossing*, McCarthy suggest a similar ecological leveling, but without the dramatic intensity or philosophical bite. As Billy and Boyd leave a brief encounter with an acting troupe, the "primadonna" watches the brothers leave through her spyglasses: "Inhabiting only that ocular ground in which the country appeared out of nothing and vanished again into nothing, tree and rock and the darkening mountains beyond, all of it contained and itself containing only what was needed and nothing more" (*TC*, 231). Both novels invoke a cosmic sense of place, the leveling landscape of the desert plains, but what was a climactic revelation of epic grandeur in *Blood Meridian* has transformed here into quiet speculation.

In McCarthy's first epic novel, *Suttree*, the photograph book becomes a symbol of the terror of the fragility and impermanence of human life as seen by the lead character. He sees his aunt's memory book not as a site of nostalgia but a "picturebook of the afflicted." He asks that the photo album of his distant ancestors be shut tight, as the photos represent the reality of these ancestors' deaths and remind him of his own mortality rather than the memory of their lives: "Put away these frozenjawed primates and their annals of ways beset and ultimate dark. What deity in the realms of dementia, what rabid god decocted out of the smoking lobes of hydrophobia could have devised a keeping place for souls so poor as this flesh. This mawky worm-bent tabernacle" (*Sut*, 130). When Billy returns in *The Crossing* to the United States after three trips to Mexico, a photo album once again seems to mock the very past it strives to preserve: "In the yellow light of the pressed glass chandelier the old photographs salvaged from some ancient removal. ... Men sitting among cardboard cactus in a photographer's studio in suits and ties with the legs of their breeches stogged into their boottops and rifles standing upright before them. The antique dresses of the women. The wary of hunted cast to their eyes. Like people photographed at gunpoint" (*TC*, 344).

There is a certain irony, one no doubt recognized by McCarthy himself, of writing books so dedicated to the construction of the past that contain so many examples of the inability to capture the past, of its ethereal and vanished nature. Even so, this commitment to creatively documenting past eras reveals McCarthy's larger sense of the passing of time, the press of modern life, and who is left behind in the transitions. Another text that evokes these longings in ways that creates an epic mood is *The Passenger*, McCarthy's final long-form novel. Bobby's attempt to inhabit a life that is simpler than the one he finds feels a lot like the desires of the central characters in *Suttree*, *All the Pretty Horses*, and *The Crossing*. However, rather than in the streets of Knoxville or the deserts of the borderlands, Bobby sees the tensions between the past and present in a physics lab that is exploring atomic secrets or a twentieth-century mathematical equation that suggests indeterminacy rather than helping solve it away, as did earlier mathematical principles. In many ways, *The Passenger* might be called the loosest and baggiest monster of them all and McCarthy's novel with the most epic intentions. It is certainly the novel of McCarthy with the most apparent non sequiturs, plot diversions, and engagements with the "big ideas" of the twentieth century. Rather than explore those here, I will save a fuller discussion of these moments until chapter 4, "The Precarious Mood," where I investigate how the press of modernity forces McCarthy in his final two novels to adopt an entirely different aesthetic sensibility, a "provisional mood" that addresses the precarious nature of our current place in the world.

II. *Moods*

The notes [in a musical composition] themselves amount to almost nothing. But why some particular arrangement of these notes should have such a profound effect on our emotions is a mystery beyond even the hope of comprehension.

—CORMAC MCCARTHY, *Stella Maris*

A great writer is always a great enchanter.... The three facets of a great writer—magic, story, lesson—are prone to blend in one impression of a unified and unique radiance, since the magic of art may be present in the very bones of the story, in the very marrow of thought.

—NABOKOV, *Lectures*

THREE

"Little More Than a Childhood Enthusiasm"
Thick Description and the Taxonomic Mood

Chapter 3 takes a turn from modes to moods, from the formal structures of language to the feelings created through language. Chapters 3 and 4 take as their cues the rhythms and musical elements of McCarthy's writing. Whereas the first two chapters chart identifiably distinctive modes of writing that are embodied in unique formal structures, the last two chapters seek to identify less mappable, but equally as important, stylistic qualities. We may not be able to locate consistent formal rules of the taxonomic feeling of his writing (the focus of this chapter) or the provisional disposition of his final two works (the focus of the fourth chapter), but we can still explore how stylistic moods work to create very real experiences for and feelings within the reader. There are impressionistic tendencies explored in these chapters, rather than structural modes of writing.

This chapter argues that McCarthy's fiction shows consistent but counterintuitive engagements with the natural world. In his novels we find unexpected moments of meticulous reconstruction of the plant life and geological processes in the settings of his novels. Rather than searching for some elusive and utopian natural purity, McCarthy uses these natural spaces to reduce the world to its "raw core of parsible entities," as he puts it in a different context (*TR*, 75). I chart McCarthy's interest in a taxonomic orientation toward the natural world that can be found since his first short stories as an undergraduate student and that persists into the final words of his last novel. Drawing loosely on theories of vegetal politics,[1] this chapter also explores McCarthy's interest in "weeds" and vegetal-human interaction. Rather than presenting a pastoral appreciation of the sublime natural world, McCarthy works more like the eighteenth- and nineteenth-century naturalists, whose commitment to scientific categorization and understanding parses the landscape before building it back up. Rather than using this knowledge to solve the world, as these earlier naturalists attempted to do, McCarthy's knowledge ultimately unsettles the world, as it leads to a consideration of the profound mysteries at the center thereof. His thick description of natural settings merges dreamlike wandering with scientific observation, and the result is a mood of both discovery and questioning.

In a 1948 issue of McCarthy's high school newspaper, *The Gold and Blue*, from Catholic High School in Knoxville, Tennessee, there is a profile of the fifteen-year-old "Charlie," as Cormac was then called, that includes a list of his favorite hobbies. While most high school students might identify sports, music, dancing, and reading as newspaper-appropriate hobbies, McCarthy's list was decidedly more idiosyncratic. He mentions his home at the "foot of Brown Mountain" as the ideal place for his explorations, describes his dreamy attitude while wandering through "a field of dove," and names the nearby Smoky Mountains as a great place for an early morning "quest" to the trout streams. The short profile ends with a distinctly McCarthy-sounding list of hobbies: "taxidermy, cartooning, painting, stamp collection, and making parts for a collection of old guns" (fig. 6). This list, with the inclusion of guns and taxidermy, immediately brings to mind some of the more macabre elements of McCarthy's fiction, including his narrators' fascination with violence. When first seeing this list, one might think of *Child of God*'s necrophiliac Lester Ballard and his obsession with guns and dead bodies, as well as the subsequent dissection of Lester's body by medical students at the novel's conclusion. However, when considered in the context of the rest of the high school profile, namely McCarthy's love of the outdoors generally and species of birds and fish specifically, taxidermy suggests his burgeoning interest in biology and a taxonomic understanding of the natural world. From this perspective, taxidermy is not a morbid fascination of death and bodies but a robust exploration aimed at understanding how the

Charlie McCarthy

Charlie finds his home at the foot of Brown's Mountain a perfect setting for his sportsman's nature. Long tramps through these hills with his dog, Joe, take up much of his leisure time. A dreamer as well, he likes to let his mind wander through fields of dove, across a smooth lake in an early morning quest for pickerel or up to the trout streams of the Smokies.

Charlie is a genuine lover of hillbilly songs. His favorite, "Valley of the Shenandoah Eve," he sings in a deep baritone voice.

His other hobbies include taxidermy, cartooning, painting, stamp collecting, and making parts for a collection of old guns.

FIGURE 6. Profile of fifteen-year-old "Charlie" McCarthy in *The Gold and Blue* newspaper, 1948.

world works, and more specifically how the animal and vegetal systems can reveal the world's mysteries.

This high school profile also reminds us of a moment in McCarthy's diptych of final novels, *The Passenger* and *Stella Maris*, which were published three-fourths of a century after the profile appeared in his high school newspaper. There exists a remarkable continuity in interest between these two texts separated by seventy-four years, especially when we look at McCarthy's depiction of Bobby Western's childhood fascinations in the final novels. These fascinations are rooted in the natural world and a desire to understand better this world and are rendered in a style that resonates with Charlie McCarthy's own early interests. When Bobby returns to Wartburg, Tennessee, to visit his grandmother Glenellen, he begins reminiscing about his time as a child and young man there. One of the most lucid and most protracted memories in the novel involves Bobby's high school science experiment, which was a biological study of a local pond. The reader learns that Bobby made it to the finals of the State Science Fair for his study of the pond. For this project, Bobby charted and drew life-size replicas of "every visible creature in that habitat, from gnats and hellgrammites through the arachnids and crustaceans and arthropods and nine species of fish to the mammals, muskrat and mink and raccoon, and the birds, kingfisher and wood duck and grebes and herons and songbirds and hawks. Like Audubon he'd had to draw the great blue heron leaning over the water because it was too big for the paper. Two hundred and seventy-three creatures with their Latin names on three forty foot rolls of construction paper." This project took Bobby two years and it did not win the contest. Soon after this experience, Bobby got "deep into mathematics and pond ecosystems were little more than a childhood enthusiasm." (TP, 164).

While mathematics and physics take up the majority of the book's attention to science, this claim of biological ecosystems being solely a "childhood enthusiasm" feels inaccurate. After Bobby ends his reminiscence about the project and his time in high school, he still views the world around him through these taxonomic glasses. As he climbs up a mountain near his grandmother's house, Bobby thinks of the muskrat and its Latin name, *Ondatra zibethicus*, and its V-shaped wake of water in the pond, as well as its construction of a beaver-like house of sticks. He notices the ilex and laurel along the trail, as well as the dead chestnut trunks left over from the blight of half a century before. He sees a broadwing hawk and he again recalls the Latin name, *Buteo platypterus*, and even its exact eye measurement of eleven millimeters. As he walks back to his grandmother's house, he observes the "fox scat" and the hardwood trees bent by the direction of the wind (TP, 163–65). Indeed, Bobby's, and I am arguing McCarthy's, interest in the physical world returns to this sense of classification that both offers understanding of individual creatures and plants and uses them to orient his characters within the world. It becomes Bobby's early sense of navigating the world with all its complexities. Just as the scientific study does not resolve the mysteries but does provide the young child a means of beginning to explore how pieces of the world fit together, McCarthy's description of Bobby's walk comes during his search for understanding and meaning in his adult life, at a time when the stability of life is called into question. This paragraph feels much like his high school project from decades earlier and connects to the very interests expressed in McCarthy's high school newspaper. Finally, this attention to detail and commitment to the cataloging of the natural environment, flora and fauna, romantic and mundane, stands as a central thematic concern and stylistic mood in McCarthy's fiction.

"LITTLE MORE THAN A CHILDHOOD ENTHUSIASM"

In his intense fascination with the labeling of the world around him, McCarthy shares an interest with another prominent wanderer of the hills of Appalachia (and the southeastern United States more generally): the eighteenth-century naturalist William Bartram. Like McCarthy, Bartram set out into the wild spaces of the U.S. South with the goal to document, and ultimately understand, the wild regions of the nation. His most famous work, now known as *Bartram's Travels*, reconstructs his journeys through the Southern colonies from 1773 until 1777. *Travels* brings a scientific commitment to the travelogue that provided a form of knowledge in the shifting sands of the Revolutionary era. Bartram was open to romantic language, such as in the second paragraph of the introduction of *Travels*, in which he writes, "This world, as a glorious apartment of the boundless palace of the sovereign Creator, is furnished with an infinite variety of animated scenes, inexpressibly beautiful and pleasing, equally free to the inspection and enjoyment of all his creatures." While McCarthy might have balked at such openly romantic and religious language, this sense of the infinite variety of the natural world that provides infinite opportunities for inspection seems closely related to McCarthy's taxonomic mood. We get an even clearer sense of a related commitment to scientific documentation in the third paragraph, in which Bartram describes the "more luxurious scenes of splendour" through scientific language, as he lets the taxonomy do the talking: "Myrtus communis, Myrt. Caryophyllata, Myrt. Pimento, Caryophyllus arotamticus, Laurus cinnam. Laurus camphor." The passage goes on to list another twenty-four species identified only through their biological names with no commentary.[2] Perhaps Bartram was writing for an audience he expected to be intimately familiar with all of these species by their taxonomic identification. More likely, the classification was a way of establishing order or expressing the beauty in the diversity of plant life, of understanding the structure behind the wildness of the rural places of the region.

More than merely intriguing anecdotes, this chapter's opening vignettes and connections to Bartram reveal McCarthy's taxonomic mood with its consistent interest in biological description and classification that runs from the first stories he published as a college student and remains throughout his entire career as a novelist. In 1959 and 1960, McCarthy published two short stories in the University of Tennessee literary magazine, *The Phoenix*,[3] the only stories he ever published. The reader notices the taxonomic mood briefly in McCarthy's first published story, "A Wake for Susan" (1959), as he situates the protagonist's dreamy engagement with history in very ecological terms. The story is propelled by Wes wandering through the natural areas around his home: "A well-worn path led through the cool shade of second growth hardwoods—oaks and hickories. The damp leaf-carpeted woodland floor was punctured haphazardly with moss-padded grey limestone. The path led past the remnants of an abandoned quarry. Wes paused to chunk a rock into the green algae covered water of the quarry hole" ("WfS," 3). Wes's childhood romp through the woods quickly moves toward a somewhat clunky metaphysical engagement with the past as he stumbles on a gravestone of a young woman who died in 1834. While this story in its entirety perhaps feels like a youthful expression by a developing author, we can see McCarthy's tendency, as with *The Passenger* and his profile in *The Gold and Blue*, to yoke childhood wandering and a scientific observation of the natural environment.[4]

With his second short story, "A Drowning Incident" (1960), published a year after "A Wake for Susan" and five years before his first novel, *The Orchard Keeper*, McCarthy's taxonomic imagination emerges in more detail and with more clarity. Once again this mood is aligned in the text with childhood wandering. In the story, the natural world and the unnamed protagonist's comprehension of it become more central to the story than the events of the plot. The story begins to reveal McCarthy's attraction to the macabre. It follows the protagonist as he finds some drowned puppies and deduces that they were killed by his father, who promised the boy that he would take them to a farm and a new home. The very short piece ends with the boy bringing a rotting body of a puppy to the house and placing it in the baby crib, tucking it in with the sleeping baby, "green entrails oozing onto the sheet as the blanket fell." The final line of the story prefigures the common theme in McCarthy's fiction of the tension between sons and fathers: "He is waiting for him to come home" ("DI," 3–4).

It would be easy to see this story as a gothic tale filled with morbid descriptions of dead animals and fraught family dynamics. To be sure, it does contain these elements. However, it is telling just how much McCarthy chooses to frame these aspects of the piece with the boy's intense and keen biological observation. While not precisely taxonomic yet in his language, McCarthy charts the intricacies of his environment through the eyes of a very attentive child. After he wanders through the backyard, where he observes a cricket and black widow, he moves past the rabbit tobacco, blackberry brambles, and a screen of willows, "lime and golden as they turned in the sun with his passage." It is then that he comes upon the creek in which he will later find the drowned puppies. But rather than moving immediately to the major plot event of discovering the dead family pets and the subsequent sense of loss and betrayal, the narrative lingers on the minute details of the creek: "The floor of the pool was mottled brown and gold as a leopard's hide where the sun seeped through the leaves and branches overhead. Minnows drifted obliquely across the slow current. Through the water-glass he watched the tiny shadows traverse the leopard's back silent and undulant as a bird's flight. He found some small white pebbles at his elbow and dropped them to the minnows; they twisted and shimmered slowly to the bottom trailing miniscule bubbles that stood in brief tendrils before rising and disappearing." It is the boy's scientific attention that is emphasized; the reader is invited into this world and inhabits the boy's experiences as he "watched" the intricacies of the movement within the microecosystem and "found" materials to help animate it and reveal its secrets. McCarthy is a novelist famous for his intense and vivid narrative descriptions, and obviously the ability to craft a scene and setting is crucial to creative writers in general. Even so, it is startling how often McCarthy turns to the natural world in these thick descriptions. His texts slow down and linger when he brings to life the biological world plant by plant and creature by creature.

When the boy finally discovers the drowned puppies, rather than focusing on his emotions or a sentimental description of the dogs' death, McCarthy once again turns to the boy's scientific curiosity. He notices the puppies in between the minnows and water spiders, and the crawfish that "shot beneath the looped bole of a cottonwood." He "*studied* the water as he went" (emphasis added). When he finally fished out a burlap sack that originally contained all the puppies, he saw just one black puppy. There are no affective descriptions of the puppy's expression or any other details that could be tied to emotion or sentimentality. Instead, McCarthy writes that "a large crawfish tunneled half through the soft wet belly" ("DI," 3–4). After retrieving the puppy, the boy returns to the house and the story ends. It is the tension of waiting for his father's reaction to his leaving the puppy in the baby's crib that becomes the final emotional piece of the story, but the story as a whole is largely devoid of this kind of dramatic suspense, and the father remains an undefined specter in the story's background. In his place is a biological study of the natural environment and the microecosystem animating the creek. Perhaps the study of the natural environment expresses a desire for understanding for the boy (and in this case, for his father's actions in the world) as much as it provides this understanding.

When Bartram finds his way to Appalachia in 1775 after wandering around the Deep South from his base camp of Charleston, South Carolina, he is so enwrapped in his biological study that he is for a long time oblivious to the brewing Revolutionary War. Similarly, his attention in his journals seems locked to the natural world at the expense of the more suspenseful aspects of his travels. At one point he is looking for a "protector and guide" to help him make contract with the "Indian settlements over the hills." He eventually does engage with the Indigenous people with which he comes into contact, but not before we get thirteen pages of intense description of the path that "led me over uneven rocky land, crossing rivulets and brooks, and rapidly descending over rocky precipices." We do eventually hear of the breakfast meal provided him by the Indigenous locals, but only after Bartram charts the flora, including "a new species of Rhododendron . . . the flaming Azalea, Kalmia latifolia, incarnate Robinia, snowy mantled Philadelphus inodorus, perfumed, Calycanthus, &c."[5] Just as one might accuse the young McCarthy of burying the lede in his story about the puppies in a plethora of naturalist description, Bartram finds the contact with rural Indigenous populations to be secondary to his charting of the natural world. He clearly relishes the deep attention to biological detail, an attention that McCarthy prizes as well.

This kind of thick description so treasured by McCarthy continues into his first published novel, *The Orchard Keeper*. Once again, it is filtered through the eyes of a young boy, John Wesley Rattner, as he wanders through the mountains south of Knoxville, Tennessee, the same mountains Cormac mentions in his high school profile. John Wesley's wandering also feels a lot like that of the unnamed narrator in "A Drowning Incident," even in the way this wandering frames the novel's major plot turns in unexpected ways. In *The Orchard Keeper*, John Wesley is a young boy who is fascinated with setting traps to catch muskrats in the foothills near his home. We might remember that Bobby in *The Passenger* singled out muskrats in his walk around his childhood home, identifying them by their Latin name. John Wesley, earlier in the novel, targeted mink (also mentioned by Bobby), but his friend Warn informs him "they ain't anymore" mink in the area. In response, John Wesley saves money, sets up a loan arrangement with the local outdoor store to purchase some traps, and finally sets traps for muskrat in the Brown Mountain environs. Rather than focus on the traps themselves or what John Wesley gains from such a pastime, McCarthy paints the picture of the natural world he encounters when studying the habitats and setting traps:

> He went on up the creek, crossed a shelf of limestone where periwinkles crowded and watercress swayed in the current [of the stream]. In a honeysuckle tunnel reeds and grasses were tramped down and a tangled sheaf of white weed stalks floated over his second trap.... The creek clattered down through green stone grottoes, over the rocks, curling, eddying under the white roots of cottonwoods where crawfish peered out with stemmed eyes. And the sun running red on the mountain, high killy and stoop of kestrel hunting, morning spiders at their crewelwork. (*OK*, 86–87)

While this detail is purportedly included to give a setting to John Wesley's checking of his traps, and we learn that there were no muskrats in any of the traps, the supposed plot once again feels beside the point and McCarthy does not seem particularly invested in depicting the catching of animals. Instead, this passage reads much like Bobby's high school project in *The Passenger*, and we get a listing of the flora and fauna that enmeshes this setting and checking of traps. The scene is visceral and detailed as one might expect from a talented novelist, but it is also taxonomic and descriptive with an intensity of identification that feels particularly unique in the twentieth and twenty-first century to the pen of Cormac.

It is not surprising that when John Wesley meets his largely positive male role model and pseudofather, Marion Sylder, he comes across Sylder's crashed vehicle and helps extract him and get him to safety only because

John Wesley is out checking his muskrat traps. Also important is the fact that Sylder was running moonshine when he crashed and John Wesley later has his traps confiscated for trapping without a license. Both of these details bring up one of McCarthy's favorite subjects—what he presents as the overreach of governmental policy that threatens individuals who desire to live largely off the grid. From this angle, it makes logical sense that Sylder is the one who "loans" John Wesley the money to buy replacement traps (*OK*, 159–60, 207–8). They are aligned in their desire to live outside of monitored society and further aligned with the wildness of nature (a theme we see developed throughout most of McCarthy's career). One scholar sees this theme as the central thread of dissent and rebellion that connects McCarthy's Tennessee novels: "The relationship between the mountaineer and the authorities that have historically dealt with him presents a classic example of Foucauldian resistance and power, one that is reflected and deconstructed in McCarthy's Appalachian novels."[6] The novel hurls toward its conclusion when John Wesley returns a dollar bounty he originally received for turning in a sparrowhawk to the government office of the city of Knoxville. The boy wonders at the abstraction of value in the bounty system, believing hawks "must have some value of use commensurate with a dollar other than the fact of their demise." After an unsatisfactory conversation with the woman at the bounty desk, John Wesley feels duped and states, "I cain't take no dollar. I made a mistake, he wadn't for sale" (*OK*, 233). This attention to the abstraction of exchange calls into question the governmental and capitalist relationship to the natural world. John Wesley, like so many of McCarthy's protagonists, comes to balk at the modern world's attempt to chart and dissect the biological world for commercial gain. These transactions in McCarthy's novels lose the inherent value and unassimilable essence of this world. Conversely, his taxonomic tendency to classify does not have an end goal and does not work toward mastery. It instead reveals and revels in the mysteries one finds.

While not alone in offering an environmental critique of the capitalist logic of the modern world, McCarthy's commitment to documenting it through a biological lens creates a distinct feel to his taxonomic mood. One of the most valuable symbols of the hard-won naturalist's knowledge in this novel is Uncle Ather's book *Trapping the Fur Bearers of North America*, a trove

"LITTLE MORE THAN A CHILDHOOD ENTHUSIASM"

FIGURE 7. "Wildcat Set."
From S. Stanley Hawbaker, *Trapping North American Furbearers* (1941).

of information and experience which the young boys keep with reverence after Ather is institutionalized toward the end of *The Orchard Keeper*. McCarthy includes the title of an actual book, written by S. Stanley Hawbaker and published in 1941. McCarthy mixed up the title of the book, as the actual name is *Trapping North American Furbearers*. The book's subtitle recalls McCarthy's high school list of hobbies and his penchant for taxonomy: *A complete guide on trapping all North American furbearers for both amateur and professional, also deer hunting, turkey hunting, bear hunting, tracks and tracking, lures and baits, skinning and handling fur, etc.* While McCarthy misremembered the title just a little, he clearly values Hawbaker's knowledge. The book is famous (at least among trappers and naturalists) for its meticulous and numerous black-and-white illustrations (see fig. 7). McCarthy goes so far as to describe one of the book's sections, "Lynx and Bobcat Sets," and he even paints an image for the reader of one of the illustrations—"a great hairy lynx sniffing at the bait on hind legs" (*OK*, 207–8).[7]

The sense of a precious and hard-earned knowledge being passed down through Hawbaker's book and its preservation of a largely lost set of skills reappears in McCarthy's fiction twenty-nine years and six novels later as

Billy Parham attempts to trap the she-wolf in *The Crossing*. This time around, McCarthy includes the correct title of the volume and includes the full name of the author (and once again decides against including the subtitle). Interestingly, *The Crossing* is set in the 1930s, before Hawbaker's book was even published. Either McCarthy is unaware of this "error" or did not mind playing loose with history to enhance the novel's themes and imperatives, as he did with the chronology of the history of Knoxville, Tennessee, in *Suttree*. In *The Crossing*, McCarthy even provides some biographical details about Hawbaker's experience, writing of Billy's sense that the book was ultimately of little use in catching a Mexican wolf: "Hawbaker was from Pennsylvania and he didn't have all that much to say about wolves" (*TC*, 40). Part of McCarthy's attention to taxonomic detail is his attention to the rhythms of the natural world and the idiosyncrasies of biological microecosystems, an attention that is the key to successful trapping.

In a setting very much at odds with Hawbaker's and John Wesley's wandering environments, Billy must rely on the passed-down knowledge of a local trapper named Echols, who specializes in trap maintenance and creating scents to bait the traps. Although we never meet Echols, his neighbors speak in awe of his wisdom and the success of his specialized scent liquids and traps, all of which are meticulously, and a bit mysteriously, cataloged and maintained in his trapper shack (see fig. 8).

While it is Echols's scents that are presented as being the most valuable, especially his #7 Matrix, which has earned a local lore connected to its effectiveness, McCarthy saves the intensity of his description for the care and specific tuning of wolf traps, this time from Billy's father: "Crouched in the broken shadow with the sun at his back and holding the trap at eyelevel against the morning sky he looked to be truing some older, some subtler instrument. Astrolabe or sextant. Like a man bent at fixing himself someway in the world. Bent on trying by arc or chord the space between his being and the world that was. If there be such space. If it be knowable" (*TC*, 22). Published in the same year as *The Crossing*, McCarthy's only published play, *The Stonemason* (1994), expresses a very similar idea that stonemasonry becomes more than a mere physical skill; it becomes a type of spiritual communing with the larger laws of the universe: "True masonry is not held together by cement," opines the mason Ben Telfair, "but by gravity. That is to say, by the

"LITTLE MORE THAN A CHILDHOOD ENTHUSIASM"

FIGURE 8. Trapping supplies.
From Hawbaker, *Trapping North American Furbearers*.

warp of the world. By the stuff of creation itself. The keystone that locks the arch is pressed in place by the thumb of God" (*Stone*, 9).[8] In much the same way, in McCarthy's hands, Billy's father is engaging not just the physics of the trap but the larger principles of the world.

McCarthy's sense of exploring the mysteries of life through an examination of the nature around us has a precursor in another foundational naturalist from the American tradition, nineteenth-century author Henry David Thoreau. Thoreau famously described his retreat to Walden Pond as a search for knowledge and through knowledge an understanding of his place in the world. It is the reduction of the world to its more fundamental, parsable elements (to echo McCarthy's phrase once more): "I went to the woods because I wished to live deliberately, to front only the essential facts of life, and see if I could not learn what it had to teach, and not, when I came to die, discover that I had not lived.... I wanted to live deep and suck out all the marrow of life, to live so sturdily and Spartan-like as to put to rout all that was not life, to cut a broad swath and shave close, to drive life into a corner, and reduce it to its lowest terms... and be able to give a true account of it in my next excursion." In this passage, Thoreau seems to almost bully nature into revealing its secrets (forcing life to say "uncle"); it becomes part of a Spartan regiment, not unlike Benjamin Franklin's strict dedication to the conquering and elimination of his bad habits expressed in his autobiography. "Simplicity, simplicity, simplicity" Thoreau presents as the goal, and then "Simplify, simplify" as the task.[9] McCarthy has no such illusions of mastery or dominion over nature. He is committed to the intense study, to the desire to eliminate social pablum from consideration, as was Thoreau. In fact, it is the study, classification, and learning of nature and life that connects him in my mind to Thoreau's retreat. But he doesn't share Thoreau's sense of command or his confidence in learning timeless and transcendental messages from this study. He is most often left with mystery.

This sense of the value of knowledge, be it Billy's father's or Thoreau's or McCarthy's, makes sense when we consider the reason for the traps in *The Crossing*. Billy is not interested in catching the wolf to destroy it. In fact, after he successfully traps it, he takes it to Mexico to try to release it safely in the mountains that he believes are the wolf's homeland. Much as the younger John Wesley eventually learns about the hawk in *The Orchard Keeper*, Billy refuses the bounty connected to the wolf's capture and death and refuses to sell it to gawkers in Mexico. As he stays with the wolf, he observes its habits, learns the comprehendible actions that lay beneath its wildness, and reveres it for this very wildness. In these moments of the novel, McCarthy revels in the taxonomic mood, as the reader, too, learns about this animal's routines and instincts. For both John Wesley and Billy Parham, then, trapping becomes a way to engage the mysteries of the natural world: to study, categorize, and learn from it. It falls in line with McCarthy's early stated hobby of taxidermy. Like McCarthy's interest in the classification of the natural world and like nearly all McCarthy's young protagonists, there is a taxonomic appreciation for wild creatures and an intense desire to learn the patterns behind the wildness, even if they only lead to more and deeper mysteries.

Desert Scopes

When *No Country for Old Men* arrived in bookstores in 2005, McCarthy scholars and readers didn't know exactly what to make of it. It felt more like a script of an action film than one of McCarthy's dense and philosophical novels, and it certainly did not appear to reflect on the surface his commitment to the natural world. Not surprisingly, it was quickly turned into a movie by Ethan and Joel Coen just two years later. In an interview with *The Guardian*, the Coen brothers talk about converting the novel to the screen and joke about how little they did to McCarthy's cinematic and dialogue-heavy text: "Joel: 'Ethan once described the way we worked together as: one of us types into the computer while the other holds the spine of the book open flat. That's why there needs to be two of us—otherwise he's gotta type one-handed. That's how you "collaborate" with someone else.' Ethan: 'Paperback novels just won't lie open properly! They flip shut.'"[10] It is no surprise to learn that McCarthy originally conceived of the novel as a screenplay. Even upon its publication as a novel, admirers of the novel, such as the Coen brothers, were drawn to its "built-in cinematic values."[11] This novel also seemed to many to be out of place for McCarthy, or at least a signal of a new direction, in its seeming adherence to the pulp territory of the neo-Western genre on the one hand and a "noir style crime narrative" on the other.[12] Early reviews of the novel accused it of containing "lackluster pulp beneath the author's standards."[13]

From another perspective, the novel registered a more compelling shift for McCarthy, one that can be traced through *No Country* (2005) to his next novel, *The Road* (2006): "The departure in *No Country for Old Men* displays a preoccupation with style itself, in all its variety and diversity, as well as with the fluid possibilities of popular literary genre."[14] When one takes this cue and looks at the novel through style instead of genre, and considers the taxonomic mood more specifically, the early scenes in the novel become more than a cinematic attempt to establish a film-like setting. They express a commitment to the kind of observation and charting we have seen throughout McCarthy's career. When the reader meets Llewelyn Moss early in the book, he is glassing the desert landscape with "a pair of twelve power german binoculars." Moss is hunting antelope, which explains his study of the terrain, but as with previous hunting scenes in McCarthy's fiction, the passage is more committed to a thick description of the landscape Moss sees through the binoculars than to the prey he is tracking. Binoculars make sense in a hunting scenario, especially where the hunter sits on top of a ridge, looking down on the grassy desert plains below. However, in the larger context of McCarthy's taxonomic mood, it brings to mind the close scientific study of the environment, more akin to a microscope than a hunting scope. The mention of the rifle's "Unertl telescopic sight of the same power as the binoculars" further suggests a scientific examination, a closer-than-usual inspection of the environment (NCfOM, 8).

When the antelope come into Moss's sight, the description of the animals is matter of fact and described with little interest: "The antelope were a little under a mile away." It is the natural landscape, especially the geological and vegetal features, that captures the narrator's interest. McCarthy writes of the angle of the sun on the desert with "the shadow of the ridge and the datilla and the rocks [that fell] far out across the floodplain below them." In previous books, namely *Child of God*, McCarthy creates a voyeuristic feel by emphasizing the character of Lester Ballard watching other people often in intimate or vulnerable positions. In *No Country*, we watch Moss examining not the humans around him but the environment. Moss "sat studying the land," watched the movement of the animals, and "scanned the country with his binoculars." While he does see the prey and eventually discovers a crime scene, once again, the narrative saves its energy for the natural formations and even weather patterns: "The pale orange dust that hung in the windless morning light grew faint and then it too was gone. The barrial stood silent and empty in the sun.... The rocks there were etched with pictographs perhaps a thousand years old. The men who drew them hunters like himself. Of them there was no other trace ... a rough trail leading down. Candelilla and scrub catclaw. He sat in the rocks and steadied his elbows on his knees and scanned the country with the binoculars" (NCfOM, 10–11). One could suggest that this scanning of the countryside stages the hunting scene and can thus stand as a metaphor for the human hunters and hunted that take up the majority of the plot of the novel. Moss's background as a sniper in Vietnam further underlines this theme. But, here at the novel's opening, McCarthy pauses. The reader watches Moss watching the intricacies of the environment and studies Moss studying the terrain in front of him. McCarthy's attention to the desert landscape stands out early in this otherwise crime/cartel novel.

His classifying mood with the Southwest ecosystems finds its most intense articulation in his first novel set in the desert, *Blood Meridian* (1985). From the perspective of McCarthy's newness to the desert ecosystems both as a writer and a resident, this intensity in the first novel about the Southwest makes sense: study of an unfamiliar landscape leads to discovery that leads to understanding with allowance for the consideration of the mysterious and undefinable. While it is McCarthy's amazing ability to create distinctive and memorable characters and unforgettable scenes of human interaction that rightfully defines this book, the novel's careful scientific descriptions of the numerous ecological landscapes, or microecosystems, feels as significant, and leads one scholar to suggest that one of the novel's chief concerns is "the consequences of not adapting to the constraints of the (desert) landscape."[15] Earlier examples of McCarthy's commitment to the natural world focus on the flora and fauna of a local East Tennessee landscape. *Blood Meridian* turns its attention to the geological and meteorological: "They rode through regions of particolored stone upthrust in ragged kerfs and shelves of traprock reared in faults and anticlines curved back upon themselves and broken off like stumps of great stone treeboles and stones the lightning had clove open, seeps exploding in steam in some old storm. They rode past trapdykes of brown rock running down the narrow chines of the ridges and onto the plain like the ruins of old walls, such auguries everywhere of the hand of man before man was or any living thing" (*BM*, 50). In this novel, the geological formations invite a deeper consideration of geological time and the relationships between the slow march of the earth's time in comparison to the chaotic race of human time, and the even shorter and less predictable span of an individual life.

The descriptive mood dominates as the group rides through mountain pine forests and malpais and lava formations, through bone-dry deserts and dusty lowcountry filled with scrub brush, through treacherous canyons and past guarded water sources. As the book takes us through such multiple bioregions within the wild spaces of the Southwestern United States and northern Mexico, the travelers ride through "moonblanched waste" and past low benches of land "where walls of dry aggregate marked an old river course," upon a trail "that ran carved along the solid stone face of a bluff a thousand feet above the clouds," with a "desert absolute" that was "devoid of feature altogether and there was nothing to mark their progress upon it" (BM, 244, 189, 295). As McCarthy becomes our scrivener for the unfolding of these explorations, he becomes not unlike his character the Judge, who is constantly recording the biological and geological and anthropological worlds in his ledger. The other riders never know what to make of the Judge, who is mysterious and seemingly all-knowing, able to pull off feats such as fashioning gunpowder out of the materials at hand in a desert lava formation. He often removes himself from the group to perform scientific studies, such as when he is seen breaking ore samples with a hammer or when he falls behind the pack to "botanize" before riding harder to catch up. When presented by a member of the group with the idea that God does not lie, the Judge responds to the gang, "No, He does not. And [holding up a rock] these are his words. He speaks in stones and trees, the bones of things" (BM, 116, 127).

When the Judge is asked why he keeps such meticulous notes of the natural landscape, he famously replies that "whatever in creation exists without my knowledge exists without my consent.... The smallest crumb can devour us. Any smallest thing beneath yon rock out of men's knowing." When the Judge states that only when a human can parse "each last entity" and is able to isolate them before him can one be "suzerain" (keeper or overlord, in the Judge's translation) of the earth, one feels that McCarthy shares the Judge's privileging of the endless quest for knowledge and understanding. McCarthy's narration does not have the will to power and devilish need for domination in such study as the Judge does, but he seems to feel, like the Judge, it is his responsibility to pay attention to the geological, biological, and anthropological "specimens" presented to us by the world. He does not share the Judge's sense that the "freedom of birds is an insult to me," but does share his sense of the importance behind "the task of singling out the thread of order from the tapestry" of the world (BM, 198–99). For all his larger-than-life and destructive qualities, I would suggest that it is the Judge's more mundane scientific curiosity that reflects

McCarthy's decision to turn to the Southwest after writing four books set in the Appalachian Mountains and the foothills nearby. It is easy to see that McCarthy's interest in the desert Southwest of the nineteenth century is wrapped up in the histories and mythologies of the Americas. As we will see in the upcoming sections of this chapter, his earlier attention to the Appalachian geography challenges decidedly different mythologies, namely the pastoral representation of the eastern mountain landscapes, a pastoral tradition which feels almost diametrically opposed to the inhospitable climates McCarthy constructs in the desert novels. If we might borrow from Nichols and characterize McCarthy's depiction in terms of "constraints,"[16] we will see that McCarthy approaches the Appalachian Mountains without the expected romanticization of their wild beauty and sustaining bioregion. McCarthy instead creates, most notably in *Child of God* and *Suttree*, what I call the "apastoral mood."

"Nothing but the Same Mountains": McCarthy's Appalachia and Apastoral Mood

As I emphasize throughout this book, McCarthy consistently reveals the precarity of life through a preciousness of language that captures beauty at the sentence level, if not always in the souls of many of his characters. He also exhibits a love of craft, of an appreciation for a well-made instrument or a well-performed skill. There is beauty to his description of masterful executions of such craft (think of Echols's traps or the pair of binoculars discussed in the previous section). Even so, he gives special loving attention to the natural world in his descriptions and taxonomic study of the minutiae of this world. In all of these examples, one might expect to find a sentimentality in McCarthy's language. While he clearly loves the natural world that he observes around him, especially that of East Tennessee and the desert Southwest, McCarthy rarely enters the realm of what we might call pastoralism. His descriptions are based in science and observation, perhaps occasioning philosophic musings, but almost never sentimental flights.

According to whom you ask, pastoralism might be defined as a mood or a mode, as a genre or a convention, limited to poetry or open to all forms of writing. In fact, pastoralism seems to be the kind of term we all think we understand but rarely agree on the definition. There seems to be at least some agreement that pastoral literature came into focus during the Western classical periods of Greece and Rome, presenting shepherds and farmers as not degraded by or at least not subsumed by the concerns of city life. Virgil's *Eclogues* is the archetypal example here. Pastoralism found a rebirth in the British Renaissance, especially with Edmund Spencer and Sir Philip Sidney, and then either largely disappeared, weakened, or transformed in the nineteenth century and beyond into something else, perhaps with a whiff of the pastoral but struggling to fit into the traditional conceptions of the term.[17] Even with this somewhat established chronology, the idea of the pastoral has evolved through what one scholar calls "representative anecdotes," rather than systematic means.[18] I might revise the terminology in this excellent observation for my purposes to say that it often operates through moods rather than systematic modes. The very diverse natures of the literature and the idea of the pastoral encourage such unsystematic classification. In an attempt to rein in the definitional chaos of the term, Terry Gifford has identified four types of the pastoral: 1) a "historical form with a long tradition," 2) an "area of content" (such as the celebration of country in contrast to the city), 3) a pejorative term meant to illuminate how unrealistic the romantic notions of the pastoral often are, and, finally, 4) "neutrally descriptive" accounts of rural farming practices in literature.[19]

The idea of Appalachian literature and literature about the U.S. mountain ranges often fits within modern articulations of the pastoral, one fitting most clearly in Gifford's second category and finding its critique of the content in his third category. The idea of Appalachia as a bucolic retreat from the cities is clearly a tradition with which McCarthy was well-versed when he sat down to write his first four Tennessee novels. Take, for example, what many scholars see as the first expression of Appalachian literature, Mary Noailles Murfree's *In the Tennessee Mountains* (1884), a book that makes liberal use of the local color convention that places "outsider" visitors and narrators into her tales about rustic Appalachian subsistence communities. In order to define what is unique about the region, Murfree leans on a romanticized conception of the natural landscape, which she calls the "majestic procession of mountains" across the eastern parts of Tennessee. The collection of short stories (all of which originally appeared in the *Atlantic Monthly*) has numerous passages that describe the mountains in rosy, water-color romantic language, such as the attention to the setting in "The 'Harnt' that Walks Chilhowee": "Floods of sunshine submerged Chilhowee in liquid gold, and revealed that dainty outline limned upon the northern horizon; but over the Great Smoky mountains clouds had gathered, and a gigantic rainbow bridged the valley." For Murfree, this natural splendor is further instantiated in the characters' actions, behavior, and morality, and her women characters are often given nicknames that align them with the splendor of the natural world: "ethereal woodland flower," "slip o'willow," brightly colored "red-bird," having eyes like "deep, limpid mountain streams," or eyes like those of a deer that expressed "something free, untamable, and yet gentle," serving as just a few illustrative examples.[20]

As the concept of Appalachian literature evolved, so, too, did the sense of the pastoral, even as the commitment to the rural splendor of the region survived. Where Murfree creates the "postcard" beauty of the Appalachian Mountains, extending this splendor to some of her favored characters, James Still relied on an even more pastoral notion of the region, the contrast between rural farming life and the encroaching industrial life discussed by Gifford. Generally understood as the second major Appalachian piece of fiction, James Still's *River of Earth* (1940) is a modernist tale that relies on a minimalist prose reminiscent of Hemingway, a prose that eschews the romantic metaphors employed by Murfree. Even so, Still represents the contrast between country and city in this novel by pitting salaried life of the coal mines, and the intermittent and alienated labor therein, against what he portrays as the natural and enriching rhythms of life on a farm. We see the comparison especially vividly from the child narrator's perspective: "Sitting there I thought I would grow up into such a man as Grampa Middleton . . . , learning to read and write, and to draw up deeds for land; and I would learn to plow, and have acres of my own. Never would I be a miner digging a darksome hole."[21]

Not only does committing to rural life in *River of Earth* connote a more educated and contemplative life of the narrator's grandfather but Still gives a McCarthy-like taxonomic accounting of the surfeit of home gardens in the good years. While Still may avoid the excessive romantic language of Murfree, many of his visions of the pastoral are romanticized in other ways. In the opening chapters, the garden is described with both glorified language connected to successful horticulture and attention to the nuances of plant growth: "The garden grew by a miracle, and the blackberry winter passed with the early April winds, doing no harm. Beans broke their waxen leaves out of hoe-turned farrows, bearing the husk of seeds with them. Sweet corn unfurled tight young blades from weed mold, timid to night chill, growing slowly and darkly . . . 'They hain't nigh ready,' Mother would say. 'When a bean snaps like you'd stroke a stick, hit's time. Wait till they've had their full growth.'" Later on, when the seven-year-old narrator learns to plow the field behind the oxen with his uncle, the action, much like the description of the hoe-turned farrows in the previous passage, seems in tune with the world, as if partaking in its natural rhythms: "The earth parted; it fell back from the shovel plow; it boiled over the share. . . . I felt like the earth flowing, steady as time." This pastoral vision is contrasted and threatened in the novel by the dirty realities of the international and industrial and filthy demands of the mines, as evidenced by the first view the family gets of the mining town Blackjack: "We reached Blackjack in the middle of the afternoon. The slag pile towering over the camp burned with an acre of oily flames. A sooty mist hung over the creek bottom. Our house sat close against a bare hill. It was cold and gloomy, smelling sourly of paint."[22] There is a moral component to much pastoralism, including in Still's novel, as the natural world aligns with a universal goodness and rightness.

There is no evidence to suggest that Cormac McCarthy saw himself as taking place within this trajectory of Appalachian literature or in conversation directly with Mary Noailles Murfree or James Still. He was much more likely to cite Melville and Dostoevsky as his literary companions. But he was doubtlessly aware of the representational typology surrounding his East Tennessee mountains. Rather than contribute to this tradition's romantic depictions, his early novels demonstrate what I like to call McCarthy's *apastoral mood*. I use this term as a more neutral description that pushes back on the negating sense of his "antipastoral" stance, offered by some.[23] In his formative book about McCarthy's engagement with the pastoral, *The Pastoral Vision of Cormac McCarthy* (2004), George Guillemin charts what he

"LITTLE MORE THAN A CHILDHOOD ENTHUSIASM"

sees as a progression in McCarthy's relation to the concept of the pastoral, from traditional pastoralism in *The Orchard Keeper* to an "antipastoralism" in *Outer Dark* to a "wilderness turn" in *Child of God*, "negative biocentrism" of *Blood Meridian*, and an "ecopastoralism" of the Border Trilogy.[24]

While such a trajectory is revealing and compelling, I will focus on a more consistent sense of McCarthy's apastoral *language*. *Child of God* presents the clearest example in McCarthy's oeuvre of this apastoral mood. In this book set in the mountains of East Tennessee, McCarthy seems to invite considerations of the pastoral tradition as early at the novel's opening pages, placing the first scene in what he oddly describes as a "mute pastoral morning" (*CofG*, 4). McCarthy does pay attention to the natural setting in this scene with an intensity and tenderness I explore in the first chapter, but very little of the description would seem to fall under any of Gifford's multiple definitions of the pastoral. The story is largely about Lester being cut off from sustaining traditions and not girded up by them. There is no romantic treatment of either the environment or farming practices that we see in Murfree and Still. Lester Ballard is living in the breathtakingly beautiful natural landscape in the rural areas of Sevier County at the border of the Tennessee side of the Great Smoky National Park. Even so, McCarthy's descriptions of the landscape are sparse, often depicting the human effects on the natural world rather than its splendor. We are more likely to see junkyards and poison ivy patches than a sublime sunset fading behind the ridges. He also at times focalizes the reader's attention through the limited interests (and perhaps intellect) of Lester, who has lived in these mountains for his entire life. Whereas Murfree as a visitor to the mountains constantly extols their sublime virtues, for Lester they are familiar and easily ignored background.[25] At one point early in the novel, Lester notices the moonshiner named Kirby looking past him toward the natural landscape. McCarthy's description of Lester's reaction exhibits an apastoral sense of the everyday: "Ballard half turned to see what he was looking at out there but there was nothing but the same mountains" (*CofG*, 11).

After Lester is forcibly removed from his repossessed house for nonpayment, he takes to sleeping wherever he can find, and he moves farther and farther from the towns of Sevier County and farther and farther into the mountains. McCarthy's narrator in these moments feels detached from

Lester's perspective. Even then, he presents a similarly detached and defamiliarized treatment of the mountain landscapes. "Alone in the empty shell of a house the squatter watched through the moteblown glass a rimshard of bonecolored moon come cradling up over the black balsams on the ridge, ink trees a facile hand had sketched against the paler dark of winter heavens." This description feels overtly aestheticized, especially in a book that relies very little on such abstract aestheticization. The description is cold: the moon is "bonecolored" and the trees drawn not by a master artist but hastily sketched by a "facile hand." The description is intriguing for the reader but it presents none of the pastoral romanticization. This mood permeates the entire novel's treatment of the natural world, such as when, out of context, the setting is described: "In the morning ... the black saplings stood like knives in the mist on the mountainside." The defamiliarization of the pastoral scenes often relies on these kinds of unexpected descriptions of human-made items, such as the mountains as knives and the geological features within a cave as "huge stone urns moist and ill-shapen" (*CofG*, 40–41, 93, 134).

In his article on the novel's distinct narrative registers, Andrew Bartlett identifies what he calls the "discourse of archeology" that appears in the novel. Bartlett's description of this discourse presents this register as diametrically opposed to any sort of romanticization or equation of the landscape with the "good." Speaking of the novel's discourse of archeology, he explains, "It positions itself at a distance from any authoritative pretensions to transcending suffering or mortality by attachment to allegorical theology or to conventional traditions of (fictional) moral decency."[26] These "authoritative pretensions" that Bartlett claims McCarthy seeks to avoid align very nicely with pastoral treatments of the natural world. Rather than connecting the natural world to a transcendent space or presenting it as symbolizing human expressions of morality, he defamiliarizes it, makes it strange and humanized and aestheticized. Just as he describes the mountains as facile sketches and knives, McCarthy follows Ballard through the mountains ravished by a recent storm: "He passed a windfelled tulip poplar on the mountainside that held aloft in the drip of its roots two stones the size of fieldwagons, great tablets on which was writ only a tale of vanished seas with ancient shells in cameo and fishes etched in lime" (*CofG*, 127–28).

This passage initially invokes with the "great tablets" images of Moses and the deliverance of divine law directly from God, thus giving voice to one of the most profound statements of the traditions of Western morality.[27] However, as opposed to a divine and immutable set of laws, on Lester's tablets the tale recorded is concerned with "vanished seas" and "fishes etched in lime." The adverb "only" undermines the reader's desire to read in this some steadfast natural laws or pastoral morality. The world leaves a record on these tables, but it is incoherent and insubstantial. The allusion in this scene to Moses and the great tablets suggests a transcendent meaning, but it is not one that the reader or Lester have much faith in its existence.[28] As the narrator informs the reader a few pages later, Lester certainly did not see a transcendent message in his environment, instead focusing on the chaos that resulted from the storm: "Given charge Ballard would have made things more orderly in the woods and in men's souls" (*CofG*, 136).

The Urban Kudzu Jungle

In his study of pastoralism in McCarthy, Guillemin originally suggests that because McCarthy's fourth book, *Suttree*, has an urban setting and "contains few natural scenes that would validate a pastoral reading,"[29] it is more properly understood as a picaresque novel. However, he further suggests the novel's attention to the "social wilderness" of the city and the "internal wilderness of the human mind" makes "it possible to discuss *Suttree* as if it were in fact a pastoral novel."[30] While I do not disagree with this argument, I would like to suggest here that the novel does, in fact, contain a great deal of attention to the natural world. When we break down the familiar if problematic conception of the divide between the rural and urban worlds and explain what geographer Derek Alderman calls the "relational entanglements" between "nature and society" and between plants and humans specifically, we see a very particular brand of pastoralism based in, of all things, urban weeds.[31]

The intimate entanglement between weeds and humans marks its presence in the opening page of McCarthy's first urban novel. As the narrator invites the reader to travel with them through the city of Knoxville, the reader is ushered "*past these corrugated warehouse walls down little sandy streets where blownout autos sulk on pedestals of cinderblock. Through warrens of sumac and pokeweed and withered honeysuckle giving onto the scored clay banks of the railway. Gray vines coiled leftward in this northern hemisphere, what winds them shapes the dogwhelk's shell. Weeds sprouted from cinder and brick. A steamshovel reared in solitary abandonment against the night sky*" (*Sut*, 3). The middle line of this quote suggests these weeds are conditioned by natural forces, the same forces as create the whorl in a snail's shell. But the particular mention of sumac and pokeweed and honeysuckle and unnamed vines growing in the city brings to mind not natural cycles but the misplaced and invasive characteristics of these weeds. They are what are in other contexts called "spontaneous urban plants" or ruderal plants (plants growing on waste ground or within refuse) that typically grow in abandoned landscapes.[32] The plants are not unusual or ill-adapted to the urban landscape; they flourish there. In McCarthy's descriptions, they are nearly inseparable from the steam shovel, the pedestals of cinderblock, the cinder bricks in which they are surrounded in this passage. *Suttree* is famous for its attention to the down-and-out citizens at the margins of the city, and one could say McCarthy grants a similar attention to the weeds growing in the cracks of the sidewalk and in the crumbling alleyways of this former textile mill town fallen upon harder times.

In her project titled "The Sanctuary for Weediness," Ellie Irons considers "vacant" lots, explaining that this name implies an emptiness that ignores the "vibrant ecosystems" cropping up in such spaces, which are quite prominent if we only pay attention. For Irons, writing in 2016, attention to the weedy spaces of Bushwick, Brooklyn, New York, becomes an invitation to examine what we often ignore or become "blind" to. Her gallery of grown and photographed ruderals becomes "an entreaty to engage the weedy and spontaneous. Beyond plant-blindness and nativism, there are functioning feral ecosystems that can lead us towards an ethic of degrowth and reinvestment in what already exists. Let the dandelions live!" Irons's perspective is decidedly anticapitalistic, asking that we engage with and preserve the abandoned spaces and forgotten land in our urban landscape. This project perfectly aligns with my sense of McCarthy's goals for *Suttree*: "*We are come to a world within the world. In these alien reaches, these maugre sinks and interstitial wastes that the righteous see from carriage and car another life dreams. Illshapen or black or deranged, fugitive of all order, strangers in everyland"* (*Sut*, 4). If blindness becomes a metaphor in this novel for what society willfully ignores in its environment, weeds are a central component of how this metaphor operates.

Whereas the "righteous" choose to ignore or root out these spontaneous and inglorious plants, McCarthy brings them to center stage. Famous for his large vocabulary, McCarthy employs the vague term "weed" and its variants more than forty times in this novel, and one is tempted to allow their appearance to fade into the background or setting of the novel, as Anna Lawrence suggests often happens with plants more generally that have "typically backgrounded designation as 'environment.'"[33] As Lawrence reminds us, these weeds become symbolic white noise in fiction that helps establish the ratty conditions of the environments in which the characters and narrator of the novel travel. McCarthy resists this tendency in precisely the way Lawrence suggests is crucial to a productive understanding of plants, from a "critical plant studies [CPS]" and/or "vegetal geography" perspective. While McCarthy frequently includes the umbrella term "weeds" in the novel, he is just as likely to name them. He writes of blackberries, reeds, sumac, ivy, milkweed, honeysuckle, burdock, pokeweed, periwinkle, creepers, many other spontaneous species that commonly crop up in urban spaces, and, of course, the most famous of southern weeds: kudzu. Lawrence writes that one of the mechanisms that makes us blind to the particularities of species is their reduction to generic and abstract groupings, such as "crops" or, in this case, "weeds": "Plant bodies have been typically obscured, made invisible by their categorization as undifferentiated collectives."[34]

Giving name to these generally invisible weeds brings them to the forefront, removes the reader's cultural blinders that train them to ignore ruderal plants. What emerges from McCarthy's taxonomic commitment to weeds in this novel is the instantiation of a feral ecosystem (to borrow from Irons again), one that captures the urban jungle of midcentury Knoxville with the botanical and metaphorical sense of that world. McCarthy emphasizes this ecosystem when Gene Harrogate is released from the county jail and crawls into the undergrowth at the margins of the city: "Harrogate came batting his way through the jungle of kudzu that overhung the bluffs above the river until he found a red clay gully of a path going down the slope. He followed along through lush growths of poison ivy and past enormous mummy shapes of vinestrangled trees, banks of honeysuckle dusted in ocher, into a brief cindery wood where grew black sumacs, pokeweeds gorged with sooty drainage whose clustered fruit gleamed small baubles of a poisonous ebon blue" (*Sut*, 91). McCarthy pays attention in this passage to the interchange between the humanmade aspects of the environment and the vegetal ones. The woods are cindery and the pokeweed is gorged with sooty drainage. Describing the pokeweeds as "gorged" suggests that they are not eking out a life in these dusty environs—they are thriving.

The passage is reminiscent of Allen Ginsberg's midcentury city poem of spontaneous urban plants, "Sunflower Sutra." In this poem, the speaker wanders with Jack Kerouac in the urban wastelands of San Francisco into a grimy railroad yard wherein sits a locomotive and an unexpected sunflower "on top a pile of ancient sawdust":

> and the gray Sunflower poised against the sunset, crackly bleak and
>   dusty with the
> smut and smog and smoke of olden locomotives in its eye—
> corolla of bleary spikes pushed down and broken like a battered crown,
>   seeds fallen
> out of its face, soon-to-be-toothless mouth of sunny air, sunrays
>   obliterated on its hairy head like a dried wire spiderweb,
> leaves stuck out like arms out of the stem, gestures from the sawdust
>   root, broke pieces
> of plaster fallen out of the black twigs, a dead fly in its ear,
> Unholy battered old thing you were, my sunflower O my soul, I loved
>   you then![35]

Like McCarthy, Ginsberg is committed in this poem to demonstrating the new urban ecosystems in which grime, machinery, and plant life exist together, in something close to harmony if not quite a symbiotic relationship. However, whereas McCarthy is apt to present the ecosystem as a predictable and organic growth of human-plant entanglement, Ginsberg is surprised by the beauty of the sunflower, a beauty which the poem presents as outside the expectations of a trainyard. The poem's conclusion suggests the deeper beauty of living things that is beneath "our skin of grime." In *Suttree*, on the other hand, the grime and the plant life are presented as imbricated equivalents living in the complex relationships of urban spaces.

As Harrogate winds his way to the "lush waste" of the junkman's fenced lot, McCarthy once again emphasizes the exchange between human industry and plant growth in ways that feel organic, part of a new natural. As with Ginsberg's poem above, McCarthy emphasizes the existence of flowers growing through the industrial waste: "The gate was weighted with a chainload of gears and closed gently behind him. The air was rich with humus and he could smell the flowers. Wild datura with pale strange trumpets and harebells among the debris. Great gangly rosebushes covered with dying blooms that collapsed at a touch. Phlox lavender and pink along a leaning wall of cinderblock and loosestrife and columbine among the iron inner works of autos scattered in the grass" (*Sut*, 93). For Irons, it is precisely these kinds of "novel ecosystems" that are worth our attention, where the "structure and function of the landscape has been so dramatically altered by humans that the changes have become irreversible." In a different context, it might make sense to distinguish between native and invasive species, between manicured and wild nature. In these urban spaces, such distinctions, suggest McCarthy and Irons, are no longer relevant. The urban centers and the establishment of these plants express a coexistence that represents the modern urban experience.

For Irons, one can see something akin to an agency of the plants in the abandoned lots when one considers how many of these weeds are non-native species: "Tough, adaptable plants from around the world have colonized the space, mirroring the shifting population of humans whose infrastructure now dominates the surrounding land."[36] I doubt McCarthy would feel comfortable with such language being applied to his novel—he is less concerned than Irons with what these plants "have to offer." Even so, *Suttree* does create some striking parallels between the downtrodden and underappreciated "underclass" of Knoxville who are the center of his novel and the resiliency of the weeds that keep showing up unwanted in urban spaces. In short, Irons's sense of the spontaneous and hardy life of these nomadic plants maps very well onto the characters of the novel. Toward the conclusion of *Child of God*, McCarthy describes the nomadic Lester Ballard as a "weedshaped onearmed human." Often in *Suttree*, the general sprawl of the weedy growth serves as a metaphor for the unconnected lives of the disconnected coterie that lingers in the shadows of the city. Lawrence describes urban weeds as unruly workers with "an innate disposition to get into the wrong place," and suggests that the "weed reveals the limits to a more-than-human ethics of care, estranged from the utilitarian valuation of productive life."[37] Once again, I do not want to suggest that McCarthy expresses interest in the agency and ethics of vegetal life exactly, but it is plain to see a connection between the description above and the unruly and estranged characters in *Suttree* who are similarly resistant to the "utilitarian valuation of productive life"—the weeds on the margins of "proper" society.

Weeds also seem central to the taxonomic mood of the novel, a mood that is often filtered through (or is filtered by) Suttree's own moods. Toward the end of the novel, as Suttree's desperation crescendos and his moorings disappear, he visits the herbalist and conjurer Mother She, who gives him potions and rituals designed to help him heal. After a confusing but largely ineffectual experience, Suttree wanders out of her house and the plant life seems to mirror his psychological mindset: "The rind of a moon lay cocked in the sky and the world looked cold and blue. He could see the stalks of dockweed dead in the yard and beyond them the barren and pestilential locust wood and the trashpapers and newsprint among the boughs like varied birds illshaped pale and restless in the wind. He wandered through the wood" (*Sut*, 429).

One final example of the weedy undergrowth of McCarthy's fourth novel: Alderman calls attention to the "relational entanglements" between humans and invasive species, paying special attention to kudzu. We might build on this by thinking about how such entanglements in *Suttree* become a way for McCarthy to explore the urban interstices, the places that are hidden and unmanageable. As Irons reminds us, from a vegetal perspective, "vacant lots" are anything but empty. They are teeming with life.[38] In *Suttree*, kudzu and other "invasive" vines provide cover for the characters of the novel, who are constantly at risk of being rounded up, harassed, and beaten by the police force that sees these people as an invasive and colonizing presence in need of eradication. Harrogate finds refuge behind the cover of the kudzu jungle, only stumbling out of it into the city on his terms. During his various journeys, he travels through a "wall of ivy" and a "mass of vines" to a "bower of honeysuckle." He crosses the railroad tracks through a "high revetment of honeysuckle and then through a patch of cane" (*Sut*, 138, 31). It is not surprising that McCarthy most commonly attaches these descriptions to Harrogate's wandering, as he is the most vulnerable to police surveillance among the white characters. (Ab Jones, the Black bar owner, is much more viciously surveilled, and McCarthy's account of the racialized police brutality that ends Jones's life is the most visceral account of such brutality written by a white author in the midcentury that I can think of, except perhaps the earlier example of Eudora Welty's story "Where Is the Voice Coming From?," a story based on her imagined recreation of the murder of civil rights activist Medgar Evers.)

Harrogate, like Ab Jones and Suttree at times and most of the characters who congregate in the dive bars near the river, needs to stay out of the sight and attention of the roaming police officers. In this way, the kudzu jungle, the wall of ivy, the mass of vines, and bower of honeysuckle become a bizarre form of antisurveillance that allows the characters to come and go, to disappear into the weeds and to reappear on their own terms. Early in the novel, as Harrogate leaves his jaunts in the watermelon patch and returns to public space, it feels natural and he works with the tangle of weeds rather than fighting against it: "He crossed the stand of cane in a series of diminishing reports and went over the top of the honeysuckle in graceful levitation and lit in the road in the lights of a car rounding the curve" (*Sut*, 33). Harrogate is called in the novel a "crazed figure," "sly rat-faced," "a convicted pervert of a botanical bent," a clown, and much worse (*Sut*, 31, 33, 54, 115). He is described as clumsy, awkward, sneaky, and clueless, so it is telling that it is when he is crossing the honeysuckle divide between civilization and the hidden undergrowth that he moves in "graceful levitation." He is adept at making such crossings. Suddenly, Irons's thoughts about colonizing weeds mirroring the shifting population of humans doesn't feel so far-fetched. Harrogate chooses his home to be under a viaduct in a "little concrete pillbox filled with pipes and conduits where you could store things and with the weeds grown about outside there was never a retreat so secluded." When Suttree visits and then leaves this "derelict fairyland," McCarthy once again connects its seclusion with the weeds surrounding it: "Suttree took a final look around and shook his head and went through the weeds *to the world*" (*Sut*, 116–18; emphasis added). Suttree leaves Harrogate's place and only after he navigates through the weeds has he reentered the city.

Suttree leaves the press of the urban spaces a few times in the novel, once to attend his son's funeral, once to help Reese and his family with mussel brailing, and memorably to escape the cycles of despair and ruination he is experiencing by fleeing to the Smoky Mountains. The reader would not be foolish to expect a return to a more recognizable pastoral note when Suttree leaves the urban jungle and takes a retreat to the natural wonders of the Great Smoky Mountains. The same reader would surely remember many examples of the restorative escape into nature in American literature—Thoreau's retreat to go to the woods in *Walden*, Ishmael's escape of society to the wild seas in Melville's *Moby Dick*, Murfree's and Still's Appalachian oases mentioned above, Tayo's embrace of the Laguna Pueblo landscape in Leslie Marmon Silko's *Ceremony*, and countless others. But as so often is the case with McCarthy's novels, the text seems to actively resist readers' conventional expectations. If one looks for Suttree's pastoral recharging in the mountains, they will be left scratching their head.

This scene, which occurs in the latter third of the book, begins with some markers of McCarthy's taxonomic mood, perhaps amended here to reflect the altered biological and geological ecosystems of the mountain environs. Suttree hikes deep into the mountains, listing flora, fauna, and fish with characteristic specificity. He even returns to his favorite trapping animal, the mink: "Scrambling up a stone throat pool to pool he saw a mink go black and bowbacked limping over the rocks. Dark mucronate droppings steaming on a shalepane replete with bones, scales, shellshards." Attention to the minutiae of the secluded mountain ecology initially feels restorative, and even what we might call semipastoral, as Suttree searches for allegory and meaning in the grandeur of the setting, a grandeur that is implicitly contrasted with the urban jungle he left: "He was moved by the utter silence of it.... In an old grandfather time a ballad transpired here, some love gone wrong and a sabledressed girl drowned in an icegreen pool where she was found with her hair spreading like ink on the cold and cobbled river floor. Ebbing in her bindings, languorous as a sea dream." (*Sut*, 282).

Such romantic language of excess and allegory reminds one of McCarthy's first published story, "Wake for Susan," which hinges on a young boy's adolescent fantasies about the former life of the young girl whose tombstone he has just discovered. There is a young and unformed style to this early story written in the 1950s, and this passage from *Suttree* feels reminiscent of the reliance on youthful fantasy to propel the story. However, the more mature writer of *Suttree* does not linger in this style for long, as McCarthy's romantic gaze finds a characteristic darker turn that focuses on the "high vast emptiness" of the mountains. The old ballad is long gone and is replaced with the "cold indifferent dark, the blind stars beaded on their tracks." Such oscillation between meaning and the absence thereof builds throughout the scene and time becomes hard to track. We know that Suttree has plunged deeper into the mountains and that his beard is now long and his clothes are falling off from a lack of sustenance. In what begins to feel like a vision quest, Suttree expresses what briefly feels a transcendent lesson through his engagement with nature: "He looked at a world of incredible loveliness. Old distaff Celt's blood in some back chamber of his brain moved him to discourse with the birches, with the oaks. A cool green fire kept breaking in the woods and he could hear the footsteps of the dead. Everything had fallen from him. He scarce could tell where his being ended or the world began nor did he care" (*Sut*, 284–86). Whether it is from a lack of food or the cold or time in isolation, Suttree appears to be hallucinating at this moment, and McCarthy's language expresses a communion with nature and the restorative potential of new insights gleaned from such communion.

As fast as McCarthy places us within a recognizable framework of the transcendence of earthly constraints through a blending with nature, the scene becomes ghastly. Suttree's hallucinations become more sinister and the communion is harder to discern. The scene becomes in Suttree's mind medieval, as he begins to see "illbedowered harlots" and "squalid merrymakers," an "eldern gnome," a mesosaur, and "nemoral halfworld inhabitants in buffoon's mockery." While these specters do not feel particularly menacing, neither do they feel productive of insight or wisdom. The promise of a transcendent bond with nature that produces sustaining wisdom has devolved in less than two pages into a carnival parade of "puckish revelers" that have nothing to offer Suttree and from whom Suttree learns nothing (*Sut*, 287–

88). Suttree initially seems to retreat to the mountains for reasons similar to those sustaining Henry David Thoreau's trek to Walden Pond a century earlier. Even so, the lack of pastoral significance in McCarthy's passage above stands in opposition to Thoreau's sense of purpose. The lack of a search for higher meaning is only highlighted when Suttree returns to Knoxville and takes up his old habits with exactly the same debauched randomness that has characterized his life experiences throughout the entire book. The pastoral discourse with the birches and oak has failed Suttree or become inaccessible to him. He returns unchanged with the same scales over his eyes as he had when he lit out to the mountains several weeks earlier.[39]

Environmental Precarity: McCarthy's Late Ecocritical Turn

For most of his career, McCarthy's interest in the ecology of the Americas tends to reflect a cognizance of political arguments of environmental peril without directly engaging the politics specifically. One can sense an ecocritical bent as early as McCarthy's first novel, *The Orchard Keeper*, which follows characters trying to exist on the fringes of society and increasingly being drawn against their wills into the routines and limitations of an industrialized society. The wild spaces that enable their ways of life are disappearing under the tighter surveillance and spread of the urban centers. This disappearance of natural or wild spaces continues to be central to McCarthy's perspective throughout his career. Think about Suttree's final fleeing of the new realities of the city and its "white concrete of the expressway [that] gleamed in the sun where the ramp curved out into empty air and hung truncate with iron rods bristling among the vectors of nowhere" (*Sut*, 471). Consider, too, the fence builders or surveyors who move like the mechanisms of a clock (escapement and pallet) across the prairies at the end of *Blood Meridian* (*BM*, 337). In both cases, workers are bringing into human cartographical and commercial order environments that throughout the book were formerly untamed wild spaces.

McCarthy's final three novels, beginning with *The Road* and culminating with *The Passenger* and *Stella Maris*, envision environmental peril differently. Humans have always been at the whim of an ever-powerful nature in McCarthy, but in these final three novels, McCarthy seems to entertain what we have taken to call "the Anthropocene"; in short, humanity's ability to affect and threaten permanently the planet and the very biological diversity that has fascinated him since he was a child. Environmental and ecocritical readings of *The Road* have dominated scholarship since that book's release in 2006.[40] Rather than rehash this scholarship and circle around an already robust field of literature, I will conclude this chapter by focusing on McCarthy's continuation of this ecological turn in the final two novels, wherein the particularly global peril of the atomic age merges with the acknowledgment of an increasingly destabilized ecology.

I began this chapter with a brief discussion of *The Passenger* and Bobby's taxonomic stroll through the woods near his grandmother's house, where he encounters the muskrat, *Ondatra zibethicus*, McCarthy tells us, and the broadwing hawk, *Buteo platypterus*. While this stroll exhibits McCarthy's interest in the classification of the natural world, the biology-minded hike is interrupted by Bobby's thoughts about the precarity of these scenes and their proximity to modern technological nightmares: "Somewhere beyond that the installation at Oak Ridge for enriching uranium that had led his father here from Princeton in 1943 and where he'd met the beauty queen he would marry. Western fully understood that he owed his existence to Adolf Hitler. That the forces of history which had ushered his troubled life into the tapestry were those of Auschwitz and Hiroshima, the sister events that sealed forever the fate of the West." On the one hand, this consideration is connected to his memory of place, as Bobby reminiscences about his childhood in this scene and his present-day walk is imbued with the past. McCarthy sandwiches this thought about the sealed fate of the West between an extended description of Bobby's high school biology study and his observation of the muskrat, and it is immediately followed by his amazement at the hawk's effortless flight, suggesting that these bucolic scenes are connected in Bobby's mind to the horrifying "forces of history" that have defined the twentieth century. It also underscores the fact that the fate of the West, including the atomic bomb's potential to obliterate all aspects of a natural landscape, has the ability, and perhaps even the probability, of rendering such taxonomy as Bobby's attention to the natural world as irrelevant or archaic. His mother's earlier memory of riding on a "school bus" being transported as a worker to the electromagnetic separation plant in the nuclear facility expresses a similar imbrication of the natural world and the modern instruments that imperil it: "she thought that she might be the only one of them [the 'calutron girls' who worked at the plant] that while she did not know what this was about knew all too well that it was Godless and that while it had poisoned back to elemental mud all living things upon that ground yet it was far from being done. It was just beginning" (*TP*, 165, 175).

Similarly, when McCarthy describes the detonation of the atomic bomb in Hiroshima, he places it within an ecocritical perspective, inverting the natural and the humanmade, the living and the destroying. The passage contains a description of a growing sporophore that defamiliarizes the traditional phrase "mushroom cloud" while also cementing that connection; the bomb's cloud is called a "mycoidal phantom" that "blooms like an evil lotus." The scene then inverts this naturalistic description of the technological violence of the bomb when describing its effects: "They saw birds in the dawn sky ignite and explode soundlessly and fall in long arcs earthward like burning party favors" (*TP*, 116). The bomb has become fungal and the birds have become party favors. In a novel full of engagement with the atomic age, this is the only description of an atomic detonation; there is no mention of the testing of the bomb, which Bobby's father would presumably have been involved with in some way, an image we see centered in Christopher Nolan's 2023 film, *Oppenheimer*.[41] McCarthy's decision to invert the natural and technological metaphors emphasizes how interconnected they are and how capable humanity is to erase the precious natural world etched into all of McCarthy's previous novels. Such an erasure revises McCarthy's earlier imagining of the catastrophic event in *The Road* wherein the destruction of the natural world is enacted by undefined forces about which the reader never learns. In *The Passenger*, conversely, the link between human technology and natural destruction is incontrovertible.

McCarthy was famously cagey when asked about the "event" that led to the end of civilization in *The Road*, tying it instead to the long history of

"LITTLE MORE THAN A CHILDHOOD ENTHUSIASM"

extinction events in our world: "A lot of people ask me [about the cause of the destruction in the novel]. I don't have an opinion. At the Santa Fe Institute I'm with scientists of all disciplines, and some of them in geology said it looked like a meteor to them. But it could be anything—volcanic activity or it could be nuclear war. It is not really important. The whole thing now is, what do you do? The last time the caldera in Yellowstone blew, the entire North American continent was under about a foot of ash."[42] In *The Passenger*, on the other hand, he seems much more intent on forcing his readers to wrestle with the realities of the atomic age, suggesting we have only seen the beginning of the evils to emerge from it, to echo Bobby's mother.

Once the precarity of the world is established, and the atomic age underlies all the uneasiness in the novel, we can see an ecocritical sensibility working throughout the entire novel. Early in the novel, Bobby notices the still-visible destruction caused by Hurricane Camille that tore through the Gulf states more than a decade earlier, reminding us all of the role of climate change in such recent disaster (*TP*, 90). In the middle of another unnamed storm, Bobby considers the migratory birds who just crossed the gulf: "Weary passerines. Vireos. Kingbirds and grosbeaks. Too exhausted to move. You could pick them up out of the sand and hold them trembling in your palm. Their small hearts beating and their eyes shuttering. He walked the beach with his flashlight the whole of the night to fend away predators and toward the dawn he slept with them in the sand. That none disturb these passengers" (*TP*, 283). This passage might remind readers of the earlier novel *Child of God*, in which Lester Ballard captures a young robin and holds it in his hand: "He caught and held one warm and feathered in his palm with the heart of it beating there just so" (*CofG*, 76). Both Bobby's and Lester's holding of the birds in their palms suggests a fragility and tenderness that is often lacking in McCarthy's prose. However, in *The Passenger*, this fragility is yoked to a larger sense of precarity—the birds are in need of protection and are already "weary."

McCarthy even invokes specifically the idea of the threat of extinction in the novel in what feels like a direct revision of his earlier obsession with bird watching and the detached study of nature. As Bobby is talking with Borman, a friend of Bobby's currently living in the "swamps east of Lafayette," Borman notices the changes in the ecological landscape: "Somewhere out here the last ivorybill died. Thirty years ago probably. I still listen to them. What sense does that make? They're gone forever."

> I didnt know you were a bird watcher.
> I'm not. I'm a forever watcher.
> Forever is a long time.
> Tell me about it. (TP, 232)

The ivory-billed woodpecker was the largest woodpecker north of Mexico and thrived in the old-growth forests of the southeast United States. With the deforestation of the region in the nineteenth century, the ivory-bill's habitat was threatened and its numbers drastically declined. It was a threatened species in the early twentieth century and is now considered to be most likely extinct. There was one alleged sighting in Arkansas in 2004, but none since then. Many more recent attempts to locate the bird have been unsuccessful.[43] McCarthy's mention of the ivory-billed woodpecker is one of the novel's most direct invocations of the ecological disasters threatened by the atomic bomb but also promulgated through technological and industrial development more generally. The fact that the ivory-bill population was decimated not by twenty-first-century climate change or atomic radiation or urban smog but by nineteenth-century deforestation underscores that, for McCarthy, our environmental precarity has been under way for a long time. Borman's refinement of "bird watching" to "forever watching" matches McCarthy's own interests. As his writing developed in the twenty-first century, and his sense of the Anthropocene hardened, environmental disasters and extinctions become yoked to human activity, and the sense of the damage being, in Borman's word, "forever" is heightened.

McCarthy's interest in the possibility of extinction and humanity's role in it has a long history, one that can be tied back to the earliest days of his time at the Santa Fe Institute, where he enjoyed his conversations with scientists and mathematicians. While it is the mathematics that may be granted special attention as readers wrestle with *The Passenger* and *Stella Maris*, McCarthy was also drawn to scientists of the biological world, such as evolutionary biologist and paleobiologist Doug Erwin, who is a senior scientist at the National Museum of the Smithsonian Institute, and external affiliated professor with the Santa Fe Institute. In a series of memorial comments dedication to the memory of McCarthy on the Institute's website, Erwin remembers McCarthy's long-standing interest in the topic of extinction:

> I was slow in realizing that Cormac was not interested in dinosaurs. In the early 2000s, Cormac developed an intense interest in the details of the bolide impact associated with the end-Cretaceous mass extinction. How large was the impactor? What would it have looked like? How long would the dust cloud have remained suspended in the atmosphere?
>
> Returning to SFI after the latest mass extinction meeting (there were many meetings then), Cormac interrogated me about the finest details, revealing what I viewed as an increasingly unhealthy interest in the event. Finally, in some frustration, I told him about a series of volumes collecting the latest modeling of dust clouds, the spread of impact debris, and the incineration of North American forests. I thought Cormac's unaccountable interest was finally satiated. They were, as we saw in the beginning of *The Road*.[44]

Perhaps Erwin had not yet read *The Passenger* when he offered these comments or perhaps he was thinking of the genesis of McCarthy's earlier novel and its particular interest in the kind of planetary catastrophes that show up in that novel, but his comments resonate with McCarthy's developing interests in his final novels in environmental peril and the delicacies of ecosystems and habitats. It feels as if rather than focusing on the "what do you do" response in *The Road*, in these final books he is more attuned to the causes, minute and massive, that lead us step by step toward mass extinction.

Up until the final novels published months before McCarthy died in June of 2023, *The Road* was his most recent book. The last paragraph in that novel has long been one of my favorites in all of McCarthy's work. Before the new books, it read as a sort of coda to McCarthy's taxonomic mood, expressing the same commitment to the charting and describing of the natural environment that had been around since his high school interest in taxidermy. The novel concludes,

> Once there were brook trout in the streams in the mountains. You could see them standing in the amber current where the white edges of their fins wimpled softly in the flow. They smelled of moss in your hand. Polished and muscular and torsional. On their backs were vermiculate patterns that were maps of the world in its becoming. Maps and mazes. Of a thing which could not be put back. Not be made right again. In the deep glens where they lived all things were older than man and they hummed of mystery. (TR, 286–87)

Brook trout are notoriously sensitive to environmental change and serve as an aquatic version of the "canary in a coal mine" idea, registering the harmful effects of acid rain and rising water temperatures especially. Whereas some species may be heartier and resistant to such differences, brook trout register the early warning signs of climate change. As Jordon Ross, the president of Trout Power, explains it, "The fish that live in (these waterways) are essentially a bio-indicator. . . . If you're going to go and catch wild, native brook trout in a stream, and they exist—that in and of itself is an indicator of a healthy ecosystem."[45]

In addition to containing an environmental warning that reinforces the sense of precarity in the novel as a whole, this final paragraph is beautiful and mournful, tragic and wistful. It is not coincidence that the final word in the paragraph and in the book is "mystery," a mystery of the natural world that is easy to overlook and that is disappearing. The mystery lies in nothing more and nothing less than the close examination of the world. Upon such inspection, the "vermiculate patterns" become legible maps. However, whereas human maps traditionally reduce mystery by offering a logical understanding, in McCarthy's hands these maps engender and reveal mystery. Whether it is brook trout, the rock formations in the Sonoran Desert, the weedy hidden pathways in urban Knoxville, or the muskrat habitats in the Tennessee mountains, it is the hum of mystery that sustains the world in McCarthy's fiction.

FOUR

The Precarious Mood
The Passenger, Stella Maris, and the Fragile Twentieth Century

Chapter 3 examined McCarthy's taxonomic mood and the ways in which his interest in classification was as likely to lead toward a sense of the uncategorizable mystery as it was to dispel such unknowns. This final chapter builds on this idea of indeterminacy, focusing on the last two novels of his career, *The Passenger* and *Stella Maris*. More specifically, this chapter explores the twinned nature of these novels and suggests that the formal composition of each novel, as well as their function as a "duality," establishes a mood of precarity. While drawing on McCarthy's newer interest in theoretical physics and abstract mathematics, both books use these scientific concepts to create new literary styles, but also to explore from a different vantage point questions that help define McCarthy's career. One aspect of *The Passenger* and *Stella Maris* that feels new and radical is that not only do they engage the philosophical and scientific implications of theories of indeterminacy and chaos but they are also formally determined by them. By this I mean the very ideas of radical indeterminacy and quantum entanglement that McCarthy's protagonists struggle to comprehend in the world of mathematics become part of the organizational structure of the twinned novels. The two novels cannot be separated, at least without losing their center. Nor can they be reduced to one novel (even as they were probably originally envisioned as one longer novel). In many ways, they present two different yet interconnected versions of the world. The characters within the novels become like Schrödinger's cat, both alive and dead in a hypothetical box. Indeed, in *The Passenger,* Alicia is dead in the first paragraph, and the novel follows her brother's attempt to come to terms with his loss. In *Stella Maris,* Alicia is very much alive, although boxed into a series of psychological interviews that spiral toward her suicide.

Toward its conclusion, this chapter switches gears somewhat, as I seek to establish the historical record of displacement in East Tennessee that haunts these novels, and one could argue McCarthy's entire career. Even though the discussion of historical record and accuracy comes to dominate in these moments, the effect is the same, as McCarthy uses the historical past in the service of a mood of precarity. As the people of East Tennessee are displaced by governmental initiative, including most notably for the subject of these novels, the Oak Ridge nuclear facilities so central to the development of the atomic bomb, the result is a lack of grounding for the people, a lack of a belief in the future, and the provisionality of the present. So while my research approach at the end of the chapter may shift a bit, the mood elicited from this research remains the same.

As McCarthy's second-to-last novel, *The Passenger,* careens toward its conclusion, the reader hears from the mathematical genius Alicia Western, who has been dead since the first page of the novel when we first read of her suicide. Throughout the novel, we learn from her brother, Bobby, and her conversations with the Thalidomide Kid that Alicia has been part of the University of Chicago PhD mathematics program since her mid-teens and has been extended a residency at the very prestigious Paris-based IHÉS (Institut des hautes études scientifiques) to work with Alexander Grothendieck—both the institute and Grothendieck are factual elements added to the fictional story. This novel and its companion, *Stella Maris,* follow Alicia's evolution as a thinker, mathematical savant, and young human (she is a child in large portions of the books).

Even with her unparalleled mathematical accomplishments as a teenager, when talking about mathematical theory, Alicia speaks in terms of doubt and unknowability, rather than mastery: "*I dont know how one does mathematics. I dont know that there is a way. The idea is always struggling against its own realization. Ideas come with an innate skepticism, they dont just go barrel-*

ing about. And these doubts have their origin in the same world as the idea itself. . . . Of course, the idea is going to come to an end anyway. Once a mathematical conjecture is formalized into a theory it may have a certain luster to it but with rare exceptions you can no longer entertain the illusion that it holds some deep insight into the core of reality." She ends her thoughts in this chapter by turning away from mathematics and toward reality more generally, specifically storytelling's ability to capture and relate this reality: "*You think that you can create a history of what has been [in a story]. Present artifacts. A clutch of letters. A sachet in the dressingtable drawer. But that's not what's at the heart of the tale. The problem is that what drives the tale will not survive the tale. As the room dims and the sound of voices fades you understand that the world and all in it will soon cease to be. You believe that it will begin again. You point to other lives. But their lives were never yours*" (TP, 297–98).

Apart from showing the suicidal and fatalistic views that defined Alicia's adult life, this passage exhibits McCarthy's lifelong interest in the social role of tales and storytelling. It also displays his late-life fascination with theoretical mathematics, such as that found in topos theory and quantum mechanics. His time as a resident, then trustee, and now "immortal trustee" of the theoretical and interdisciplinary Santa Fe Institute has left an undeniable imprint on his late fiction. As David Krakauer, president of the Institute, puts it, McCarthy is an "aficionado on subjects ranging from the history of mathematics, philosophical arguments related to the status of quantum mechanics as a causal theory, comparative evidence bearing on non-human intelligence, and the nature of the conscious and unconscious mind."[1]

It is this chapter's contention that it is not so much that his time at the SFI has changed McCarthy's orientation to the world but that it has shifted the language he uses to explore the world. He has pondered the indeterminacy of reality, the meaning of life, and the illusory notion of transcendent Truth ever since the opening pages of his first novel. So, rather than seeing his turn to science in his later years as a fundamental shift, it makes sense to think about the ways he weaves theoretical mathematics and physics into these long-held considerations. Bryan Giemza, in his book *Science and Literature in Cormac McCarthy's Expanding Worlds*, suggests that McCarthy's interaction with science and complexity theories within science more specifically fits well with the kinds of questions readers of McCarthy have been asking all along: "In honoring the spirit of McCarthy's work, and the mutual reinforcement of scientific and humanistic discourses, our inquiries come to resemble the stuff of Santa Fe's big questions, and in framing those queries carefully, we become, in the broadest sense, a band of merry scientists."[2]

McCarthy proves deeply committed in *The Passenger* and *Stella Maris* to offering a complex representation of indeterminacy in the form of the novels. The two books are interwoven in an intricate manner that McCarthy never attempted before, not even with his Western Border Trilogy published in the 1990s, where characters traverse in and out of multiple books. At the first international conference dedicated to these novels held by the Cormac McCarthy Society in September 2023, less than a year after the novels' publications, there were several early attempts to define and name the intricate relationship between the two novels; a dyad, a diptych, sibling novels, contrapuntal, and the quantum gothic were terms bandied about as descriptors, as well as their formal affinity to various mathematical principles, such as entanglement theory and complexity theory.[3] The novels have elsewhere been compared to a double act, the double-faced Janus, and Johann Sebastian Bach's *Goldberg Variations*. Like Bach's fugues and variations, the separate tales/melodies within the novels are independent, yet remain fundamentally inseparable.[4]

While the novels entertain questions McCarthy had been exploring his entire literary career, they are focused through McCarthy's more recent thinking about science as seen in his nonfiction essay "The Kekulé Problem," published in *Nautilus* (an interdisciplinary scientific journal) in 2017. McCarthy was surely working on or at least thinking about *The Passenger* and *Stella Maris* as he penned this essay. The most direct parallels to "The Kekulé Problem" in the novels are voiced by Alicia. Perhaps no other character in his canon is as closely aligned with McCarthy's own expressed ideas as is Alicia. It might be surprising that he puts his thoughts into the mouth and brain of one of his few women protagonists. That she is also a misunderstood and alienated genius may be less surprising.

In "The Kekulé Problem," McCarthy entertains both his intense interest in a scientific accounting of the world and his love of language. The essay focuses on what he presents as the odd and incredible work that the unconscious does as "a machine for operating an animal." He is fascinated, as many others in the past have been, with the ways our brains can resolve problems while we are sleeping or otherwise occupied, when we are not "thinking" about the problems. McCarthy believes this unconscious machine has been around much longer than language, so it must speak to the conscious mind through symbols and dreams. August Kekulé becomes McCarthy's symbol for this dynamic, as legend has the German chemist figuring out the structure of the benzine molecule while asleep, dreaming of the ouroboros forming the shape of a ring. It was this dream that allowed Kekulé to understand the structure of the benzine molecule as a ring. Thinking, in this kind of experience, is for McCarthy "largely an unconscious affair." In fact, for McCarthy, language creates as many problems for us as it provides solutions: "Did [language] meet some need? No. The other five thousand plus mammals among us do fine without it."[5] These ideas are repeated very closely, at times almost verbatim, by Alicia in her discussions with the psychiatrist Dr. Cohen in *Stella Maris*.[6]

Both McCarthy in "The Kekulé Problem" and Alicia in the novels question the primacy of language and both search for older human forms of cognition rooted in the unconscious and dreams. For Alicia, an accomplished classical violinist, music seems more closely aligned with the prelinguistic. She explains, "The notes [in a musical composition] themselves amount to almost nothing. But why some particular arrangement of these notes should have such a profound effect on our emotions is a mystery beyond even the hope of comprehension. Music is not a language. It has no reference to anything other than itself" (*SM*, 38). It is intriguing, then, that McCarthy would seek to enact these principles through fiction, through language itself. One way to understand this apparent paradox is to see McCarthy as decentering and frustrating the rules of language and narrative in these novels as a way to approach the mystery of musical expression, thus tapping into the unconscious mind's tendency to speak to the conscious mind through symbols and dreams. McCarthy encourages us to engage these novels as a type of dreamscape—not so much as the hallucination-filled dream visions of Lewis Carroll's *Alice's Adventures in Wonderland* or Samuel Taylor Coleridge's poem "Kubla Kahn," but as attempts to tap into the realms of human experience not captured by the conscious and rational part of our brains. McCarthy's final books seek to communicate to the reader on a level that is at times beneath the rules of language and the rationality of the conscious mind and at others residing alongside but apart from the conscious and traditional mechanisms of expression.

The Eponymous Passenger, the Thalidomide Kid, and Other Literary Frustrations

Even if the reader is able to master highly theoretical mathematics and quantum mechanics, and if this reader is able to absorb fully McCarthy's Kekulé metaphors in the novels, the books still remain difficult to comprehend. There is the relationship of the two books, which seem paired but also unique to themselves. There is in *The Passenger* a number of stunted plotlines—the airplane crash, the missing passenger, and the governmental surveillance—that are never fully explained. There are unexpected and disconnected forays into major moments of twentieth-century history, including the development of the atomic bomb, the JFK assassination, the Vietnam War, and many others. *The Passenger* begins as a potboiler, a thriller about espionage, and ends with a man alone wandering the beaches of a Spanish island. There is very little connective tissue weaving it all together. Fold in *Stella Maris*, which is comprised entirely of a recorded conversation between the psychiatrist Dr. Cohen and the residential patient Alicia, and the connections are even less apparent.

One review calls the books "deliberately frustrating,"[7] and this description feels like a fair way to characterize them. Like Alicia's mathematical ideas that she claims lose power as they become formalized into theories, the confusion created by these novels and their fragmented stories is not resolved as we better understand them. Instead, we are asked to balance multiple stories, realities, and frames of reference together. As much as abstract theoretical mathematics become key elements of the novels' structure, so, too, is the fragmentation of ideas, storylines, character arcs, and the like. The promise of a predictable whodunit offered in the opening pages of *The Passenger* is never realized. The frustration of the standard narrative arcs (and more than a few readers) is yet another means of creating the precarious mood—we often don't know where we are in the books or even at times what we are reading. Some readers have characterized the novels as being sloppy, a sloppiness generally attributed either to the fact that McCarthy had been working on them since the early 1980s or to the fact that they were finished by an author in his late eighties. Neither of these explanations for the fragmented nature of books feels entirely right to me. Instead, the novels feel incredibly intricate and meticulously orchestrated. The texts present a surfeit of philosophical and mathematical ideas about uncertainty, but the most radical and fearless element of the books is McCarthy's courage to represent this uncertainty formally, through the structure and plotlines of the conjoined novels.

One of the most mysterious aspects of the books is the role of the character known as the Thalidomide Kid, a character who appears to Alicia when she is alone, usually in her bedroom. Doctors in the novels go to some lengths to diagnose the Kid and his cohorts (or 'horts for short) as products of Alicia's paranoid schizophrenia with "a longstanding aetiology of visual and auditory hallucinations" (*SM*, 3). The Kid similarly describes himself to Alicia in the opening pages of *The Passenger* as a figment of the imagination: "Not every ectromelic hallucination who shows up in your boudoir on your birthday is out to get you" (6). However, the books seem to resist such a singular understanding of this character as merely a hallucination in at least a couple of ways. First, at one point the Kid appears to Alicia's brother, Bobby, who has mental health issues but no signs of hallucinatory conditions, eight years after she dies. This "fact" of the novels is impossible if we write the Kid off as residing solely in Alicia's imagination. Second, the novel includes passages where the descriptions of the Kid are outside of Alicia's experience and perspective. This, too, would be impossible in a straightforward presentation of her hallucinations. Neither does McCarthy want to dispel the possibility of the Kid and the 'horts being imagined. In fact, they refer to themselves in this way at times, seeming to corroborate the doctors' diagnoses. Rather, McCarthy encourages his readers to hold at the same time the possibility that the Thalidomide Kid is real and that he is imaginary, an entity with superhuman powers and a hallucination, alive in the novel and dead outside of Alicia's mind. We are left, once again, thinking of Schrödinger's metaphor of the cat that is both dead and alive in the box.

Real or not, the Kid is certainly odd. He is called a "dwarf" and described as having flippers, "sort of like a seal has," and wears "funny oar-like shoes." He has a "pale keloidal skull" that is "eggshaped" with "visible commissures of the plates through the papery skin" and "chewed-looking ears" (TP, 5, 272, 55, 275). In many ways, he is a diminutive version of the Judge in *Blood Meridian*, whose lack of melanin and a similarly egg-shaped head evoke the description of him as a "great pale deity" (BM, 92). While the Thalidomide Kid does not suggest such greatness, as he fumbles and stammers precisely where the Judge is composed, he does seem supernatural. His description as a hallucination attests both to the possibility of his emerging from Alicia's mind and of his otherworldly qualities. Real or not, he clearly does not fit comfortably into our reality.

As mentioned above, McCarthy keeps the fictional conceit that the Kid might actually exist in play through narrative shifts, where the narrator steps outside Alicia's perspective and describes the Kid apart from her own impressions. While these shifts are subtle and easy to overlook, they create the sense of the Kid operating independently, outside of Alicia's perhaps hallucinogenic mind. The first instance of this kind of separation happens in chapter 4 in *The Passenger*, as the Kid is visiting Alicia in her attic bedroom. As they discuss Alicia's closeness to her brother, the narrative shifts away from dialogue: "*The Kid had paused and was standing in the dormer window looking out over the darkening countryside. The wind sheared thinly along the tin eaves and the glass rattled in the sash and was still again. The girl watched him. . . . She turned to the mirror and for a moment she thought he was gone but he was there in the glass*" (TP, 113). Perhaps one could account for all of this within Alicia's mind, but it encourages us to see him as independent. He is looking out the window, observing the wind's shearing along the house. Alicia thinks he is gone, but he remains there. This unsettling of narrative perspective and narrative "truth" is another example of McCarthy's commitment to rendering instability and uncertainty at the formal level of these novels.

An even more pronounced moment of separation between Alicia's perspective and the narrative description happens in chapter 7, when the Kid appears to Bobby long after Alicia had died. Once could suggest that Bobby is now imagining the Kid as his sister did, perhaps even as an attempt to keep her alive through his memory or imagination. This suggestion works to a certain extent. But McCarthy describes the Kid once again as a real being, independent from Bobby's and Alicia's minds. When Bobby first meets the Kid, the encounter is narrated as real: "He was much as she'd described him. The hairless skull corraded with the scars perhaps come by at his unimaginable creation. The funny oarlike shoes he wore. His seal's slippers splayed on the arms of the chair" (*TP*, 272). The reader is both encouraged to believe Bobby is imagining him "much like" his sister described to him and to see the Kid as independent and, in the book's universe, real. Indeterminacy is coded into the novel, even at the level of character development.

Finally, there is the odd name: the Thalidomide Kid. Thalidomide is a compound developed by the West German pharmaceutical company Chemie Grünenthal GmbH. It was initially intended as a sedative or tranquilizer but also became a widely prescribed drug of the 1950s and 1960s to treat morning sickness in pregnant women. The manufacturers and scientific community tested the drug before its release, but did not include tests involving pregnant subjects. The resulting "Thalidomide tragedy" led to more than ten thousand babies being harmed by the effects of the drug. These effects included infant mortality and perhaps most famously severe birth abnormalities, especially phocomelia (malformation of the limbs).[8] These details about the harmful effects of the drug help to explain parts of the Kid's appearance—the "chewed-looking ears" and his "flippers." The facts, however, do not help the reader to understand *why* he is connected to this pharmaceutical scandal or *how* it helps us to understand his appearance in the novel. His birth story is never given, nor is an explanation of his misshapen limbs. Undoubtedly, part of the role of the Thalidomide Kid is his ability to blur the line between reality and unreality in the novel or to suggest the idea of multiple realities. Furthermore, in a point I will return to shortly, the allusion to the Thalidomide tragedy also places the books within a context of twentieth-century technology and science, emphasizing the dangers of a too-eager confidence in the power of these technological advancements. This misplaced confidence in scientific and technological discovery looms over both novels and becomes part of the precarious mood that colors them. In 1935, DuPont adopted its famous advertising slogan "Better Living through Chemistry," a slogan it would use until 1982. That the Thalidomide Kid's "deformations" come out of the spirit captured so poignantly in this slogan is a reality that becomes part of the book's affective centering on the provisionality of knowledge.⁹

Conspiracy and Information in a Modern World

One way to begin to envision throughlines between the various plot elements of the two books is to see them as expressing McCarthy's interest in one of the defining legacies of the twentieth century—the growing belief in conspiracies that give the public a way to understand increasing governmental and corporate surveillance.¹⁰ These conspiracies question the basic reality of what in other contexts is considered reliable and truthful. The attention to conspiracy theories in these novels creates a mood of paranoia that becomes hard to shake. The paranoid mood extends beyond the characters and settles into the novel's narrative structure. This formal commitment to such a paranoid perspective can be found in the fact that all of the major "asides" to the plot and family story relate to issues in the twentieth century that have created conspiratorial buzz. The secrecy behind the atomic project, the uncertainties about U.S. engagement in Vietnam, and especially the assassination of John F. Kennedy all enacted huge conspiracy theories, and they all show up unexpectedly in *The Passenger*. I will explore the atomic age in greater detail in a few pages, but both the Vietnam engagement and the JFK assassination appear in this novel as what at first seems like throwaway bar banter, or McCarthy's awkward attempt to engage the key moments of the twentieth century. However, I am suggesting they are not "sloppy" plot moments of pastiche or lazy writing; they become key formal elements that work to shake the foundation of the novel's structure(s).

We also see McCarthy's attention to the ways paranoia affects his novels' characters. In this light, rather than a banal recounting of the history of these events, we get personal stories therein. With the Vietnam War, Bobby grills his good friend Oiler about his experience in the war. Reluctant to provide details, Oiler hedges with comments such as, "You can make up your own story. You wont be far off." When Bobby pushes Oiler on his role in the war, Oiler responds, "You dont even know enough to ask" (*TP*, 35). It becomes clear that Oiler's perspective is a familiar one; translating the "war experience" to those who haven't been there is a difficult and often fruitless process. The gap of knowledge and experiences is too great.

But behind this give-and-take about Oiler's experiences as a "door gunner" on a military helicopter in Vietnam is a meditation on the knowability of the war at all. The confusion about the mission or purpose in Vietnam only creates a heightened sense of uncertainty in these asides. In 1971, Daniel Ellsberg reported on and leaked information about what would become known as *The Pentagon Papers*. These documents about the Vietnam War were originally classified and were produced by the Vietnam Study Task Force, comprised of thirty-six analysts, commissioned by Secretary of Defense Robert McNamara to create an "encyclopedic history of the Vietnam War."[11] These papers became so monumental and so controversial because they provided glimpses underneath the official governmental reports that had heretofore been delivered. The papers suggested, among other things, that the U.S. military was operating in Laos, in opposition to the claims and rules of engagement, and that the government (all the way up to President Lyndon B. Johnson) had consistently lied to the American public about key facts and policies in the war, U.S. involvement in the South Vietnamese coup that led to the assassination of President Diệm, and countless other aspects of the nation's involvement in Southeast Asia since World War II. In this light, Oiler's comment "You dont even know enough to ask" can serve as a commentary on the war more generally, and our ability to know and trust the histories that are handed down. The conspiracies about governmental manipulation and orchestration of global political landscapes suddenly had a byline with these papers, and the information was appearing in the *New York Times*, the *Washington Post*, and *Time Magazine*. The paranoid mood here is eventually supported by the mainstream media.

In *The Passenger*, rather than pursue a line of questions about rules of engagement or military policy, Bobby is quick to ask Oiler lurid personal questions. "How many times were you wounded?" quickly escalates to "Did you kill a lot of people?" to which Oiler can only respond, "Jesus" (*TP*, 36–38). As the line of questioning intensifies, Bobby seems not so dissimilar from the barroom acquaintance Angelica whom Vietnam vet and Louisiana poet Yosef Komunyakaa writes about in the prose poem "Nude Interrogation":

DID YOU KILL ANYONE OVER THERE? Angelica shifts her gaze from the Janis Joplin poster to the Jimi Hendrix, lifting the pale muslin blouse over her head. The blacklight deepens the blues when the needle drops into the first groove of "All Along the Watchtower." I don't want to look at the floor. *Did you kill anyone? Did you dig a hole, crawl inside, and wait for your target?* Her miniskirt drops into a rainbow at her feet. Sandalwood incense hangs a slow comet of perfume over the room. I shake my head. She unhooks her bra and flings it against a bookcase made of plywood and cinderblocks. *Did you use an M-16, a hand-grenade, a bayonet, or your own two strong hands, both thumbs pressed against that little bird in the throat?* She stands with her left thumb hooked into the elastic of her sky-blue panties. When she flicks off the blacklight, snowy hills rush up to the windows. *Did you kill anyone over there? Are you right-handed or left-handed? Did you drop your gun afterwards? Did you kneel beside the corpse and turn it over?* She's nude against the falling snow. Yes. The record spins like a bull's eyes on the far wall of Xanadu. Yes, I say. *I was scared of the silence. The night was too big. And afterwards, I couldn't stop looking up at the sky.*[12]

There is a lurid voyeurism in both Angelica's line of questions and Bobby's. McCarthy suggests a further connection in how romantic interest and war fascination are often linked by responding to Bobby's questions by saying he had never been asked these questions "by a man" (*TP*, 39). Both interrogators want to know the very information that veterans are often loathe to discuss or traumatized by the retelling. They are searching for foundational knowledge and understanding where there is none. Oiler continuously articulates his resistance to telling these stories. At one point, he directly states, "Gimme a break. That's it, Bobby, I'm done" (*TP*, 41). As we will shortly see, this exchange mirrors the testy exchanges in *Stella Maris* between Alicia Western and her aggressive interviewer, Dr. Cohen. Just as Alicia is reluctant to share her private traumas in a psychiatric setting and often requests a break from the interviews, so, too, does Oiler recoil from Bobby's insistent questioning.

Rather than giving the questioning Angelica what she wants, the voice in Komunyakaa's poem speaks of loneliness and fear instead of the expected barbarity and violence. Similarly, when Bobby asks Oiler about his biggest regret about the war, he speaks not of killing Viet Cong or of raiding villages but of the death of elephants roaming the Southeast Asian jungles: "Where we flew out of Quang Nam we'd see these elephants in the clearings and bulls would back off and raise their trunks and challenge us. Think about that. That's pretty fucking bold. . . . [The rockets on the helicopters] could go anywhere. So maybe we thought what the fuck. They've got a chance. But we never missed. And it would just blow them up. They'd just fucking explode. I think about that, man. They hadnt done anything. And who were they going to see about it? So that's what I think about. That's what I regret. All right?" (TP, 42). While this story does not exactly resonate with the larger conspiracies revealed in *The Pentagon Papers*, it does invoke the silent and alternative history—the parts of the war that were "sliding off into the toilet," in Oiler's words—that was repressed or concealed from the public because of its barbarity and abandonment of what the U.S. public liked to think were the purpose and rules of a very confusing war. Oiler's war story interrupts *The Passenger*'s principal plotline to take the reader on a temporary aside to the Vietnam conflict, this disruption of plot a reminder of McCarthy's resistance to a formal wholeness or continuity in his final novels.

Bobby's interaction with the private investigator Kline brings up the notion of conspiracy in a manner that proves more central to the plot, as Kline helps Bobby investigate who is following, surveilling, and curtailing his life. It seems certain that the agents harassing Bobby are from the government—they are capable of freezing his bank accounts and seizing his property. They also seem to have resources that have enabled them to learn a lot about him, especially given his out-of-the-way job as a salvage diver. Bobby and Kline suspect at certain points that the men in black suits are from the IRS, and there are elements in the novel that suggest their investigation is nothing more than an examination of Bobby's unclaimed wealth, which the reader knows comes from his grandparents burying of gold coins in the basement of their house. Even his grandparents' decision to bury hundreds of thousands of dollars' worth of gold in lead tubes in their basement resonates with the mood of paranoia, and the more Kline and Bobby explore, the more the conversation hinges on conspiracies, big and small. There is a paranoid feel to Bobby and Kline's conversations, and McCarthy's depiction of Bobby's experiences more generally.

This unsettling context provides a way to approach the somewhat odd inclusion in the novel of Kline's extended digression about the assassination of John F. Kennedy. Even this diatribe follows another consideration of alleged governmental conspiracy, the possible cover-up of Ted Kennedy's vehicular homicide of one of his brother Robert's campaign workers, Mary Jo Kopechne, in 1969 on Chappaquiddick Island, Massachusetts. Although information about the crash is still limited, according to most reports, Ted allegedly drove off a bridge with the two of them in the car and plunged into a river, where Mary Jo drowned. The accident was not reported to authorities until the morning, and there were reports of Kennedy's alcohol consumption being a factor and of a subsequent governmental cover-up. There are to this day books being written on the accident accelerated by the recent release of original FBI files of an investigation from 1969.[13] The event will be familiar to fans of the HBO series *Succession*, which fictionalizes the event in the finale of its first season in 2018.[14]

McCarthy embeds Kline's diatribe about the JFK assassination within Bobby's panic over the covert surveillance of his person, possibly related to the plane wreck and possibly related to his personal finances. Such a narrative structure points to McCarthy's conspiratorial mood in the book, his interest in the coexistence of multiple versions of truth and reality that ultimately undermine any claim to a primacy of a coherent reality altogether. Beginning with the assertion that he doesn't believe that Lee Harvey Oswald was responsible for Kennedy's death, Kline goes into flabbergasting detail (for a book with nothing to do with the assassination) about the shooting. He mentions the ballistics of the ammunition found on site and the capabilities of the weapon Oswald abandoned: "The Carcano [6.5 Mannlicher-Carcano rifle] could no more have done that than a BB gun." He analyzes Jackie Kennedy's actions on the trunk of the car to consider the angle of the shot and the likelihood of Kennedy being hit by a "frangible" hollow-point round. He turns to the famous Abraham Zapruder film, vital to so many conspiracy theories about the assassination, at one point singling out frame 313 of the 8 mm, 26-second home-movie recording of the shooting (*TP*, 338–44). As those who have spent time with this film and its backstory are aware, this frame was originally withheld from the public, ostensibly because it was too graphic, and wasn't released to the public until twelve years after the assassination. Many viewers are inclined to believe the idea that the suppression of the frame makes sense as a gesture of restraint that the public expects to see in coverage of the murder of its president. For others, including Kline, the image has been withheld because it challenges the official history of who shot JFK. For these people, where the shot came from, the required marksmanship, and a host of other evidence prove that Oswald could not be the assassin. As this multipage digression concludes, Kline returns to 1980 and the reason for Bobby's visit—his need to change his identity and get supporting documents that will allow him to escape his own entanglement in a governmental secret mission. Once again, we are presented multiple coexisting realities, and the result is a feeling of the precarious nature of reality itself.

As was the case with Oiler and the Vietnam discussion, Bobby and Kline's conversations tend to happen in bars and restaurants, unannounced and unexpected public meetings that would make electronic or in-person eavesdropping less likely. The 1990s TV show *The X Files* would be proud of their work to cover their tracks from spying governmental agents. The book never definitely takes a stand on whether Bobby's sense of conspiracy regarding his own life is delusional or paranoid or accurate. It is yet another one of those unresolved elements of the book, like the missing passenger, the looted airplane, the missing black box, and the bizarre and quickly terminated investigation of the plane wreck. What seems to tie all these fragmented portions of the novel together is the paranoid sense of unknowability being a fundamental aspect of post–World War II America, the relativity of truth and history to invoke both quantum physics and postmodern critical theory. It creates a mood of precarity, where everything is provisional and nothing makes complete sense. Just as McCarthy uses the fragmentation of his plot and the insertion of the Thalidomide Kid in this plot to fracture a coherent narrative, he examines the late twentieth century's fascination with conspiracy and cover-ups to return to his favorite topic—the conditional basis of all history, truth, and language. It is a mood that creates a feeling of unease and a sense of uncertainty that might, from other perspectives, feel like a clumsy organization of the novel or lack of editorial direction. As a gesture of transparency, I feel I should reveal that as I was doing some Internet research on the suppression of facts in the Mary Jo

Kopechne case, my perfectly fine and relatively new laptop went completely haywire and ceased working to the point I couldn't even shut it down for several minutes. Conspiracy? I'll let you, Kline, Mulder, and Scully, decide.

The Kid and the Entertainment of an Earlier Era

I have argued above that *The Passenger* is firmly committed to the exploration of mid-twentieth-century history, including conspiracy-laden history and the hushed history of complex and controversial wars, but in a way that fractures the reader's sense of this history. These moments in the text, which are generally centered around Bobby and his wandering around New Orleans bars and his conversations therein, are interrupted throughout the novel with italicized exchanges between the Thalidomide Kid and Alicia. Not only are these interruptions outside of the present of the novel—Alicia, as we know, has been dead since page one—but they also provide a different grid of references than does the rest of the novel. Bobby's concerns are post–World War II paranoia. The Kid's actions are based in prewar forms of entertainment, namely a slew of vaudeville acts and skits that Alicia rarely finds entertaining or even bearable. But he draws on this entertainment with the goal of saving Alicia's life by talking her out of her suicidal ideations. He aims to distract her, to entertain her, but the goal is always to alter her mood, even if it is through irritation or provocation. So, one might ask, why does McCarthy create a mediator to this history in the Thalidomide Kid, who relies on routines and bits taken from the vaudeville shows of a bygone era?

The first time we meet the Kid at the beginning of *The Passenger*, he is described as having mannerisms like "a villain in a silent film," and thus is immediately placed in a long tradition of the American entertainment industry. This initial introduction, which comes before any mention of Bobby or the airplane or the book's present, is an extreme example of an in medias res beginning to the novel, except it is even more confounding precisely because what we are thrown into the middle of makes so little sense. The Kid carries an enormous phone that appears like a gag prop and speaks in misstatements seemingly designed for entertainment. He constantly mixes up common sayings: "Two wrongs don't make a riot," "dining on fatback and harmony grits." He tells bawdy jokes and messes up the punchline, such as the one about Minnie Mouse and her affair, which typically ends with the line "She's fucking Goofy" and not "she's fucking nuts," as the Kid delivers it. He speaks of the "old Chautauqua stuff" that he hopes Alicia will like because she "always had a taste for the classics" (TP, 5, 10–14).

These kinds of exchanges between the Kid and Alicia appear at the beginning of each chapter, and we get ten performances in all. The Kid often brings his cohorts, or 'horts, as he calls them, to help stage the entertainment. At the beginning of chapter 2, the Kid and his 'horts appear in blackface and conduct jokes in dialect; in chapter 3, they perform the classic song and dance "Shuffle Off to Buffalo" from the stage musical 42nd Street. In chapter 7, a rakish wooden dummy named Puddentain comes out of a trunk, looking "cocky and slightly dangerous," and performs a typical brand of bawdy vaudeville (TP, 53, 76, 239). As scholars of the history of the stage remind us, vaudeville is often seen as throwaway "vapidity." David Monod suggests alternatively that it is actually an "engagement with modern life," both in terms of its ability to reach a national audience through the distribution of acts and in its seeming banality, which served "a therapeutic function" that battled the emptiness and discontinuity of modern life.[15]

While the vaudeville skits are largely ineffective at distracting Alicia, the Kid's sense of their possible therapeutic benefits seems to diagnose her emptiness and her sense of the "discontinuity" of modern life. In fact, his role often feels more helpful than the official "therapeutic" members of the mental institution who "grope" Alicia, sexualize her in their descriptions and diagnoses, and exploit her genius for their own research. There is a tenderness in the Kid's attempt to distract Alicia from her suicidal plans, and the tenderness is reciprocated at several points in the novels. At one point in the first chapter, when Alicia mocks the 'horts' acts, the Kid expresses his pain: "We really put ourselves out for you you know." Alicia quickly apologizes. At other times, it is Alicia who recognizes the considerable efforts the Kid goes to in order to stage these performances, even when she takes issue with them: "You're just totally bogus. . . . Don't you think I can see that this is all just for my benefit. . . . You're just a pain in the ass. You and your entertainments. Your shopworn Chautauquas." The Kid replies, "How about cutting me some slack? It's not like there's a playbook here." At another point, she cuttingly calls him a "dwarf" and then offers a series of sincere apologies (*TP*, 12, 106, 127–28). They have a consistent and enduring relationship, even as it is often strange and possibly exists only in her head.

The Kid is clearly grasping for straws throughout much of his interaction with Alicia. He struggles to figure out how to help her in a manner that is not unlike Black in *The Sunset Limited*, who is desperate to keep White from committing suicide. As their exchanges become increasingly tender, Black comes to realize and lament the fact that he wasn't given the words to change White's mind. There builds in the relationship between Alicia and the Kid a similar tenderness based around her growing ideations of suicide. In what is their final exchange in italics of the novel, they discuss Alicia's growth and her current suffering. The Kid begins,

> *But you stopped crying.*
>   *As a baby.*
>   *Yes.*
>   *Yes. Actually I think I got pretty quiet.*
>   *Do you cry now?*
>   *Yes. I cry now.* (*TP*, 354)

While they are fragmentary and disruptive to the plot of *The Passenger*, the offset exchanges between the Kid and Alicia provide the reader with almost everything we know about her. She is endlessly mythologized by her brother, Bobby, so what we learn from him are mostly ethereal memories. But hearing Alicia speak to the Kid, a possible hallucination, actually provides a very clear sense of her as a girl growing into an adult. We learn of her precollege years in Wartburg, Tennessee, how she frightened her grandmother and eventually moved to the attic in almost monastic retreat. We learn that she didn't enroll in the local university as planned, eventually found her way to Chicago and the University of Chicago, only to take a leave of absence and move to Tucson, where she worked in a bar. We learn that she was institutionalized for mental health issues and was groped and abused by the doctors. We learn she received electroshock therapy in the mental facilities; the Kid and 'horts were burn victims as a result (*TP*, 72, 112, 290, 293, 292, 125, 130). So, in a way that feels very fitting with McCarthy's commitment to multiple realities and the uncertainties of the world as explained by theoretical mathematics, the Kid is both a hallucination and a very real interlocuter; he is both extremely unreliable with his out-of-date minstrelsy and vaudeville humor and a keen observer of Alicia, as well as quite possibly the character who understands her the best.

In chapter 6 of the novel, in what appear to be Alicia's final days alive, the Kid attempts to interest her in some old family movies. Rather than giving much attention to the family dynamics and potential for nostalgia, the section focuses on the mechanisms of the recording: the "antique" film projector, the 8-mm film that runs at 24 frames per second, the shaky footage shot from a "handcranked Kodak" (*TP*, 189, 195). In some ways, this scene appears to be another example of the Kid's obsolete entertainment. But it feels different here. Film, we must remember, is what killed the vaudeville show, as the showhouses converted into movie theaters and variety show audiences moved on to double features. Also, the attention to a hand-shot, 8-mm film brings to mind the discussion of Zapruder's filming of the JFK assassination. Even the Kid becomes frustrated at the medium as the home movie comes to an end: "It's all a murky business anyway. Take a bunch of stills and run them tandem at a certain speed and what is this that looks like life? Well, it's an illusion" (*TP*, 194). In the end, the Kid calls attention to the artifice of the films and thus the nostalgia for the family past. This sense of the illusion of the supposed factual medium of film shares much with McCarthy's precarious mood more generally. From this perspective, at least, the Kid appears reliable.

McCarthy had long been haunted by photographic representations of the family past that bring back to life those who have long departed. In *Suttree*, Cornelius visits his aunt and uncle only to be terrified by their photo album, "confronting figures out of his genealogy": "Old distaff kin coughed up out of the vortex, think and cracked and macled and a bit redundant too, recurring unchanged as if they inhabited another medium than the dry pilgrims shored up on them. Blind moil in the earth's nap cast up in an eyeblink between becoming and done. I am, I am. An artifact of prior races." As Suttree continues to consider his ancestors in the photos, the album becomes a testament to the impermanent nature of life, rather than lasting memories. He thinks, "What deity in the realm of dementia . . . could have devised a keeping place for souls so poor as is this flesh. This mawky wormbent tabernacle" (*Sut*, 126–30). Alicia seems to share Suttree's trepidation of the images of the family past, and these images end up questioning the past rather than capturing it. She explains to the Kid: "[The people in the family movies are] not entertaining. They're sad. The dead are not loved long. . . . I [opened] my heart. And this is what I got. And anyway some things cant be fixed. And history is not for everybody" (*TP*, 188–89). If images promise the ability to "fix" the past, to provide a steady and reliable history of that past, McCarthy's characters are mocked by this promise. He uses twentieth-century technologies of entertainment, film, and photography to emphasize his long-standing commitment to exposing the fallacy of just such promises.

Making Bombs in the Hinterlands: The Manhattan Project and East Tennessee

The previous sections of this chapter have explored McCarthy's commitment to fragmentation, often at the formal level of the construction of plot, or as we might have put it in the 1980s, its (de)construction. The remainder of this chapter will shift a bit and rely on a somewhat sturdier sense of history to build the forgotten stories of the "secret city" of Oak Ridge, Tennessee, during World War II. Even with this shift, McCarthy's focus in his final two novels on how experimental governmental programs, such as the atomic bomb project based partially in Oak Ridge, led predictably and consistently to the displacement of East Tennessee populations. This focus creates an ominous if different kind of precarity, the precarious nature of preindustrial, rural communities in the face of "modernization."

With the recent popularity of films and TV shows about the atomic age, most notably Christopher Nolan's *Oppenheimer* and the Emmy-winning HBO series *Chernobyl*, McCarthy's treatment of the subject in his two 2022 novels feels both timely and relevant.[16] This interest also pulls at a thematic thread that has been embedded in his fiction since before the turn of the century. McCarthy's first widely popular Western novel, *All the Pretty Horses* (1992), takes place not in the frontier of the nineteenth century, when you might expect to find a desert horseback thriller. Rather, it is set in "the era of Heisenberg, *Invisible Man*, and John Wayne," as James Lilley aptly puts it.[17] So the Western topic of the book is in many ways an elegy for a culture already gone or an escape from the pressing realities of the atomic age. The protagonists, John Grady Cole and Lacey Rawlings, clearly see their trip to Mexico in this way, as an escape from the city and modern notions of respectability and responsibility. A couple of days into the trip, camping by a fire, Rawlings romantically muses, "I could get used to this life" (*AtPH*, 35).

McCarthy again contrasts the southwestern rancher life with the rush of twentieth-century technology in *Cities of the Plain* (1998) when he mentions how the country had in one man's lifetime gone from the horse and buggy to the "atomic bomb" (106). Without a doubt, McCarthy has been interested in the massive changes in people's lives in the twentieth century and beyond for his entire career, and generally this interest concerns the ways that technological advances and governmental institutions threaten the freedom of human experience. In *The Passenger* and *Stella Maris*, the surname of the central character, Bobby Western, might initially appear to be a nod to these earlier novels and their interest in the wild frontier, but in these twinned novels the atomic age takes center stage as McCarthy explores the key role that his childhood home of the greater Knoxville, Tennessee, area played in the building of nuclear weapons. While his surname, Western, suggests an older history, Bobby conceives of his life in this global context: "Western fully understood that he owed his existence to Adolf Hitler. That the forces of history which had ushered his troubled life into the tapestry were those of Auschwitz and Hiroshima, the sister events that sealed forever the fate of the West" (*TP*, 165). This short passage begins with "Western" and ends with "West," perhaps signaling McCarthy's sense that we should consider the surname in the context of Western science and culture, as well as the global technological tensions and clashes often enacted by these pillars of science and culture.

The East Tennessee setting within sections of these novels is no bucolic getaway or backwater remnant of an earlier era, as it often was in McCarthy's Tennessee period of his first four novels. Instead, McCarthy places his characters in the World War II "secret city" of Oak Ridge, Tennessee, twenty-five miles north of Knoxville. Oak Ridge's national laboratories produced enriched uranium that played a central role in the Manhattan Project and the city was built by the federal government almost overnight in 1942 to fast-track the nation's weapons projects during the war. In a matter of months, Oak Ridge went from a rural farming community to a city with over thirty thousand workers, and by 1945 the city's population had ballooned to over seventy thousand. The laboratory's nuclear facilities had similarly appeared almost overnight. As Eleanor puts it in *The Passenger*, "It looked as if they had just somehow emerged out of the ground. The buildings. There was no accounting for them" (*TP*, 173). It is, in this context, the rapid changes to the novel's community that feels particularly precarious.

From a biographical perspective, it makes sense that McCarthy would turn his attention to the East Tennessee portion of the Manhattan Project to tell his story of a family of scientific stars and the burdens of being a mathematical genius. McCarthy must have been keenly attuned to the role that Oak Ridge played in the national atomic story, a story his late-career interest in quantum physics and theoretical mathematics, as well as in the technological horrors of the twentieth century, would have led him to naturally. However, from a literary perspective, the interest in this location north of Knoxville marks a radical departure from his other Tennessee novels, which are centered in the downtown area or in the rural foothills and mountains to the south of the city. There is no evidence that McCarthy had much connection to the Oak Ridge or Wartburg areas of East Tennessee. Ray Smith, the historian for the city of Oak Ridge and former historian of the Y-12 National Security Complex, where he worked for forty-seven years, told me that much of McCarthy's information in the novels about the uranium enrichment process was gathered not by long-standing knowledge or personal historical research but was provided through his brother Dennis, who went on a fact-finding mission to Oak Ridge in September 2011. During this visit, Ray gave Dennis a personal tour of the Y-12 enrichment facility and taught him the term "calutron girls," a term McCarthy would use to describe Bobby and Alicia's mother, Eleanor, who worked in the plant.[18]

THE PRECARIOUS MOOD

Technology and Displacement in East Tennessee

McCarthy chooses the unfamiliar location of Oak Ridge to tie his narrative into the modern horror of an atomic age, a new concern in his work as a focus of sustained attention. He also used this historical moment to return in his last novels to a very familiar theme in his fiction—governmental overreach and its detrimental effects on those less connected to the power hierarchies associated with the government. There are scarcely any bigger governmental initiatives in the nation's history than the Oak Ridge and Los Alamos projects during World War II, where the government developed world-class laboratories, uranium-enrichment plants, nuclear bombs, and testing facilities out of nothing in some of the most isolated and geographically daunting places in the nation.

When Bobby visits his childhood home of Wartburg in *The Passenger*, his grandmother recounts a long history of displacement and regional planning enacted by the federal government. "I know they was families got thowed off their farms back in the thirties by the TVA and come to Anderson County and got thowed off all over again. They was even families had been removed from their homesteads in the Great Smoky Mountains National Park in the thirties, TVA in the thirties again, and the atom bomb in the forties. By that time they didn't have nothing" (*TP*, 174). Granellen's story depicts an accurate history of East Tennessee's remarkable role at the center of early twentieth-century social planning and experimentation, especially the kind that aimed to bring "premodern" rural spaces into modern America through technological innovation and regional restructuring. This history reveals both the brazen confidence in nation building of the era and the ways in which these "improvements" were often built at the expense of members of vulnerable rural communities. As Granellen's story highlights, in a thirty-year period the residents of East Tennessee's rural communities experienced three moments of federal social experimentation that led to the displacement of local citizens: the formation of the Great Smoky Mountains National Park, the TVA river-damming projects, and the formation of the Oak Ridge nuclear facility that was a key part of the Manhattan Project in

World War II. That McCarthy would represent these citizens' experiences as provisional and under attack is no surprise.

During World War II, the Manhattan Project developed rapidly and the Oak Ridge facilities eventually employed more than 75,000 people.[19] The project's goal to produce U-235 in unprecedented amounts allowed Oak Ridge to transform from rural farmland to the fifth largest city in Tennessee in three years (1942–1945),[20] an almost unfathomably rapid growth, given the fact that the site was chosen in part because of its rural, out-of-the-way location. In *The Passenger*, McCarthy characterizes the facility's odd relationship to the rural area even decades later: "[Bobby] could see his grandmother's house and the barn and the road and the adjoining small farms beyond, the pieced fields and the fencelines and woodlots. The rolling hills and ridges to the east. Somewhere beyond that the installation at Oak Ridge for enriching uranium that had led his father here from Princeton in 1943 and where he'd met the beauty queen he would marry" (*TP*, 165).

The Oak Ridge installation that Bobby imagines just over the hills was established in 1942 and the enriched uranium produced there fueled the August 6, 1945, nuclear strike in Hiroshima, Japan. Oak Ridge's role in the nation's atomic project was to put into production cutting-edge and theoretical science and technology designed to isolate and produce this weapons-grade uranium. The compound incorporated four facilities and three means of processing uranium. The first facility, Y-12, was an electromagnetic facility that separated the uranium by capturing the U-235 as it was injected into a magnetic field, which, because of the difference in mass, produced a slightly different path than the U-238. The second principal building, named K-25, was built for gaseous diffusion, which combined uranium with fluorine gas and forced the gas through a barrier capable of separating the lighter U-235 from the heaver U-238 isotopes. Both facilities were enormous, requiring vast amounts of electricity and space. In 1945, the K-25 building was the largest building in the world under one roof. The third facility was S-50, a thermal diffusion plant that used heat generated by a steam plant to separate the uranium isotopes. The compound also housed a graphite reactor, X-10, that originally proved that plutonium could be created in a uranium reactor, and the facility abandoned plans for another plant for the centrifugal capturing of U-235.[21] The "Manhattan Project's Clinton Engineer Works," as it was initially called, employed 100,000 workers at its peak in May 1945, 50,000 construction workers, 40,000 employees in the nuclear production plants, and 10,000 involved in the management and oversight of the facilities and newly constructed town.[22]

In *The Passenger* and *Stella Maris*, Eleanor, Bobby and Alicia's mother, worked as a "calutron girl" at the Y-12 plant, monitoring the electromagnetic readings and radiation levels. McCarthy documents the mixture of tedium, consequence, and secrecy the position entailed, going back in the novel's time to 1942 (a rare instance of time traveling in this historically bound novel) and reconstructing Eleanor's experience for the reader: "She entered a guardhouse with the others and was given a badge with her photograph in a small black metal frame and two black pens. She had already passed her security and health inspections.... No one was told what it was that they were doing. They were given simple instructions and they sat for eight hours a day at their stations under the glare of the fluorescent lights, watching a dial and turning a knob. If you spoke to anyone you could be terminated. You could even be jailed. The pens were radiation dosimeters" (*TP*, 176). Eleanor is not a major character in this book, as she has long been dead before the present of 1980 in the novel. She is generally relegated to her children's memories of her, hazy recollections of a distant past. But in this passage, the 1940s becomes the present and the narrative perspective follows the young women as they began working at this mysterious and complex and frightening facility that seemed to emerge out of nowhere. Such a temporal and narrative shift calls attention to McCarthy's investment in this history and East Tennessee's role in the bombing at Hiroshima "that sealed forever the fate of the West."

The term "calutron girl" is a phrase that Ray Smith coined in 2004 but that shows up in *Stella Maris* as a contemporaneous term used to describe Eleanor and her coworkers. The accepted designation in the 1940s would have been "cubicle operators," and the operators were not allowed to talk with one another, even on the bus to and from the facility.[23] Secrecy became tied to national security and gave Oak Ridge its nickname, "The Secret City" (see fig. 9). We know now that their task was to monitor the uranium-separation process and to adjust the beam current as needed for the process,

FIGURE 9. A billboard encouraging secrecy in Oak Ridge, Tennessee, during World War II.
Wikipedia.

but the largely untrained and often uneducated calutron operators would have known no such thing. Even so, the fact that they were required to wear dosimeters that measured radiation levels certainly emphasized that something new and important and dangerous was happening there. Even though the calutrons were designed to be operated by those with PhDs in scientific fields, according to Manhattan Project engineer Theodore Rockwell, the young women who operated the equipment in Oak Ridge "did extraordinarily well," surprising the scientists.[24] Like the factory workers crystalized in the symbol of Rosie the Riveter, the women of rural East Tennessee were crucial components of the national "war effort."

A glance at the famous Ed Westcott photograph of the calutron facility (fig. 10) demonstrates the rationale for the term "cubicle operator" and evokes the tension and tedium that these positions clearly held. This photograph is so evocative that it became the inspiration for Denise Kiernan's 2014 book about women's role in the Oak Ridge war effort, *The Girls of Atomic City: The Untold Story of the Women Who Helped Win World War II*.[25] It stands to reason that McCarthy would have had this photo and others of their kind in

FIGURE 10. Calutron operators at the Y-12 plant in Oak Ridge (1944). Wikimedia Commons.

mind as he wrote about Eleanor. One can imagine the scene in the novel in which Alicia and Bobby's father strolled down the corridor in this photo and introduced himself for the first time to their mother, Eleanor. In the novel, he slips her a note with his phone number, an interaction that constituted a violation of the code of secrecy that would certainly have been more of a threat to the local calutron operator than the world-renowned scientist from Princeton. This mixture of personal story that explains the family history of the Westerns and the factual (and hard to come by) information about the previously secretive Y-12 facility is yet another prominent incorporation of specific twentieth-century technological detail in these imbricated novels.

As audiences of the recent film *Oppenheimer* no doubt recall, the production of small amounts of uranium-235 had been successfully accomplished before, but never military-grade uranium in such quantities. The calutron used to produce the uranium was developed by Ernest O. Lawrence at the Radiation Laboratory at Cal-Berkeley, which gave it the name (from California University Cyclotron). The scientists at the Oak Ridge laboratory created, developed, and experimented with the largest magnet in existence, which was ready for use in May 1942. General Electric was brought onboard for electrical equipment and controls, and the Allis-Chalmers Company, a manufacturing business out of Milwaukee, was in charge of the magnets.[26] Just as the atomic project more generally was truly an international collaboration between scientists and machinists from all over the world, Oak Ridge, heretofore an unincorporated rural area outside of the small town of Clinton, Tennessee, became the nexus of the international technology used to produce weapons-grade uranium. McCarthy's interest in this process is understandable, especially in terms of the subject of these final novels. The atomic project allows McCarthy to merge his lifelong interest in the precarious lives in rural East Tennessee and his newer passion for theoretical mathematics and physics. His time at the Santa Fe Institute toward the end of his life no doubt sharpened his interest in this hidden history, but anyone growing up in the Knoxville area in the second half of the twentieth century was keenly aware of the vague outlines of this history. Children were reminded several times a year when they would be ushered out into the hallways of their schools to put their heads between their knees against the lockers in a drill of nuclear bomb preparation known as the "duck and cover." Teachers would stress to local children the proximity of Oak Ridge and its likelihood as a primary target for the Soviet Union's nuclear missiles as an inducement or fear tactic to get children to take the drills seriously. The paranoid mood expanded to include local school safety drills.

Bobby and Alicia's father and his colleague Robert J. Oppenheimer remain optimistic about the prospects of their work, and McCarthy emphasizes their clear consciences regarding the construction of the atomic bomb. Alicia mentions her father's lack of guilt in *Stella Maris*, suggesting that such a lack of a guilty conscience would be a surprise to most people (61). In *The Passenger*, Oppenheimer is presented as a chain-smoking genius, enamored of the science: "A lot of very smart people thought [Oppenheimer] was possibly the smartest man God ever made." McCarthy questions this detached logic by adding the phrase, "Odd chap, that God" (*TP*, 115). If many could dissociate the war effort and the rapid acceleration of technological development from the destructive realities of the atomic bomb, these novels never do. Despite her relative cluelessness about the work being done at Oak Ridge, Eleanor saw portents of evil therein: "She looked at the other women on the bus but they seemed to have abandoned themselves and she thought that she might be the only one of them that while she did not know what this was about knew all too well that it was Godless and that while it had poisoned back to elemental mud all living things upon that ground yet it was far from being done. It was just beginning" (*TP*, 175). While Eleanor appears for only a few pages in these novels, she is in many ways the moral center of it, checking the optimism of scientific breakthroughs and nationalist pride. McCarthy links the notion of Oppenheimer being the "smartest man God ever made" to Eleanor's sense of the godlessness of it all to expose the bankruptcy of the type of logic that detaches the science from its aftermath.

While the specter of atomic weapons gives voice to the novel's provisional mood, so, too, does the inevitable displacement of rural peoples that was part of this construction of a massive federal nuclear facility. The Oak Ridge portion of the Manhattan Project displaced approximately three thousand people from their East Tennessee homes in order to make room for the sixty thousand acres of requisitioned land necessary for the project: "Although secrecy was a major factor in selecting project sites, complete isolation was not possible. Generations of families, farmers, and Native Americans resided in these chosen 'isolated' areas. As a result of the Manhattan Project, these people were forced to abandon their homes and land, often without sufficient or even any compensation. The displacement had economic and emotional repercussions, as well as long-term environmental consequences."[27]

Residents began to be notified in November of 1942, often with just a couple of weeks to relocate. Many of the landowners were forced to move off their land even before purchase arrangements were completed.[28] As is the case with many of these governmental requisitions, homeowners were typically given far below the market value for their land, with residents many times getting less than half of the actual value for their farms. They were often forced to move without the typical moving resources. Smith explains, "Many of them did not have automobiles. They did not have trucks to move their belongings. If they had an automobile, they might not be able to buy gas for it or tires. Those things were rationed." As Johnson and Jackson put it in *City Behind a Fence*, "things fast became a nightmare."[29]

The usual story of the development of the atomic bomb is understandably focused on a group of misfit but brilliant scientists, many of whom escaped Hitler's antisemitic policies in Europe. This version of the story of the atomic bomb is situated in Chicago and at the University of California at Berkeley with road trips to Los Alamos. Oppenheimer and Einstein and General Groves. The centrality of the uranium production in Oak Ridge, represented by the dropping of marbles into a fishbowl in the film *Oppenheimer*, is lost in this version. It is a story that was not lost on East Tennessean Cormac McCarthy.

In *The Passenger* and *Stella Maris*, McCarthy places this history in a larger narrative of dispossession in East Tennessee. He does so by intentionally conflating in the novels the region's displacement of folks from related but independent social engineering projects in the region, seemingly combining the TVA electricity projects of the early to midcentury *and* the 1940s displacement to make room for the new atomic city, Oak Ridge. What ties these histories together, apart from the displacement of rural farmers, is the way the nation and federal government saw the area as a perfect place for social experimentation. The poverty, lack of modern development, and dearth of recent technological innovation identified East Tennessee as the ideal place for such experimentation. McCarthy's thematic conflation of these distinct historical events makes sense when we consider the role that Bobby and Alicia's father played in the science that enacted the Oak Ridge displacements, especially when we consider it alongside McCarthy's own father's role as general counsel for TVA, in charge of the earlier displacements in East Tennessee. Fathers have always been difficult figures in McCarthy's fiction, but here the link between governmental overreach and its effects on the powerless feels particularly acute. This storyline in these novels thus illuminates a tension between alternative histories, the official and international story of the atomic bomb, and the regional story of the provisional lives of poor working and farming families, whose displacement played a key role in the nation's expansion into a global power.

You only need to read a few pages into McCarthy's career as a novelist, when we see Arthur Ownby shooting up a "fat, bald, and sinister" governmental installation in *The Orchard Keeper* (93), to pick up on the antigovernment and antidisplacement stance that is so prevalent in his work. We see McCarthy's return to this topic in *The Passenger* most notably when Bobby visits Wartburg and listens to his grandmother recount the family's history. We learn from Granellen that her grandfather and uncle built a house in Anderson County in 1872. Both Granellen's and Alicia's versions of this house construction are filled with McCarthy's love of expert manual labor and attention to craft that runs throughout his career. Granellen states, "I don't know how they knew to do what they done, Bobby. I want to say that they could of done anything.... That house was the most beautiful house I ever saw. Ever floor in it was solid walnut and some of them boards was close to three foot wide. All of it hand planed. All of it at the bottom of a lake" (*TP*, 173–74).

Alicia in *Stella Maris* offers a similar version of the story: "I've seen photographs of [the house] and it was quite beautiful. They'd never built a house before. I'm not sure they'd ever even seen one built. What if they could have seen eighty years into the future? That's not very long. The simplest undertaking is predicated upon a future that has no warrant" (70). We can hear in Alicia's story echoes of Sheriff Bell in *No Country* and the father in *The Road* in this question about the role of craft and beauty in a world so precarious that it has outlived a belief in its future. We later learn that this treasured house was lost as part of the requisitioning of land for the Manhattan Project in the rural area that would soon be called Oak Ridge. Granellen places this family loss in a larger framework of what she sees as governmental imposition leading to the dispossession of local residents: "We tried to hold on to it. But they just took it.... You had two weeks' notice. Then you had to be gone. You wasn't even supposed to take the furniture but most did. They'd leave out in the middle of the night. Like thieves.... It was hard" (*TP*, 174).

This recounting once again overlaps with Alicia's, this time in *The Passenger*, as we get a flashback to her sitting at "the dressingtable which had belonged to her greatgrandmother and which had been taken out of the house in Anderson County at night even as the waters were rising. In the drawer of the dressingtable was a packet of letters tied with a blue silk ribbon. Antique stamps and a script in brown ink penned with a quill. Addressed to a house whose stones now lay in the silt at the bottom of a lake" (105). This sense of an ancient and unrecoverable family history (represented by the letters penned with a quill) suggest that more than an edifice was lost in this removal. In some ways, the overlap between Granellen's story in *The Passenger* and Alicia's in *Stella Maris* makes sense—they are drawing from the same family lore, the same batch of stories. But on the other hand, these two characters see the world quite differently, and McCarthy goes out of his way to suggest that they share some of the same values despite their differences, or at least share an appreciation for the vanished family history.

But more important to my argument here, in these scenes Granellen and Alicia merge without distinction four moments of twentieth-century governmental displacement of East Tennessee citizens in their telling of the history of the family home—1) the displacement caused by the 1930s flooding as a result of the damming the local rivers by the TVA , 2) the claiming of family lands to create the Great Smokies National Park (also in the 1930s), 3) the claiming of land necessary to make the uranium-enrichment laboratories in Oak Ridge in the 1940s, and 4) the subsequent loss of property connected to the flooding caused by the Melton Hill Dam in the 1960s, again engineered by the TVA. All of these upheavals were engineered by the federal government, and all of them sanctioned under the banner of national progress and pride. The Melton Hill Dam is the only act of requisition that could have sentenced the family home in *The Passenger* to "the bottom of a lake." There was no flooding of lands as part of the Oak Ridge displacement and earlier TVA flooding did not happen in this area. It should be noted that historian Ray Smith says that such flooding of a home would be extremely unlikely even with this 1960s damming.[30] Even so, it fits McCarthy's narrative about dispossession and the submersion of the past quite well, historical accuracy be damned. What makes Granellen's story so confusing from a historical perspective is that the memories of four separate moments of governmental claims of imminent domain become almost indistinguishable. Indeed, distinguishing between them seems to almost miss the point. When we read the passage, it seems as if they lost the family home during the Manhattan Project, but the mention of the house being underwater draws one to the TVA's prominent flooding of the area in the 1930s, which doesn't make sense, since we know they lost the house in the 1940s.

So, to untangle Granellen's imbricated representation of history in the novels in a way that stay true to the region's history, we can surmise that the family lost their home in 1942, moved to a rental property near Clinton, Tennessee, and then were forced to relocate to Wartburg (farther west and outside of the nuclear project's domain). Then, two decades after they were kicked off the land, the house was flooded by the TVA Melton Hill project of the 1960s. More likely, McCarthy did not care to specify such details. Either way, this forced relocation is the moral center of Bobby and Alicia's maternal family history, and it is symbolized by the family home at the bottom of a lake. Even as McCarthy turns to new territory with the interest in theoretical mathematics and atomic science, he emphasizes a theme that has been around since Uncle Ather was dislodged from his home and went up Harrikan Mountain in *The Orchard Keeper*—the ways in which our technological development and governmental policies created precarious realities for lower- and middle-class working folk.

In *The Passenger* and *Stella Maris*, these personal and familial stories that are told by Bobby, Alicia, and Granellen can be contrasted with another history, one with which Bobby is equally well-versed, and which appears in the novel as a sort of prologue to Granellen's story: "Somewhere beyond [his grandmother's community in Wartburg], the installation at Oak Ridge for enriching uranium that had led his father here from Princeton in 1943 and where he'd met the beauty queen he would marry. Western fully understood that he owed his existence to Adolf Hitler. That the forces of history which had ushered his troubled life into the tapestry were those of Auschwitz and Hiroshima, the sister events that sealed forever the fate of the West" (*TP*, 163). We see it even earlier in the novel, as Western again thinks of his father's legacy in modern technology and modern warfare, in this case about the detonation of an atomic bomb: "In that mycoidal phantom blooming in the dawn like an evil lotus and in the melting of solids not heretofore known to do so stood a truth that would silence poetry a thousand years" (*TP*, 116). As with the case of Alicia's questioning of the beauty of the house after World War II, these passages nod to *The Road* and the Adorno-inspired questioning of the role of art in such a destructive age. "To write poetry after Auschwitz," penned Adorno in 1947, "is barbaric."[31] We see it again in Alicia's thoughts in *Stella Maris*, when she thinks of her father witnessing the first test detonation of an atomic weapon: "The thing I remember my father saying was that he put his hands over his goggles against the initial flare of light and that was when it came he could see the bones in his fingers with his eyes closed. There was no sound. Just this searing white light. And then the reddish purple cloud rising in billows and flowering into the iconic white mushroom. Symbol of the age" (113).

Early in *The Passenger*, as John Sheddan and the bartender Bianca are discussing the hard-to-understand Bobby, Bianca asks, "Does Knoxville produce crazy people or does it just attract them?" Sheddan responds, "Interesting question. Nature nurture. Actually the more deranged of them seem to hail from the neighboring hinterlands" (32). Like that of Marion Sylder and Arthur Ownby in McCarthy's first novel and Gene Harrogate in the fourth, Bobby's maternal family hails from these neighboring hinterlands, and as is the case with these characters, McCarthy's attention and empathy consistently turn toward the folks off the beaten path and their provisional stories so often left out of our nation's, our region's, and our city's histories.

As Granellen's conflation of different moments of social engineering in the region makes evident, there were multiple such projects and the Tennessee Valley Authority's electricity and river damning and social engineering project of the 1930s to 1960s is one program that surely matched the upheaval and ambition of the Manhattan Project. These two federal projects are further linked by the fact that Oak Ridge was identified as a prime location for the Manhattan reservation in part because of the abundance of affordable and reliable electricity; this electricity was produced by the hydroelectric processes that came from a nearby TVA project, Norris Dam, completed in 1936, just six short years before the construction of Oak Ridge began. So similar were the projects from the locals' perspective that when the federal officers began showing up to begin surveying for the nuclear facilities it was a very familiar scene: "When the 'strangers' first showed up with their transits and survey rods, local people assumed they were simply more TVA men."[32]

Like Oak Ridge, the TVA Norris project was fueled by an abstract idealism centered around the control and use of natural features, changing the earth's powerful forces into monetizable resources. Also like the Oak Ridge atomic facilities, TVA was framed and justified by the idea of ushering an out-of-touch region into the modern world. As David Lilienthal put it in 1944, "A new and modern task requires new and modern tools; a spirit of enterprise and a creative modern outlook.... What the TVA set out to do was such a new and modern task."[33] Later historians of the development of TVA further defined what the modern outlook meant for the local citizens: "To say that TVA was an agent of modernization means basically that TVA possessed the instrumentality and productivity, through programs like regional planning and power productivity, to transform wholly or in part a population removed from the mainstream of American life."[34]

The optimism surrounding TVA was embodied by its biggest supporter, Franklin D. Roosevelt, who oversaw the creation and management of the huge agency: "Before I came to Washington, I had decided that for many reasons the Tennessee Valley—in other words, all the watershed of Tennessee and its tributaries—would provide an ideal land use experiment on a regional scale embracing many states." In other places, Roosevelt referred to the action as a "social experiment," rather than one about land use.[35] The recurring idea of regional experimentation feels abstracting, and in the case of the TVA it threatened to dehumanize the changes. It also placed the upheaval in terms of resources and future gains at the expense of the people living in the basin. From this perspective, humans, like timber and waterpower, are countable resources. As the other Knoxville Pulitzer Prize–winning novelist, James Agee, put it in his 1933 article in *Fortune*, "Such is the laboratory for a great experiment. Such as the raw materials good and ill from which TVA prepares to fashion a civilization which, in a certain way, is new and is significant to all the U.S.... At least that is the way the Authority looks at it."[36]

As Granellen's story in *The Passenger* makes clear, the development of the Norris Dam and Basin Area was received very differently by the local residents. It proceeded quickly without much warning to those residents. The land was purchased through limited negotiation and, if that failed, eminent domain. The lands purchased were typically the more nutrient-rich valley lands worked by families, both landowners and tenants, in lifestyles considered "essentially premodern." More families were displaced in this first East Tennessee TVA project than any other dam the Authority subsequently constructed, and feelings of tension and ill will were a part of the process from the beginning.[37]

Charles McCarthy, father of Cormac, worked for TVA as assistant general counsel, and his primary responsibilities in this position initially involved the "condemnation of the Norris Reservoir" and the relocation of the residents impacted by the federal government's land acquisition.[38] It was this job that brought the McCarthys to Knoxville when Cormac was just four years old. Like Roosevelt and many federal workers, Charles McCarthy saw the operation in terms of the maximizing of resources and future gains. While he was responsible for the relocation of the dispossessed communities and seemed to work hard for what he believed as their best interest, his writings demonstrate an autocratic sense of national good that minimized the voices of local resistance. In the end of his 1950 article "TVA and the Tennessee Valley," Charles McCarthy speaks of a national democracy and the TVA work in abstract language that must have rung empty to the displaced residents:

> In a democracy, the happiness and well-being of the citizen are accepted as the ultimate end of government and the citizen is recognized as a man whose human dignity is worth preserving. The man who has lifted himself and his family from poverty and disease to health and financial independence by action taken on his own initiative, and as a result of his own conscious choice, has gained much more for himself and for the Nation than the man who has been forced by governmental fiat to adopt methods of operation which he does not understand and in which he does not believe. The initiative of its people is the greatest resource which the United States possesses. The TVA program is designed to see to it that that resource is used to the fullest.[39]

While Charles's son Cormac would likely agree with the notion that governmental fiat tends to rob an individual of their own initiative, he differed from his father on how one should understand social engineering projects such as the TVA dam construction. Charles did think in terms of the "common good," but it was a very abstracted sense of this good. Cormac, on the other hand, focused on the lives of those most adversely affected by these actions, and he tended to characterize governmental actions as the very example of fiat his father claimed he wanted to avoid. What felt democratic to Charles seemed autocratic to his son. In a 1935 follow-up to his original *Fortune* article on TVA, Agee captured the tension between these versions of TVA's impact while describing Charles's principal job (without naming him): "The job of buying this land . . . from farmers and helping them move elsewhere and of removing the graves of their forefathers involves what people who have no interest in human beings like to call human interest."[40]

This suspicion of large governmental planning is enmeshed in McCarthy's novels from the beginning. In McCarthy's first novel, *The Orchard Keeper*, it is represented from Uncle Ather's inability to live in the wilderness as he had for decades. It is represented in John Wesley Rattner's refusal of a governmental bounty on sparrowhawks, when he says at the novel's conclusion, "I cain't take no dollar. I made a mistake, he wadn't for sale" (*OK*, 233). It is there in the government's pursuit of off-the-grid moonshiners, especially the coprotagonist Marion Sylder. It is also seen in the government's installation of a mysterious metal apparatus in the former apple orchard, which McCarthy describes as "a great silver ikon, fat and bald and sinister" (*OK*, 93). This installation is secretive and protected by government officials who come and go in "olive-painted trucks with gold emblems on the doors, passing in and out of the gate, the men in drab fatigues, locking and unlocking the chain sedulously" (*OK*, 96). These images serve as precursors to the 1980s cinematic iconography used to represent the totalitarian USSR. It is the resistance against authority of this kind that leads one critic to see it as the salient feature of McCarthy's portrayal of Appalachia and its people.[41]

As Agee foregrounds above, perhaps one of the most controversial and dehumanizing results of TVA's land use experimentation was the removal and relocation of graves that would fall below the new dammed waterline. At least five thousand graves from various family burial grounds and churchyards were disinterred and reburied in higher grounds. Agee cites the number as six thousand and mentions that local undertakers received twenty dollars per grave to complete the task.[42] For Charles McCarthy and supporters of TVA, such occurrences were unfortunate side effects of a larger good and could be improved through negotiation about where to rebury the bodies. Charles believed that open communication with the landowners and family members of the interred could lead to positive impressions of the larger project: "The experience of TVA with these policies establishes that a land acquisition program can be a source of positive benefit to a regional agency, instead of a source of conflict with the landowners."[43] For other members of the community who reflected on the displacement, and especially the grave removal, the outlook was not as sanguine, and TVA was accused of "disrespect, autocratic activity and a disregard for personal feeling."[44] Charles and other TVA administrators certainly knew of the resistance and the feelings of locals about autocratic fiat but tended to minimize these drawbacks and looked to the utopian possibilities in the experiment. Agee once again beautifully captures in real time this tension: "TVA knows that it is, among other things, a passel of smart Yankees descended to improve a tetchy people; knows also the limits of its power; knows also that the more independently a man helps himself, the better off he will be."[45]

Perhaps due in part to his knowledge of the sordid history of relocated grave sites caused by regional hydroelectrical projects, McCarthy's early novels exhibit a fascination with disturbed graves, especially graves that are disturbed by governmental social experiments or urban spread. *The Orchard Keeper* is framed with opening and concluding chapters that detail a cemetery that is being swallowed up by modern development. In *Child of God*, the bodies being kept by the serial killer and necrophiliac Lester Ballard are somehow even further desecrated when the government finds them and removes the bodies from their resting place in caves. Before they are discovered, the bodies are described as being left by Lester in "attitudes of repose." Once the governmental agencies get hold of them, they are dehumanized, as the hands of "puppeteers" raise the bodies that are now "bound in muslin like enormous hams" that have been stamped as "Property of the State of Tennessee" (*CofG*, 195–96).

Governmental planning and the displacement of human beings, dead and alive, is met with suspicion and often animosity in McCarthy's work. He most often plumbs this issue through the figure of a rural farmer (whether it be in Tennessee or Texas or Mexico) in tension with larger societal forces. Rather than moving beyond this trope in his final work about abstract mathematics, theoretical physics, and the atomic age, McCarthy returns to it, and the image of the family house underwater registers as a tragedy. McCarthy does not suggest it is on the same magnitude of larger twentieth-century atrocities, especially the "twinned" horrors of Hiroshima and Auschwitz. Rather, he personalizes the story of regional loss and asserts its relevance in a larger story about the horrors of the twentieth century. McCarthy's novels continuously assert that such profound loss absolutely belongs in a conversation about the precarious nature of existence in the century.

Aaron Purcell writes that "from the 1920s through the 1960s, the federal government sponsored an unprecedented number of removal and relocation projects [in the Appalachian South].... Loss is a recurring theme when studying any of the government-sponsored removal projects in the [region] during the mid-twentieth century."[46] Cormac McCarthy's final two novels end with a sense of a peaceful if uneasy subsidence—perhaps the end of a career and a writing trajectory that spanned six decades. Attention to the displacement of Bobby and Alicia's maternal family and to the families uprooted by the formation of the Great Smoky Mountains National Park, the Tennessee Valley Authority, and the Oak Ridge nuclear facilities suggests that *The Passenger* and *Stella Maris* complete the circle of McCarthy's career, tying us back to the lost characters in his opening novel that are displaced and uprooted in very similar and precarious ways.

Echoes of a Life

This chapter began with the contention that *The Passenger* and *Stella Maris* marked a continuation of McCarthy's exploration of the indeterminacy of reality and the precarity of history. Abstract mathematics and theoretical physics became a new vocabulary to explore these themes but did not represent a fundamentally different examination. In many other ways, these books also feel like a calling together of a life's work. The reader will hear hundreds of echoes of McCarthy's books in this diptych, and they feel like a culmination of a career's exploration. We see his love for the conversations of law officers reemerge in these novels that call back to *The Orchard Keeper*,

Child of God, and *No Country for Old Men*. He revisits an older depiction of trans characters, as Debussy/Debbie in *The Passenger* feels like McCarthy's attempt to bring up to date the character of Dripping Through the Dew in *Suttree*. The bawdy banter of the barrooms in New Orleans is reminiscent of the back-and-forth of locals in the taverns of McCarthy's early novels. Bobby's high school biology project reflects McCarthy's own childhood interests in the outdoors and taxonomic categorization.[47]

The reader notices that his tender attention to the rock quarries around Knoxville in *The Orchard Keeper* and *Child of God* returns in Alicia's childhood performance of Medea in the "amphitheater" of the quarry, describing the dynamite holes as "featherdrills," the exact language he used to describe the quarry in *Child of God*. The final pages of both *The Passenger*, with Bobby living out his last days in a windmill on a Spanish island that McCarthy spent time on as a young man, and *Stella Maris*, with Alicia's dream of returning to wander her ancestral mountain homeland, create a mood of subsidence, one that starkly contrasts the precarity of the modern age or perhaps as a recognition of its inevitability. Both Alicia in her final thoughts in *Stella Maris* and Bobby in his last days in *The Passenger* return to simpler times, and these times look a lot like McCarthy's own childhood days in the foothills of the Smoky Mountains in East Tennessee. It would be inaccurate to suggest these novels were simply McCarthy's dying final words. He had been working on some version of them for more than four decades before he died. But the return to characters from Knoxville, the local landscape, and the sense of a simpler time in the mountains offer one answer to the precarity of the modern age. It isn't an answer that resolves anything or helps us move beyond the precarity, but it does provide a moment for tenderness that suggests something other than this precarity, and, in that regard, feels a lot like Janie's pulling in the horizon at the end of Zora Neale Hurston's *Their Eyes Were Watching God*: "Here was peace. She pulled in her horizons like a great fish-net. Pulled it from around the waist of the world and draped it over her shoulder. So much of life in its meshes. She called in her soul to come and see."[48]

Epilogue
"Them Old Dreams"

McCarthy is famous for attaching prologues and epilogues to his novels, often separating them from the text proper through the use of italics. Think of the lyrical opening to Suttree or the men moving like clockwork in the epilogue of Blood Meridian. Some readers find McCarthy's detached endings frustrating or distracting or too stylized. I have always found them fascinating. I offer this epilogue to How Cormac Works as a tribute to McCarthy's literary innovation. While I will invoke the spirit of McCarthy by including an italicized, and slightly tangential, ending, I do not dare try to imitate his ... style. (See fig. 11.)

For me, one of the enduring and endearing aspects of McCarthy's long and varied opus is his affection for local voices and regional stories. From everything we know from those who were close to McCarthy, he used to love to sit around with acquaintances and swap stories—this is as true in the dive bars in Knoxville as in the hallowed halls of the Santa Fe Institute. This love of local stories crossed state and national borders in his fiction. We find it in his Appalachian plotlines and his Mexican ones, from the voices of his Texas lawmen and the barkeep in Formentera, Spain. Dianne Luce has called our attention to the fact that McCarthy used to keep folders of local stories that he had written.[1] He would not necessarily connect them to any particular novel originally and would rearrange these stories, trying them out in different novels and contexts. The stories had for McCarthy a life outside the plot of his novels, even as he sought to infuse the novels with the life he saw in them. His imagination consistently gravitated to the stories people tell. His careful

HOW CORMAC WORKS

FIGURE 11. Self-portrait, by Cormac McCarthy.
Reproduced with permission of the McCarthy Estate.

attention to detail and the rhythms and sounds of the talented storyteller captured what made these voices unique and special.

McCarthy seemed to have a special affinity for jokes and amusing anecdotes. To capture the humor he saw in the world, McCarthy tended to incorporate aspects of the real-life characters he met into his bigger-than-life fictional characters, often drawing on experiences he had decades earlier. One such example is the real-life person from East Tennessee, John Sheddan, who later became the fictional character of the same name in The Passenger.[2] John utters some of the funniest lines in the novel, including his account of meeting an old girlfriend in Knoxville while out of jail on parole: "Why John, she says, is that you? I havent seen you in ages. Where have you been? And I said: My dear, I have been in durance vile. And she said: Really? You know my sister married a boy from Winston-Salem. And I thought to myself: I really need to get out of this town" (TP, 25). The joke, of course, lies in the woman mistaking the archaic term "durance vile," which means a long prison sentence, for a town in North Carolina. As with this quote, many of John Sheddan's more humorous moments come at the expense of the educational level and questionable sanity of the citizens of East Tennessee.

It turns out we can trace this joke back to McCarthy's correspondence from 1980, when he exchanged letters with Memphis-based writer John Fergus Ryan.[3] Over the course of a series of letters, McCarthy arranges an introduction of Ryan to the real-life "Squire" John Sheddan. When Ryan finally meets Sheddan, he comments, "John is an especially interesting person. From listening to his own tales of his lifestyle, I seriously fear the young man may one day run afoul of the law."[4] A few years later in 1980, McCarthy recounts Sheddan's time in jail and drug rehab, as well as his imaginary plea to a judge: "Your honor it was them drugs made me do all the bad stuff."[5] This humorous "plea" reminds us of Suttee's hallucinatory confession toward the end of Suttree, once again suggesting McCarthy's blending of real-life experiences and the fictional scenes he creates:

> Mr. Suttree it is our understanding that at curfew rightly decreed by law and in that hour wherein night draws to its proper close and the new day commences and contrary to conduct befitting a person of your station you betook yourself to various low places within the shire of McAnally and there did squander several ensuing years in the company of thieves, derelicts, miscreants, pariahs, poltroons, spalpeens, curmudgeons, clotpolls, murderers, gamblers, dawds, whores, trulls, brigands, topers, tosspots, sots and archsots, lobcocks, smellsmocks, runagates, rakes, and other assorted and felonious debauchees.
>
> I was drunk, cried Suttree. (457)

The letters between Ryan and McCarthy also discuss McCarthy's local friend Gary Goodman. In the same letter as Sheddan's imaginary plea above, McCarthy relates that Gary told him a story about a "lady friend," who, after he used the term "durance vile," said she had never been to North Carolina.

While the interplay between McCarthy's lived experiences with actual friends and his often absurd fictional scenes is fascinating, it is the appreciation for the well-turned phrase, the funny line, that is most pertinent here. This throwaway anecdote told by Gary Goodman to Cormac McCarthy, who then relayed it to John Ryan Fergus in a letter, remained in his drafts of The Passenger for more than four decades, or perhaps it remained in a folder of amusing anecdotes for a long time before McCarthy pulled it out for inclusion in a new draft of his 2022 novel. Either way, we see the enduring legacy of these voices and stories. We see this love for humorous side stories in Child of God, when a local citizen tells of his time in the carnival boxing match and another recounts the boy who lit a fire under some stubborn oxen only to have the oxen move three steps forward, causing the wagon to catch fire. We see it in the various escapades and stories involving Gene Harrogate and the cast of characters hunched around a fishbowl of beer in Suttree.[6] In the Border Trilogy, it is there in Jimmy Blevins's peculiar way of seeing and characterizing the world and the rich stories of the philosophical Mexican ascetics. We see McCarthy's adoration of the local expression in No Country for Old Men with Ed Tom Bell's wry exchanges with his deputies and in his more wistful personal thoughts. We see it everywhere in each of McCarthy's novels, plays, and screenplays.

It only seems fitting to conclude by returning one last time to the "character" of John Sheddan, who delivers one of the funniest and memorable lines in The Passenger: "Does Knoxville produce crazy people or does it just attract them," asks Bianca from across the bar after hearing another one of Sheddan's crazy stories. He replies, "Interesting question. Nature nurture. Actually the more deranged of them seem to hail from the neighboring hinterland (32). McCarthy always had a deep affinity for those seen by many as "deranged" and from the "hinterland." He listened to them, he captured their voices and stories, and he placed them prominently and consistently within his novels, as different as these novels were. It was their language, the style of their delivery, that gave McCarthy and his readers so much joy. These are the dreams that were "only in his head" until he shared them with the public.

Notes

Introduction

1. Nabokov, "On a Book Entitled *Lolita*," 315; Mitchell, *Mere Reading*, 46; Jacobs, *The Pleasures of Reading in an Age of Distraction*, 13–25.
2. Franco, dir., *Child of God*.
3. Mendelsund, *What We See When We Read*, 7, 30, 41.
4. Mitchell, *Mere Reading*, 46.
5. See, for example, Bannon and Vanderheide, *Cormac McCarthy's Violent Destinies*; Cooper, *Cormac McCarthy and Complexity Theory*; Giemza, *Science and Literature in Cormac McCarthy's Expanding Worlds*; Greve, *Shreds of Matter*; Holloway, *The Late Modernism of Cormac McCarthy*; Potts, *Cormac McCarthy and the Signs of Sacrament*.
6. Quoted in Luce, *Embracing Vocation*, 90.
7. Best and Marcus, "Surface Reading: An Introduction," 2, 9, 9–13, 1–4.
8. Aubry, *Guilty Aesthetic Pleasures*, 4. For Aubry's discussion of New Formalism, see especially his introduction, where he places Sharon Marcus, Stephen Best, Heather Love, Bruno Latour, Rita Felski, and Franco Moretti within this recent tradition.
9. Johnson, "Teaching Deconstructively," quoted in Mitchell, *Mere Reading*.
10. Felski, *The Limits of Critique*, 3, 5, 159, 151.
11. For a great collection that explores these issues within Southern culture, see *The Tacky South*, edited by Katharine Burnett and Monica Carol Miller.
12. Errett, *Elements of Taste*, 14.
13. Felski, *Limits*, 157–58.
14. Felski, *Hooked*, 1.
15. Mitchell, *Mere Reading*, 3.
16. Felski, *Limits*, 152.
17. This study is informed loosely by narrative theory, affect theory, and reader response theory. Books from these fields that have been formative in my imagining of this project, among many others, include *Compassion: The Culture and Politics of an Emotion* by Lauren Berlant; *Elements of Taste: Understanding What We Like and Why* by Benjamin Errett; *What We See When We Read* by Peter Mendelsund; *Our Aesthetic Categories: Zany, Cute, Interesting* by Sianne Ngai; *Experiencing Fiction: Judgments, Progressions, and the Rhetorical Theory of Narrative* by James Phelan.

18. I am thinking here of classic texts such as *Narrative Discourse: An Essay in Method* by Genette and Booth's *The Rhetoric of Fiction*. For excellent introductions to the field, see the more recent collections *The Cambridge Introduction to Narrative* and *Narrative Theory: Core Concepts and Critical Debates*. For a more in-depth look into the uneasy relationship between language and the speaker of that language, see Ann Banfield's theory of "unspeakable sentences," by which she means sentences that do not bear any explicit marker nor any implicit indication of a first person, and which are "not interpretable as the expression of a speaker's subjectivity," as described by Sylvia Patron in *Describing the Unobserved and Other Essays*, 1. This line of inquiry is particularly useful when thinking about McCarthy's wandering narrative perspective and his vacillation between narrative modes, which I explore especially in chapter 1.

19. Phelan both acknowledges his indebtedness to Seymore Chatman's *Story and Discourse* (1978) and emphasizes the distinctiveness of his model. See Phelan, "Authors, Resources, Audiences: Towards a Rhetorical Poetics," *Style* 52, nos. 1–2: 1–34.

20. Phelan, "Authors, Resources, Audiences," 2.

21. For a compelling take on an individual author's evolving style, see Edward Said's sense of "late style." For Said, as artists reach the end of their writing lives, they tend to produce writing in two distinct styles: 1) masterworks that "crown a lifetime of aesthetic endeavor" and 2) a "deliberately unproductive productiveness, a going against," which resists totality and are defined by "apartness and exile and anachronism" (1, 3). Said's interest rests with the second late style, which he sees in the work of artists as disparate as Beethoven, Lampedusa, and Cavafy. The article I am citing here was later developed into an expanded argument with the book *On Late Style: Music and Literature against the Grain* (2009).

22. Macé and Jones, "Ways of Reading, Modes of Being," 214.

23. Hale, "'On Beauty' as Beautiful? The Problem of Novelistic Aesthetics by Way of Zadie Smith," 814, 822–23.

24. Jacobs, *The Pleasures of Reading*, 13.

25. Nabokov, as recalled by a student and repeated by John Updike in the introduction to Nabokov's *Lectures on Literature*, xxiii.

26. Nabokov, *Lectures on Literature*, 5–6.

27. Guy Davenport, quoted in Frye, *Understanding Cormac McCarthy*, 30; Thane Ritalin, quoted in Luce, *Embracing Vocation*, 98; Kay Boyle, quoted in Luce, 89; David Craig, quoted in Luce, 172.

28. James, "Critical Solace," 483.

29. Hoberek, "Cormac McCarthy and the Aesthetics of Exhaustion," 493.

30. Alter, *Pen of Iron*, 172.

31. Cooper, *No More Heroes*, 3.

32. Cooper, *No More Heroes*, 5, 15.

33. Bartlett, "From Voyeurism to Archaeology: Cormac McCarthy's *Child of God*," 4.

34. Nabokov, "On a Book Entitled *Lolita*," 315.

35. Aubry, *Guilty Aesthetic Pleasures*, 11.

36. See, for example, the diatonic charts, such as the one on the website for Beyond Music Theory, https://www.beyondmusictheory.org/the-diatonic-modes/.

37. Melton, "What Are Modes in Music?"
38. For these phrases, see Gugin, "The Blood of a Nomad: Environmental Stylistics and *All the Pretty Horses*," 84, and Noble, "The Bible," 99.
39. A different version of this concept appears in my article "Cormac McCarthy's Fearless Approach to Writing," *The Conversation*, https://theconversation.com/cormac-mccarthys-fearless-approach-to-writing-207709.
40. Frye, *Unguessed Kinships*, 2.
41. https://www.allmusic.com/moods.
42. Nuzzolo, "Music Mood Classification."
43. Anonymous review in *Time*, quoted in Luce, *Embracing Vocation*, 196.
44. For example, Derek Alderman's "Toward a Historical Geography of Human-Invasive Species Relations" (2018), Lucia Argüelles and Hug March's "Weeds in Action: Vegetal Politics Ecology of Unwanted Plants" (2022), and Leslie Head et al., "Vegetal Politics: Belonging, Practices, and Places" (2014).
45. Mendelsund, *What We See*, 20.

1. Unexpected Registers

1. I have written elsewhere about this narrative tendency and stylistic attribute. See "Cormac McCarthy's *The Road* and 'a World to Come.'"
2. See, for example, Nisly's "'The Sacred Idiom Shorn of Its Referents': An Apophatic Reading of *The Road*," *Christianity & Literature* 68, no. 2: 311–24.
3. Bell, *The Achievement of Cormac McCarthy*, 53.
4. Bartlett, "From Voyeurism to Archaeology: Cormac McCarthy's *Child of God*," 4.
5. Lydia Cooper has written consistently on McCarthy's language and its relation to morality. In her book *No More Heroes*, Cooper points out that at first glance McCarthy's dire subject matter seems to produce his narrative style in which "an omniscient narrator alienates readers from fictional characters" through a narrative distance from these characters (3). In her more recent work *Cormac McCarthy: A Complexity Theory of Literature*, Cooper explores what she understands as McCarthy's narrative system that "is uniquely capable of making chaotic and complex systems imaginable" (2).
6. The quote comes from Richard Helm, "Take Show Goddess Meets Mr. End of the World," *Edmonton Journal* (6 June 2007). This reference is cited in Stacey Peebles, *Cormac McCarthy and Performance: Page, Stage, and Screen*, 1.
7. Quoted in Woodward, "Cormac McCarthy's Venomous Fiction."
8. See, for example, Brewton's "The Changing Landscape of Violence in McCarthy's Early Novels and the Border Trilogy"; Gill's *Spaces of Violence*; and the collection *Sacred Violence*, edited by Hall and Wallach.
9. McCarthy writes of dead babies hanging in trees in *Blood Meridian* (57), arterial blood in *Child of God* (69) and *Blood Meridian* (179, 274), and the splitting of Glanton's head "to the thrapple" (275) again in *Blood Meridian*.
10. See Brickner, "A Hero Cast Out, Even by Tragedy," https://archive.nytimes

.com/www.nytimes.com/books/98/05/17/specials/mccarthy-child.html?scp=50&sq=hill%20country&st=cse.

11. For an argument of how McCarthy borrows from the monstrous depiction of Grendel in the medieval text *Beowulf*, see Sarah Yancey's "Child of Grendel, *Child of God*: Cormac McCarthy's Appalachian Retelling of *Beowulf*," *Medieval Perspectives* (2022): 109–23.

12. James, "Critical Solace," 483.

13. Pound, "In a Station of the Metro."

14. See Tokushige's webpage, honebana.com, for examples and discussion of these works of art. http://honebana.com/honebana_base/honebana_introduction_en.html

15. McCarthy has previously used this image from religious iconography, this time with the description of a sleeping Billy Parham in *The Crossing*: "He fell asleep with his hands palm up before him like some dozing penitent" (126).

16. See Ellis, *No Place for Home*, 50; Brinkmeyer, "Cormac McCarthy and the Craftsman Hero"; Bellini, "Cormac McCarthy's *The Stonemason* and the Ethic of Craftsmanship"; and Cooper, *Cormac McCarthy: A Complexity Theory of Literature*, 7.

17. Brinkmeyer, "Cormac McCarthy and the Craftsman Hero," *Unsteadily Marching On: The U.S. South in Motion* (2013): 59, 66.

18. At one moment in *Child of God*, as Lester is searching for a new home, he nearly drowns in a flooded creek. As he struggles to keep above water, McCarthy addresses the reader: "He could not swim, but how would you drown him? His wrath seemed to buoy him up" (156).

19. I'm thinking here of Bill Brown's notion of "things" in his 2003 book, *A Sense of Things*, where he explores our attachment to material objects, at one point through a series of questions: "What desires do objects organize? What fantasies did they provoke? Through what economies were they assigned new value? Through what epistemologies were they assigned meaning? Today, how do we ask material objects to represent us, comfort and help us, to change us?" See Brown, *A Sense of Things*, 12.

20. Flannery O'Connor, "Some Aspects of the Grotesque in Southern Fiction" (1960), http://www.en.utexas.edu/amlit/amlitprivate/scans/grotesque.html.

21. For a wonderful extended engagement with these concerns, see Steven Frye's 2023 book, *Unguessed Kinships: Naturalism and the Geography of Hope*. In this work, Frye suggests that naturalism becomes a lens through which we might view McCarthy's mixture of darkness and hope: "McCarthy and his forebears in the naturalist tradition explore other possibilities and realms; they suggest that no mere description can capture the totality of the human condition. It is in this space that McCarthy's work charts a redemptive cartography and a geography of hope" (18). See, too, Marcel DeCoste's *Professing Darkness: Cormac McCarthy's Catholic Critique of American Enlightenment*.

22. Alter, *Pen of Iron: American Prose and the King James Bible*.

23. Alter, *Pen of Iron*, 175–77.

24. Dawn Coleman, *Preaching and the Rise of the American Novel*.

25. Andre Deutsch, "Wandering the Warrens," *Times Literary Supplement* (1970).

26. McCarthy, *Outer Dark*, 215.

27. King James Version was published in 1611.

28. Matthew 8:9–12, King James Bible.

29. Thomas Lask, *New York Times*, September 23, 1968.

30. Stacey Peebles believes that this subtitle was "probably not McCarthy's idea" and mentions that he unambiguously calls himself the text's playwright. See chapter 3 of Peebles's *Cormac McCarthy and Performance*, as well as her note to this effect on page 133.

31. John Cant, *Cormac McCarthy and the Myth of American Exceptionalism*, 124; Peter Josyph, "Older Professions: The Fourth Wall of *The Stonemason*," in *Myth, Legend, Dust: Critical Responses to Cormac McCarthy*, ed. Rick Wallach, 120; Stacey Peebles, *Cormac McCarthy and Performance*; Oprah Winfrey interview with Cormac McCarthy, https://www.oprah.com/oprahsbookclub/oprahs-exclusive-interview-with-cormac-mccarthy-video, accessed September 14, 2023.

32. I am indebted here to Nicholas Monk's argument in *True and Living Prophet of Destruction: Cormac McCarthy and Modernity*. In this book, Monk suggests that in *The Stonemason*, McCarthy explores the familiar topic of the premodern versus the modern (70).

33. Cormac McCarthy, *The Stonemason*, 6.

34. Carl Friedrich Gauss, Letter to Farkas Wolfgang Bolyai (2 September 1808). Quoted in G. Waldo Dunnington, *Carl Friedrich Gauss: Titan of Science*, 416.

35. For an entertaining treatment of the myriad ways the play is difficult to stage (and perhaps never designed to be staged), see Peter Josyph, "Older Professions."

36. See "Allegory and Allusion in Cormac McCarthy's Tennessee Novels" (2020).

37. Mike Hale, "After Saving a Jumper, The Chat That Ensues," accessed September 27, 2023.

38. Stacey Peebles finds a parallel to the brevity and fragmentation of the play in Marsha Norman's 1983 play *'night Mother*. See *Cormac McCarthy and Performance: Page, Stage, Screen*, 73–75. There have also been studies aligning McCarthy's drama to Samuel Beckett and *Waiting for Godot*. See, as examples, Dianne Luce, "Cormac McCarthy's *The Sunset Limited*: Dialogue of Life and Death (A Review of the Chicago Production)" *Cormac McCarthy Journal* 6 (Autumn 2008): 13–21, and Lydia Cooper's "'A Howling Void': Beckett's Influence in Cormac McCarthy's *The Sunset Limited*," *Cormac McCarthy Journal* 10, no. 1 (2012): 1–15.

39. These readings are supported by the most important early scholarly work on McCarthy, Vareen Bell's *The Achievement of Cormac McCarthy*. Bell describes McCarthy's novels as containing what he calls "an ambiguous nihilism."

40. For examples of these "breaks," see *Stella Maris*, 59, 104, 109, 116, 164, 190.

41. In an interview with the *Paris Review*, Hemingway famously stated, "If it is any use to know it, I always try to write on the principle of the iceberg. There are seven-eighths of it under water for every part that shows. Anything you know you can eliminate and it only strengthens your iceberg. It is the part that doesn't show. If a writer omits something because he does not know it then there is a hole in the story." *The Writer's Chapbook*, 120–21.

42. William Covino, *Forms of Wondering: A Dialogue on Writing, for Writers*.
43. T. S. Eliot, "The Lovesong of J. Alfred Prufrock," line 34.
44. Peter Mendelsund, *What We See When We Read*, 302, 135.

2. "Large Loose Baggy Monsters"

1. Virgil, *The Aeneid*, trans. Robert Fitzgerald.
2. Safer, *The Contemporary American Comic Epic* (1988), 13. For other examples in addition to Safer's account, see Quint's *Epic and Empire: Politics and Generic Form from Virgil to Milton* (1993), Steinberg's *Twentieth-Century Epic Novels* (2005), and Wofford's *The Choice of Achilles: The Ideology of Figure in the Epic* (1992). I have written elsewhere of Walt Whitman's engagement with the epic tradition: "Walt Whitman and the Epic Tradition: Political and Poetical Voices in 'Song of Myself'" (2000).
3. Quint, *Epic and Empire*, 360, cited in Steinberg, *Twentieth-Century Epic Novels*, 22. See the first essay in Bakhtin's *The Dialogic Imagination* (1981).
4. Steinberg, *Twentieth-Century Epic Novels*, 19.
5. James's famous continental preferences show up in his list of baggy novels. We might add to this Eurocentric list the numerous earlier American novels with epic gestures, such as those by James Fenimore Cooper, William Gilmore Simms, and Herman Melville, just to name a few. Melville's *Moby Dick*, for example, would fit perfectly into James's notion of the "large, loose, baggy monster."
6. See James's 1909 preface to his previously published novel *The Tragic Muse*. Interestingly, James's former mentee H. G. Wells memorably and hilariously compared the extraordinary accretion of detail in many of James's own long novels to reading about a hippopotamus trying to pick up a pea: Wells claimed that a novel by James is "like a church lit but without a congregation to distract you, with every light and line focused on the high altar. And on the altar, very reverentially placed, intensely there, is a dead kitten, an egg-shell, a bit of string. . . . It is leviathan retrieving pebbles. It is a magnificent but painful hippopotamus resolved at any cost, even at the cost of its dignity, upon picking up a pea, which has got to the corner of its den." https://slate.com/news-and-politics/2004/10/the-vogue-for-henry-james.html.
7. Crews, *Books Are Made Out of Books*, 2.
8. See Harold Bloom's *Anxiety of Influence: A Theory of Poetry* (1973).
9. Woodward, "Cormac McCarthy's Venomous Fiction," https://www.nytimes.com/1992/04/19/magazine/cormac-mccarthy-s-venomous-fiction.html.
10. See Dianne Luce's excellent work on the archives in McCarthy's Tennessee period, especially "The Archives of the Tennessee Years" and "Tall Tales and Raw Realities."
11. Jones, *Strange Talk*, 141–50.
12. Quoted in Jones, *Strange Talk*, 1.
13. Jones, *Strange Talk*, 139.

14. See cummings's poem, "[In Just-]," https://www.poetryfoundation.org/poems/47247/in-just.

15. For an extended analysis of McCarthy's commitment to intertextuality in *Suttree*, see Scott Yarborough's "The Intertextual 'Suttree': Walker Percy, Cummings, and Community."

16. Shakespeare, *Hamlet*, act 5, scene 2.

17. Shakespeare, *Macbeth*, act 5, scene 5.

18. See John Grammer, "A Thing against Which Time Will Not Prevail: Pastoral and History in Cormac McCarthy's South"; Wes Morgan, "A Season of Death and Epidemic Violence"; and Matthew Guinn, "Ruder Forms Survive: Cormac McCarthy's Atavistic Vision."

19. Frye, *Understanding Cormac McCarthy*, 153.

20. This piece was so popular and moving that it was put to music by the composer Samuel Barber, who created a work for voice and orchestra that used for its libretto passages from this prologue. Barber's "Knoxville: Summer of 1915, Op. 24" premiered in 1948 with the Boston Symphony Orchestra.

21. Agee, *Death in the Family*, 7.

22. For an extended treatment of *Suttree*'s connection to the epic (via James Joyce's *Ulysses*) and James Agee's *Death in the Family*, see Rick Wallach's "Ulysses in Knoxville: Suttree's Aegean Journey."

23. One of the earliest and most consistent commentators on the disparity between Agee's vision and the published version of *Death in the Family* has been Victor Kramer. See "A Death in the Family and Agee's Projected Novel" (1973) and *Agee: Selected Literary Documents* (1996).

24. Agee, *Death*, ix–x.

25. In his restored edition, Michael Lofaro places "The Dream Sequence" as the introduction to *A Death in the Family*, arguing that it would have most likely been Agee's choice had he been alive to oversee the publication. See Lofaro's "Restoration," 4–13.

26. Wallach, "Ulysses in Knoxville," 78.

27. Agee, *Death*, 3.

28. Agee, *Death*, 7.

29. Palmer III, "Encampment of the Damned," 145–47.

30. The phrase appears on the front page of the December 29, 1980, edition of the *Wall Street Journal* in Susan Harrigan's article "What If You Gave a World's Fair and Nobody Came?" The city eventually embraced the title, with several businesses and apparel lines using the catchphrase "Scruffy City."

31. McCarthy, *Suttree*, 4.

32. Crews, *Books*, 65.

33. Alighieri, *Inferno*, 383.

34. Shaviro, "The Very Life of the Darkness," 147.

35. See, for example, Charles Thomas's "*Blood Meridian*'s Chronotopic Gates" and John Sepich's *Notes on Blood Meridian*. The latter includes Sepich's physical map,

which has since been reproduced and colorized on Biblioklept: https://biblioklept.org/2010/09/30/a-map-of-blood-meridian/.

36. Whitman, *Leaves of Grass*, 38–39.
37. Steinberg, *Epic Novels*, 29.
38. Safer, *The Contemporary American Comic Epic*, 13.
39. Steinberg, *Epic Novels*, 31.
40. Mendelsund, *What We See*, 7, 16, 26.
41. Mendelsund, *What We See*, 31.
42. See, for example, recent articles on the novel that deal with an ecomasculinism, ontological dynamism, fallen communion, and cross-border inequality. See the works of Vahit Yasayan, Jonathan Elmore and Rick Elmore, Marcel De Coste, and Peter Arnds.
43. For a consideration of how the wolf's agency fits into an animal studies perspective, see Malewitz, "Narrative Disruption."
44. Anzaldúa, *Borderlands*, 3.
45. Anzaldúa, *Borderlands*, 3, 5, 21.
46. Anzaldúa, *Borderlands*, 4.
47. The passages are translated by Lt. Jim Campbell and can be found here: https://www.cormacmccarthy.com/wp-content/uploads/CrossingTrans.pdf.
48. Kelly, "The Epic Ballads of Mexico's Corridos."
49. For a consideration of this scene in relation to Badiou's Lacanian notions of the Real and the role of aesthetics, see Cameron MacKenzie's "A Song of Great Order."
50. The Spanish can be translated as "Hair so blonde. Gun in his hand. What are you looking for, young man. That you get up so early?"
51. The corrido can be translated as "Town of Bachinava / April was the month / Armed horsemen / the six arrived / If he was afraid / you could not see it in his face / so many arriving / the white one waits for them."
52. The reader can find another similar passage in *The Crossing* in the description of a Mexican fair that brings together workers and families of Mexicans, Mennonites, Tarahumara, Mormons, Yaquis, and Apache, all leading to the appearance of a "shabby circus." As is the case with the extended discussion of the Tarahumara, this scene lacks the exotic descriptors and imaginative excess of the passage from *Blood Meridian*. See *The Crossing*, 105.

3. "Little More than a Childhood Enthusiasm"

1. For example, Derek Alderman, "Toward a Historical Geography of Human-Invasive Species Relations" (2018); Lucia Argüelles and Hug March, "Weeds in Action: Vegetal Politics Ecology of Unwanted Plants" (2022); and Leslie Head et al., "Vegetal Politics: Belonging, Practices, and Places" (2014).
2. Bartram, *Travels*, 13–14.
3. *The Phoenix* has been continuously published since the first issue in 1959, in which McCarthy's first story appears. His second story appears in issue 2 in 1960. The

University of Tennessee has digitized most of the issues, including the two in which McCarthy's stories appear. https://digital.lib.utk.edu/collections/islandora/object/collections%3Aphoenix?display=grid.

4. This chapter was inspired by two scholars of McCarthy's work. The first is Wesley Morgan, who spoke of one day hopefully building a memorial garden to Cormac McCarthy in Knoxville, Tennessee, which would contain the flora mentioned in his Knoxville novel *Suttree*. The second is a PhD student (now graduate) and friend John Nichols, whose work on the role of bioregions in American twentieth-century literature serves as a model of such exploration. Both Wes's and John's interests turned my attention to how McCarthy delves into microregions and specific places of biodiversity.

5. Bartram, *Travels*, 274–76.

6. Rikard, *Authority and the Mountaineer*, 25.

7. This precise image is not in the primary edition of this book, although Hawbaker also published smaller pamphlets for specific animal trapping. Many of the illustrations in the book and pamphlets are drawn by Edward Isenhour, a sketch artist from the Appalachian mountain area of North Carolina.

8. To see a related discussion of McCarthy's treatment of and appreciation for craft, see chapter 1 of this work.

9. Thoreau, *Walden*, 135–36.

10. Patterson, "We've Killed a Lot of Animals," *The Guardian*, December 21, 2007, https://www.theguardian.com/film/2007/dec/21/coenbrothers.

11. Peebles, *Cormac McCarthy and Performance*, 134. For an incredibly thorough and engaging tale of the process of adaption from McCarthy's novel to the Coen brothers' film, see "Tragic Success Stories," the fifth chapter of Peebles's book.

12. This phrase comes from Steven Frye's *Understanding Cormac McCarthy*, 152.

13. Favero, "You don't have to do this," 157.

14. Frye, *Understanding McCarthy*, 154.

15. Nichols, *Bioregional Ethics*, 111–12.

16. Nichols, *Bioregional Ethics*, 10.

17. For wonderful and thorough treatments of the idea of the pastoral and the pastoral tradition, see Paul Alpers's *What Is Pastoral?* and Terry Giffords's *Pastoral*.

18. Alpers, *What Is Pastoral?*, 16.

19. Gifford, *Pastoral*, 2–3.

20. Examples taken from stories from *In the Tennessee Mountains*, in order of appearance here, "The Star in the Valley" (70, 65), "Drifting Down Lost Creek" (7), "The Romance of Sunrise Rock" (102), and "The 'Harnt' that Walked Chilhowee" (152). For a longer discussion of Murfree in relation to the local color tradition, see the introduction to *In the Tennessee Mountains* by Bill Hardwig.

21. Still, *River of Earth*, 21.

22. Still, *River of Earth*, 13–14, 135, 184.

23. See, for example, Andrew Bartlett's sense of the "antipastoral" demonic Lester Ballard in *Child of God*: "From Voyeurism," 14.

24. Guillemin, *The Pastoral Vision of Cormac McCarthy*, 3. This study was published

before McCarthy released *The Road*, which surely would have figured prominently in the argument.

25. Guillemin reads this relationship between Lester and his environment as representative of an internal and external wilderness. "It is a novel about wilderness inside and out, or, to be more precise, a representation of wild nature as reflected in a psyche gone wild." Guillemin contrasts the primal wilderness in the book with other examples of "meaningful pastoral space" (37).

26. Bartlett, "From Voyeurism to Archeology," 9.

27. Exodus 20.

28. I have written elsewhere of McCarthy's use of allegory and allusion and the ways that his use of these literary motifs often resist providing the meaning we expect them to. See Hardwig, "Allegory and Allusion."

29. Guillemin, *The Pastoral Vision of Cormac McCarthy*, 3–4.

30. Guillemin, *The Pastoral Vision of Cormac McCarthy*, 13.

31. Alderman, "Toward a Historical Geography of Human–Invasive Species Relations," 6. See also Alderman's other work on the "regional symbolic capital" of kudzu: "When the Exotic Becomes Native: Taming, Naming, and Kudzu as Regional Symbolic Capital," *Southeastern Geographer* 55, no. 1 (2015): 32–56.

32. For more information on these terms, see Irons's "Sanctuary for Weediness."

33. Lawrence, "Listening to Plants," 641.

34. Lawrence, "Listening to Plants," 631.

35. Ginsberg, "Sunflower Sutra," 36.

36. Irons, "Sanctuary for Weediness," https://ellieirons.com/projects/sanctuary-for-weedy-species/.

37. Lawrence, "Listening to Plants," 640–41.

38. Alderman, "Toward a Historical Geography of Human–Invasive Species Relations," 7, 10; and Irons, "Sanctuary for Weediness," https://ellieirons.com/projects/sanctuary-for-weedy-species/.

39. I allude here to two very different textual moments. The first is Paul's conversion to Christianity in the KJV Bible: "And immediately there fell from his eyes as it had been scales: and he received sight forthwith, and arose, and was baptized" (Act 9:18). The second is Mark Twain's account of Huck Finn's attempt to find freedom outside the presses of the town and familial obligation in the novel's final passage: "I reckon I got to light out for the territory ahead of the rest." Both suggest the possibility of a revelation and newfound freedom that fails to materialize for Suttree.

40. See, for example, recent publications such as Shannon Lodoen, "Post-Apocalyptic Fiction and the Limits of Optimism: A Pessimistic Reading of Cormac McCarthy's *The Road*," *Critique: Studies in Contemporary Fiction* 64, no. 1 (2023): 85–97; Tyler Austin Harper, "Cannibal Nihilism: Meat and Meaninglessness in the Anthropocene Imaginary," *Science Fiction Studies* 49, no. 2 [147] (July 2022): 304–21; Parisa Changizi, "The Human, Nonhuman, Inhuman in Cormac McCarthy's *The Road*," *Ostrava Journal of English Philology* 14, no. 2 (2022): 21–33; Nandita Mahajan, "Reading Climate Change in the Palimpsest: The Ecocritical Potential of Novel-to-Film

Adaptation," *Adaptation: The Journal of Literature on Screen Studies* 14, no. 2 (August 2021): 243–59; Octavia Cade and Meryl Stenhouse, "Humans as Ecological Actors in Post-Apocalyptic Literature," *MOSF Journal of Science Fiction* 4, no. 1 (2020): 47–59; and Adeline Johns-Putra, *Climate Change and the Contemporary Novel*.

41. Christopher Nolan, dir., *Oppenheimer*.

42. Cormac McCarthy, interview in John Jurgensen's "Hollywood's Favorite Cowboy."

43. Cornell Labs, "Ivory-Billed Woodpecker," https://www.birds.cornell.edu/home/the-search-for-the-ivory-billed-woodpecker/.

44. This quote is taken from the Santa Fe Institute's memorial webpage to McCarthy, "In Memoriam: Cormac McCarthy," https://www.santafe.edu/news-center/news/memoriam-cormac-mccarthy.

45. Krempa, "State pauses brook trout stocking to study acid rain recovery."

4. The Precarious Mood

1. Introduction to McCarthy's "The Kekulé Problem," *Nautilus*, April 17, 2017.

2. Giemza, *Science and Literature in Cormac McCarthy's Expanding Worlds*, 8.

3. The symposium was held at Creighton University in Omaha, Nebraska, September 21–23, 2023. For the archived symposium program with paper titles, see the Cormac McCarthy Society website: https://www.cormacmccarthysociety.com/omaha-program.

4. See, for example, the review by Beejay Silcox, "Stella Maris by Cormac McCarthy review—a Slow-Motion Study of Obliteration," *Guardian*, December 7, 2022; Constance Grady, "Cormac McCarthy's Two New Novels Are Deliberately Frustrating," *Vox*, October 26, 2022; and John Jeremiah Sullivan, "Cormac McCarthy's New Novel: Two Lives, Two Ways of Seeing," *New York Times*, October 19, 2022.

5. McCarthy, "The Kekulé Problem."

6. See, for example, McCarthy, *Stella Maris*, 28, 38, 79, 100, 129, 132, 173.

7. Grady, "Cormac McCarthy's Two New Novels."

8. The Science Museum, "Thalidomide," December 11, 2019, https://www.sciencemuseum.org.uk/objects-and-stories/medicine/thalidomide.

9. For a discussion of DuPont's slogan and the recent history of the relationship between business, morality, and science, see Livia Gershon's "What We Mean by 'Better Living,'" in JSTOR Daily, July 13, 2019, https://daily.jstor.org/what-we-mean-by-better-living/.

10. I would like to credit Brian Schill, who spoke on this idea of conspiracy being central to the book in the Q&A portion of his excellent talk "Cormac, Foucault, and Antipsychiatry," delivered at the Cormac McCarthy's *The Passenger* and *Stella Maris* Symposium in Omaha Nebraska, September 21–23, 2023.

11. Quoted in David Rudenstine, "The Day the Presses Stopped: A History of the Pentagon Papers Case," *Washington Post*, https://www.washingtonpost.com/wp-srv/style/longterm/books/chap1/daythepr.htm.

12. Komunyakaa, "Nude Interrogation."

13. See the documents on the FBI's page: https://vault.fbi.gov/Mary%20Jo%20Kopechne%20%28Chappaquiddick%29%20/Mary%20Jo%20Kopechne%20%28Chappaquiddick%29%20Part%201%20of%202/view.

14. Jesse Armstrong, dir., *Succession*.

15. David Monod, *Vaudeville and the Making of Modern Entertainment*, 2, 103, 145.

16. Christopher Nolan, dir., *Oppenheimer*; Craig Mazan, dir., *Chernobyl*.

17. James Lilley, "The Hands of Yet Other Puppets," in *Myth, Legend, Dust; All the Pretty Horses*.

18. Interview with Ray Smith, March 1, 2023. McCarthy uses the term in Alicia's account of her mother's history in *Stella Maris*, 72.

19. https://ahf.nuclearmuseum.org/ahf/history/civilian-displacement-oak-ridge-tn/.

20. Johnson and Jackson, *City Behind a Fence*, xx.

21. Interview with Ray Smith, March 1, 2023.

22. Johnson and Jackson, *City Behind a Fence*, 29–30.

23. For a wonderful account of the "calutron girls" and their contribution to the Oak Ridge facilities, see Denise Kiernan's *The Girls of Atomic City*. The term "calutron girl" appears in *Stella Maris*, 72.

24. See an interview with Theodore Rockwell in "Operating Oak Ridge's Calutrons," https://www.y12.doe.gov/sites/default/files/assets/document/08-01-03.pdf.

25. For other examples of Westcott's photography, see the Atomic Photographers website. This amazing site calls itself a "visual archive documenting the development and cultural impact of the atomic bomb and its use in Hiroshima and Nagasaki, subsequent bomb tests, nuclear disasters and the devastating effects to the environment and local populations." https://atomicphotographers.com/photographers/ed-westcott/.

26. https://www.y12.doe.gov/sites/default/files/assets/document/07-09-27.pdf.

27. Smith, Kiernan, and Holmberg, "Civilian Displacement," https://ahf.nuclearmuseum.org/ahf/history/civilian-displacement-oak-ridge-tn/.

28. Johnson and Jackson, *City Behind a Fence*, 41.

29. Johnson and Jackson, *City Behind a Fence*, 39.

30. Melton Hill Dam, which was initiated in 1960 and completed in 1963.

31. Written in 1947 and published in 1951 in *Cultural Criticisms and Society*.

32. Johnson and Jackson, *City Behind a Fence*, 39.

33. Cited in Brandon Story, "A New and Modern Task: The Tennessee Valley Authority and Appalachian Modernism."

34. McDonald and Muldowny, *TVA and the Dispossessed: The Resettlement of Population in the Norris Dam Area*, 8.

35. Quoted in McDonald and Muldowny, *TVA and the Dispossessed*, 11, 263.

36. James Agee, "Tennessee Valley Authority," 13.

37. McDonald and Muldowny, *TVA and the Dispossessed*, 8, 4.

38. William Prather, "'The Color of Life Is Water': History, Stones, and the River in *Suttree*," 42.

39. Charles McCarthy, "TVA and the Tennessee Valley," 30.

40. Agee, "T.V.A.: Work in the Valley," cited in *James Agee: Selected Journalism*, ed. Paul Ashdown, 62.

41. Gabe Rickard, *Authority and the Mountaineer in Cormac McCarthy's Appalachia*.

42. Agee, "T.V.A.: Work in the Valley," 62.

43. Charles McCarthy, "Land Acquisition Policies and Proceedings in TVA—A Study of the Role of Land Acquisition in a Regional Agency," *Ohio State Law Journal* 10 (1949): 63.

44. McDonald and Muldowny, *TVA and the Dispossessed*, 208.

45. Agee, "T.V.A.: Work in the Valley," 62.

46. Purcell, ed., *Lost in Transition: Removing, Resettling, and Renewing Appalachia*, 5.

47. See chapter 3 of this book for an extended discussion of McCarthy's interest in taxidermy and taxonomy.

48. Hurston, *Their Eyes Were Watching God*, 193.

Epilogue

1. Luce, *Embracing Vocation*, 204.

2. Wes Morgan has done conducted some excellent scholarship between John Sheddan the person and John Sheddan the fictional character. He presented some of his early findings at the American Literature Association Conference in 2023, "Long John Sheddan in *The Passenger*: The Actual and the Fictitious."

3. This correspondence is available at the University of Tennessee Hodges Library in the Betsey B. Creekmore Special Collections Library in Knoxville in the boxes "Cormac McCarthy Correspondence, 1976–1985."

4. Fergus, letter to Cormac McCarthy, November 23, 1976.

5. McCarthy, letter to John Ryan Fergus, February 1980.

6. Russell Hillier has spoken and written about McCarthy's use of humor, especially in *Suttree*. See his short piece "Something Like Amusement" on the topic.

Bibliography

Abbott, H. Porter. *The Cambridge Introduction to Narrative*. 2nd ed. Cambridge University Press, 2008.
Adorno, Theodore. "Cultural Criticisms and Society." *Prisms: Cultural Criticisms and Society*. Neville Spearman, 1967.
Agee, James. *A Death in the Family*. Vintage Books, 1998.
———. "Tennessee Valley Authority." *James Agee: Selected Journalism*. Edited by Paul Ashdown. Knoxville: University of Tennessee Press, 2005.
———. "T.V.A.: Work in the Valley," cited in *James Agee: Selected Journalism*. Edited by Paul Ashdown. Knoxville: University of Tennessee Press, 2005.
Alderman, Derek H. "Toward a Historical Geography of Human–Invasive Species Relations: How Kudzu Came to Belong in the American South." In *The American Environment Revisited: Environmental Historical Geographies of the United States*. Edited by Geoffrey Buckley and Yolanda Youngs. Rowman & Littlefield, 2018, 3–18.
Alighieri, Dante. *Inferno: Volume I* from *The Divine Comedy*. Translated by Mark Musa.
Alpers, Paul. *What Is Pastoral?* Penguin Books, 1984. Reprint, University of Chicago Press, 1996.
Alter, Robert. *Pen of Iron: American Prose and the King James Bible*. Princeton University Press, 2010.
Anzaldúa, Gloria. *Borderlands/La Frontera*. Aunt Lute Books, 1987.
Argüelles, Lucia, and Hug March, "Weeds in Action: Vegetal Politics Ecology of Unwanted Plants." *Progress in Human Geography* 46 (2022): 44–66.
Armstrong, Jesse, dir. *Succession*. HBO, 2018.
Arnds, Peter. "Tracking Wolves: A Metaphor for Cross-Border Inequality: Cormac McCarthy's Novel *The Crossing*." In *Inequality*. Edited by Kimberly Drake. Salem Press, 2018, 144–57.
Aubry, Timothy. *Guilty Aesthetic Pleasures*. Harvard University Press, 2018.
Bakhtin, M. M. *The Dialogic Imagination: Four Essays*. University of Texas Press, 1981.
Banfield, Ann. *Unspeakable Sentences: Narration and Representation in the Language of Fiction*. Routledge Press, 1982.

Bannon, Brad, and John Vanderheide, *Cormac McCarthy's Violent Destinies: The Poetics of Determinism and Fatalism*. University of Tennessee Press, 2018.

Bartlett, Andrew. "From Voyeurism to Archaeology: Cormac McCarthy's *Child of God*." *Southern Literary Journal* (1991): 3–15.

Bartram, William. *Travels and Other Writings*. Edited by Thomas P. Slaughter. Library of America, 1996.

Bell, Vareen. *The Achievement of Cormac McCarthy*. Louisiana State University Press, 1988.

Bellini, Federico. "Cormac McCarthy's *The Stonemason* and the Ethic of Craftsmanship." *European Journal of American Studies* 12 (2017): 1–15.

Berlant, Lauren. *Compassion: The Culture and Politics of an Emotion*. New York: Routledge, 2004.

Best, Stephen, and Sharon Marcus. "Surface Reading: An Introduction." *Representations* 108, no. 1 (Fall 2009): 1–21.

Bloom, Harold. *Anxiety of Influence: A Theory of Poetry*. Oxford University Press, 1997.

Booth, Wayne. *The Rhetoric of Fiction*. 2nd ed. University of Chicago Press, 1983.

Brewton, Vince. "The Changing Landscape of Violence in McCarthy's Early Novels and the Border Trilogy." *Southern Literary Journal* 37, no. 1 (2004): 121–43.

Brickner, Richard P. "A Hero Cast Out, Even by Tragedy." *New York Times*, January 13, 1974. https://archive.nytimes.com/www.nytimes.com/books/98/05/17/specials/mccarthy-child.html?scp=50&sq=hill%20country&st=cse.

Brinkmeyer Jr., Richard. "Cormac McCarthy and the Craftsman Hero." *Unsteadily Marching On: The U.S. South in Motion*. University of Valencia, 2013.

Burnett, Katharine, and Monica Carol Miller. *The Tacky South*. Louisiana State University Press, 2022.

Cant, John. *Cormac McCarthy and the Myth of American Exceptionalism*. Routledge Press, 2007.

Chabon, Michael, "After the Apocalypse." *New York Review of Books* 54, no. 2 (2007). https://www.nybooks.com/articles/2007/02/15/after-the-apocalypse/.

Coleman, Dawn. *Preaching and the Rise of the American Novel*. Ohio State University Press, 2013.

Cooper, Lydia. *Cormac McCarthy: A Complexity Theory of Literature*. Manchester University Press, 2023.

———. *No More Heroes: Narrative Perspective and Morality in Cormac McCarthy*. Louisiana State University Press, 2011.

Cornell Labs. "Ivory-Billed Woodpecker." *All About Birds*. https://www.allaboutbirds.org/guide/Ivory-billed_Woodpecker/overview#.

Covino, William. *Forms of Wondering: A Dialogue on Writing, for Writers*. Heinemann Press, 1990.

Crews, Michael Lynn. *Books Are Made Out of Books: A Guide to Cormac McCarthy's Literary Influences*. University of Texas Press, 2017.

cummings, e. e. "[In Just-]." https://www.poetryfoundation.org/poems/47247/in-just.
DeCoste, Marcel D. "'One Among and Not Separate From': Fallen Communion and Forfeit Community in Cormac McCarthy's *The Crossing*." *Christianity & Literature* 69, no. 4 (2022): 439–58.
———. *Professing Darkness: Cormac McCarthy's Catholic Critique of American Enlightenment*. Louisiana State University Press, 2023.
Deutsch, Andre. "Wandering the Warrens." *Times Literary Supplement*, 1970.
Dunnington, G. Waldo. *Carl Friedrich Gauss: Titan of Science*. Mathematical Association of America, 2004.
Eliot, T. S. "The Lovesong of J. Alfred Prufrock." https://www.poetryfoundation.org/poetrymagazine/poems/44212/the-love-song-of-j-alfred-prufrock.
Ellis, Jay. *No Place for Home: Spatial Constraint and Character Flight in the Novels of Cormac McCarthy*. Routledge, 2006.
Elmore, Rick, and Jonathan Elmore. "The World as Tale: Ontological Dynamism and Metaphysical Unity in Cormac McCarthy's *The Crossing*." *Mississippi Quarterly* 75, no. 1 (January 2022): 61–78.
Errett, Benjamin. *Elements of Taste: Understanding What We Like and Why*. Tarcher/Perigee, 2017.
Erwin, Doug. "Cormac interrogated me about the finest details." *In Memoriam: Cormac McCarthy*. Santa Fe Institute website. https://www.santafe.edu/news-center/news/memoriam-cormac-mccarthy.
Favero, Douglas. "'You don't have to do this': Cormac McCarthy's *No Country for Old Men* and the Courage to Be." *Cormac McCarthy Journal* 19, no. 2 (2021): 157–77.
Felski, Rita. *Hooked: Art and Attachment*. University of Chicago Press, 2020.
———. *The Limits of Critique*. University of Chicago Press, 2015.
Fergus, John Ryan. Letter to Cormac McCarthy. University of Tennessee Special Collections, November 23, 1976.
Franco, James, dir. *Child of God*. Rabbit Bandini Productions, 2014.
Frye, Steven. *Understanding Cormac McCarthy*. University of South Carolina, 2009.
———. *Unguessed Kinships: Naturalism and the Geography of Hope in Cormac McCarthy*. University of Alabama Press, 2023.
Genette, Gérard. *Narrative Discourse: An Essay in Method*. Cornell University Press, 1980.
Giemza, Bryan. *Science and Literature in Cormac McCarthy's Expanding Worlds*. Bloomsbury Academic, 2023.
Gifford, Terry. *Pastoral: The New Critical Idiom*. Routledge, 1999.
Gill, James. *The Spaces of Violence*. University of Alabama Press, 2006.
Ginsberg, Allen. "Sunflower Sutra." *Howl and Other Poems*. City Light Books, 1956.
The Gold and Blue. Knoxville Catholic High School Newspaper. 1948.
Grady, Constance. "Cormac McCarthy's Two New Novels Are Deliberately Frus-

trating." *Vox*, October 26, 2022. https://www.vox.com/culture/23423262/passenger-stella-maris-review-cormac-mccarthy.

Grammer, John M. "A Thing against Which Time Will Not Prevail: Pastoral and History in Cormac McCarthy's South." *Perspectives on Cormac McCarthy*. Edited by Edwin Arnold and Dianne Luce. University of Mississippi Press, 1999: 29–44.

Greve, Julius. *Shreds of Matter: Cormac McCarthy and the Concept of Nature*. Dartmouth College Press, 2018.

Gugin, David. "The Blood of a Nomad: Environmental Stylistics and *All the Pretty Horses*." In *Cormac McCarthy's Borders and Landscapes*. Edited by Louise Jillett. Bloomsbury Academic, 2016: 83–94.

Guillemin, Georg. *The Pastoral Vision of Cormac McCarthy*. Texas A&M Press, 2004.

Guinn, Matthew. "Ruder Forms Survive: Cormac McCarthy's Atavistic Vision." In *Myth, Legend, Dust: Critical Responses to Cormac McCarthy*. Edited by Rich Wallach. Manchester University Press, 2000: 108–15.

Hale, Dorothy. "'On Beauty' as Beautiful? The Problem of Novelistic Aesthetics by Way of Zadie Smith." *Contemporary Literature* 53, no. 4 (Winter 2012): 814–44.

Hale, Mike. "After Saving a Jumper, the Chat That Ensues." *New York Times* (Febuary 11, 2011). https://www.nytimes.com/2011/02/12/arts/television/12sunset.html.

Hall, Wade, and Rick Wallach, eds. *Sacred Violence: A Reader's Companion to Cormac McCarthy*. Vols. I and II. Texas Western Press, 1995.

Hardwig, Bill. "Allusion and Allegory in McCarthy." *Cormac McCarthy in Context*. Cambridge University Press, 2020: 107–17.

———. "Cormac McCarthy's Fearless Approach to Writing." *The Conversation*. June 16, 2023. https://theconversation.com/cormac-mccarthys-fearless-approach-to-writing-207709.

———. "Cormac McCarthy's *The Road* and the 'World to Come.'" *Studies in American Naturalism* (Summer 2013): 38–51.

———. Introduction to *In the Tennessee Mountains*, by Mary Noailles Murfree. Edited by Bill Hardwig. University of Tennessee Press, 2008: x–xl.

———. "Walt Whitman and the Epic Tradition: Political and Poetical Voices in 'Song of Myself.'" *Walt Whitman Quarterly* 17, no. 4 (Spring 2000): 166–88.

Hawbaker, S. Stanley. *Trapping North American Furbearers: a complete guide on trapping all North American furbearers for both amateur and professional, also deer hunting, turkey hunting, bear hunting, tracks and tracking, lures and baits, skinning and handling fur, etc*. S. Stanley Hawbaker and Sons, 1974.

Head, Leslie, et al. "Vegetal Politics: Belonging, Practices, and Places." *Social and Cultural Geography* 15, no. 8 (2014): 861–70.

Helm, Richard. "Talk Show Goddess Meets Mr. End of the World." *Edmonton Journal*, 6 June 2007.

Herman, David, et al., eds. *Narrative Theory: Core Concepts and Critical Debates.* Ohio State University Press, 2012.
Hillier, Russell. "'Something Like Amusement': Comedy and Humor in Cormac McCarthy's *Suttree.*" *ANQ: A Quarterly Journal of Short Articles Notes and Reviews* (2024): 1–8.
Hoberek, Andrew. "Cormac McCarthy and the Aesthetics of Exhaustion." *American Literary History* 23, no. 3 (2011): 483–99.
Holloway, David. *The Late Modernism of Cormac McCarthy.* Greenwood Press, 2002.
Hurston, Zora Neale. *Their Eyes Were Watching God.* Perennial Classics, 1990.
Irons, Ellie. *Sanctuary for Weediness: A Winter Respite for Urban-Dwelling Plants and Humans.* Feral Landscape Lobby. https://ellieirons.com/projects/sanctuary-for-weedy-species/.
Jacobs, Alan. *The Pleasures of Reading in an Age of Distraction.* Oxford University Press, 2011.
James, David. "Critical Solace." *New Literary History* 47, no. 4 (2016): 481–504.
James, Henry. Preface to *The Tragic Muse,* 1909. http://www.online-literature.com/henry_james/tragic-muse/0/.
Johnson, Barbara. "Teaching Deconstructively." In *Writing and Reading Differently.* Edited by G. Douglas Atkins and M. J. Johnson, 140–48. University of Kansas Press, 1986.
Johnson, Charles W., and Charles O. Jackson. *City Behind a Fence: Oak Ridge, Tennessee, 1942–1946.* University of Tennessee Press, 1981.
Jones, Gavin. *Strange Talk: The Politics of Dialect Literature in Gilded Age America.* University of California Press, 1999.
Josyph, Peter. "Older Professions: The Fourth Wall of *The Stonemason.*" In *Myth, Legend, Dust: Critical Responses to Cormac McCarthy.* Edited by Rick Wallach. Manchester University Press, 2000.
Jurgensen, John. "Hollywood's Favorite Cowboy." *Wall Street Journal,* November 29, 2009. https://www.wsj.com/articles/SB10001424052748704576204574529703577274572.
Kelly, Cynthia C. "Design of the Y-12 Calutrons." Department of Energy Database. https://www.y12.doe.gov/sites/default/files/assets/document/07-09-27.pdf.
———. "Operating Oak Ridge's 'Calutrons.'" Department of Energy Database. https://www.y12.doe.gov/sites/default/files/assets/document/08-01-03.pdf.
Kelly, M. J. "The Epic Ballads of Mexico's Corridos." *Medium,* August 6, 2023. https://medium.com/fronteras/the-epic-ballads-of-mexicos-corridos-6cca98115ed2.
Kiernan, Denise. *The Girls of Atomic City: The Untold Story of the Women Who Helped Win World War II.* Touchstone, 2013.
Komunyakaa, Yusef. "Nude Interrogation." In *Thieves of Paradise.* Wesleyan University Press, 1998.

Krakauer, David. Introduction to "The Kekulé Problem," by Cormac McCarthy. *Nautilus*, April 17, 2017. https://nautil.us/the-kekul-problem-236574/.

Kramer, Victor, ed. *Agee: Selected Literary Documents*. Whitston Pub. Co., 1996.

———. "A Death in the Family and Agee's Projected Novel." *Proof: Yearbook of American Bibliographical and Textual Studies* 3 (1973): 139–54.

Lilley, James. "The Hands of Yet Other Puppets." In *Myth, Legend, Dust: Critical Responses to Cormac McCarthy*. Edited by Rich Wallach. Manchester University Press, 2000.

Krempa, Francesca. "State pauses brook trout stocking to study acid rain recovery." *Adirondack Explorer*, June 22, 2020. https://www.adirondackexplorer.org/stories/state-pauses-brook-trout-stocking-to-study-acid-rain-recovery.

Lawrence, Anna M. "Listening to Plants: Conversations between Critical Plant Studies and Vegetal Geography." *Progress in Human Geography* 46, no. 2 (2022): 629–51.

Lofaro, Michael. *Death in the Family: A Restoration of the Author's Text*. University of Tennessee Press, 2007.

Luce, Dianne C. "The Archives and the Tennessee Year, II: *Child of God*, *The Gardener's Son*, and *Suttree*." In *Cormac McCarthy in Context*. Edited by Steven Frye. Cambridge University Press, 2020.

———. *Embracing Vocation: Cormac McCarthy's Writing Life, 1959–1974*. University of South Carolina Press, 2023.

———. "Tall Tales and Raw Realities: Late-Stage Deletions from Cormac McCarthy's *Suttree*." *Resources for American Literature Study* 38 (2015): 213–56.

Macé, Marielle, and Marlon Jones. "Ways of Reading, Modes of Being." *New Literary History* 44, no. 2 (Spring 2013): 213–29.

MacKenzie, Cameron. "A Song of Great Order: The Real in Cormac McCarthy's *The Crossing*." *Cormac McCarthy Journal* 13 (2015): 100–120.

Malewitz, Raymond. "Narrative Disruption as Animal Agency in Cormac McCarthy's *The Crossing*." *Modern Fiction Studies* 60, no. 3 (2014): 544–61.

Mazin, Craig, dir. *Chernobyl*. HBO, 2019.

McCarthy, Charles. "Land Acquisition Policies and Proceedings in TVA—A Study of the Role of Land Acquisition in a Regional Agency." *Ohio State Law Journal* 10 (1949): 46–63.

———. "TVA and the Tennessee Valley." *Town Planning Review* 21, no. 2 (July 1950): 116–30.

McCarthy, Cormac. *All the Pretty Horses*. New York: Vintage International, 1993.

———. *Blood Meridian*. New York: Vintage International, 1992.

———. *Child of God*, New York: Vintage International, 1993.

———. *Cities of the Plain*. New York: Vintage International, 1999.

———. *The Crossing*. New York: Vintage International, 1995.

———. "A Drowning Incident." *The Phoenix* (Spring 1960): 3–4.

———. "The Kekulé Problem: Where Did Language Come From." *Nautilus*, April 17, 2017. https://nautil.us/the-kekul-problem-236574/.
———. Letter to John Ryan Fergus. University of Tennessee Special Collections, February 1980.
———. *No Country for Old Men*. New York: Vintage Movie Tie-In, 2007.
———. *The Orchard Keeper*. New York: Vintage International, 1993.
———. *Outer Dark*. New York: Vintage International, 1993.
———. *The Passenger*. New York: Alfred A. Knopf, 2022.
———. *The Road*. New York: Vintage International, 2006.
———. *Stella Maris*. New York: Alfred A. Knopf, 2022.
———. *The Stonemason*. New York: Vintage International, 1995.
———. *The Sunset Limited*. New York: Vintage Books, 2006.
———. *Suttree*. New York: Vintage International, 1992.
———. "A Wake for Susan." *The Phoenix* (Fall 1959): 3–5.
McDonald, Michael J., and John Muldowny. *TVA and the Dispossessed: The Resettlement of Population in the Norris Dam Area*. University of Tennessee Press, 1982.
Melton, James. "What Are Modes in Music? 7 Music Modes Explained." March 1, 2023. https://www.learnjazzstandards.com/blog/what-are-modes-in-music/.
Mendelsund, Peter. *What We See When We Read*. New York: Vintage Books, 2014.
Mitchell, Lee Clark. *Mere Reading: The Poetics of Wonder in Modern American Novels*. Bloomsbury Academic, 2017.
Monod, David. *Vaudeville and the Making of Modern Entertainment, 1890–1925*. University of North Carolina Press, 2020.
Morgan, Wes. "Long John Sheddan in *The Passenger*: The Actual and the Fictitious." American Literature Association Conference. Boston, MA, 2023.
———. "A Season of Death and Epidemic Violence." *Cormac McCarthy Journal* 4, no. 1 (Spring 2005): 195–209.
Murfree, Mary Noailles. *In the Tennessee Mountains*. Edited by Bill Hardwig. University of Tennessee Press, 2008.
Nabokov, Vladimir. *Lectures on Literature*. Harcourt Brace Jovanovich, 1980.
———. "On a Book Entitled *Lolita*." In *Lolita*, 50th Anniversary Edition. Vintage Press, 1997.
Ngai, Sianne. *Our Aesthetic Categories: Zany, Cute, Interesting*. Harvard University Press, 2015.
Nichols, John. "Bioregional Ethics in the Literature of the United States: A Literary Survey of Four Major United States Bioregions." PhD diss., University of Tennessee, 2020.
Nisly, L. L. "'The Sacred Idiom Shorn of Its Referents': An Apophatic Reading of *The Road*." *Christianity & Literature* 68 no. 2 (2019): 311–24.
Noble, O. Alan. "The Bible." In *Cormac McCarthy in Context*. Edited by Steven Frye. Cambridge University Press, 2020.

Nolan, Christopher, dir. *Oppenheimer*. Syncopy and Atlas Entertainment, 2023.

Nuzzolo, Michael. "Music Mood Classification." *Electrical and Computer Engineering Design Handbook: An Introduction to Electrical and Computer Engineering and Product Design by Tufts ECE Students*. https://sites.tufts.edu/eeseniordesignhandbook/2015/music-mood-classification/.

Palmer III, Louis. "'Encampment of the Damned': Ideology and Class in *Suttree*." In *You Would Not Believe What Watches: Suttree and Cormac McCarthy's Knoxville*. Edited by Rich Wallach and Dennis McCarthy. Louisiana State University Press, 2014.

Patron, Sylvie. Introduction to *Describing the Unobserved and Other Essays: Unspeakable Sentences after Unspeakable Sentences*, by Ann Banfield. Cambridge Scholars Publishing, 2019.

Patterson, John. "'We've Killed a Lot of Animals': Joel and Ethan Coen Have Never Shied Away from Death, and Their Latest Film Is One of Their Bloodiest—and Best." *The Guardian*, December 21, 2007.

Peebles, Stacey. *Cormac McCarthy and Performance: Page, Stage, and Screen*. University of Texas Press, 2017.

Phelan, James. "Authors, Resources, Audiences: Towards a Rhetorical Poetics." *Style* 52, nos. 1–2: 1–34.

Pound, Ezra. "In a Station of the Metro." https://www.poetryfoundation.org/poetrymagazine/poems/12675/in-a-station-of-the-metro.

Potts, Matthew L. *Cormac McCarthy and the Signs of Sacrament: Literature, Theology, and the Moral of Stories*. Bloomsbury Academic, 2015.

Prather, William. "'The Color of Life Is Water': History, Stones, and the River in *Suttree*." *Cormac McCarthy Journal* 4, no. 1: 39–73.

Purcell, Aaron. Introduction to *Lost in Transition: Removing, Resettling, and Renewing Appalachia*. Knoxville: University of Tennessee Press, 2021.

Quint, David. *Epic and Empire: Politics and Generic Form from Virgil to Milton*. Princeton University Press, 1993.

Rikard, Gabe. *Authority and the Mountaineers in Cormac McCarthy's Appalachia*. McFarland Press, 2013.

Rivera, Tomás. *. . . y no se lo tragó la tierra*. Quinto Sol, 1971.

Rudenstine, David. "The Day the Presses Stopped: A History of the Pentagon Papers Case." *Washington Post*, 1996. https://www.washingtonpost.com/wp-srv/style/longterm/books/chap1/daythepr.htm.

Safer, Elaine. *The Contemporary American Comic Epic*. Wayne State University Press, 1988.

Said, Edward. "Thoughts on Late Style." *London Review of Books* 26, no. 15 (2004). https://www.lrb.co.uk/the-paper/v26/n15/edward-said/thoughts-on-late-style.

Schill, Brian. "Cormac, Foucault, and Antipsychiatry." The Cormac McCarthy's *The Passenger* and *Stella Maris* Symposium. Omaha, Nebraska, September 21–23, 2023.

The Science Museum. "Thalidomide." December 11, 2019. https://www.science museum.org.uk/objects-and-stories/medicine/thalidomide.
Sepich, John. *Notes on* Blood Meridian. University of Texas Press, 2008.
Shakespeare, William. *Hamlet. The Complete Works of Shakespeare*. 3rd ed. Edited by David Bevington. Scott, Foresman & Company, 1980.
———. *Macbeth. The Complete Works of Shakespeare*. 3rd ed. Edited by David Bevington. Scott, Foresman & Company, 1980.
Shaviro, Steven. "'The Very Life of the Darkness': A Reading of *Blood Meridian*." In *Perspectives on Cormac McCarthy*. Edited by Edwin Arnold and Dianne Luce. University Press of Mississippi, 1999.
Smith, Ray. Personal Interview with Bill Hardwig. March 1, 2023.
Smith, Ray, Denise Kiernan, and Reba Holmberg. "Civilian Displacement: Oak Ridge, TN." Atomic Heritage Foundation, July 17, 2017. https://ahf.nuclear museum.org/ahf/history/civilian-displacement-oak-ridge-tn/.
Steinberg, Theodore. *Twentieth-Century Epic Novels*. University of Delaware Press, 2005.
Still, James. *River of Earth*. Reprint, University of Kentucky Press, 1978.
Story, Brandon. "A New and Modern Task: The Tennessee Valley Authority and Appalachian Modernism." *Journal of East Tennessee History* 95 (2023): 4–29.
Thomas, Charles. "*Blood Meridian*'s Chronotopic Gates: Reading Cormac McCarthy through the Lens of a Literary-Historical GIS." *International Journal of Humanities and Arts Computing* 17, no. 2 (2023): 187–222.
Thoreau, Henry David. *Walden* and *Civil Disobedience*. Penguin Classics, 1986.
Tokushige, Hideki. "Honebana." www.honebana.com.
Updike, John. Introduction to *Lectures on Literature*, by Vladimir Nabokov. Harcourt Brace Jovanovich, 1980.
Wallach, Rick. "Ulysses in Knoxville: Suttree's Aegean Journey." In *You Would Not Believe What Watches:* Suttree *and Cormac McCarthy's Knoxville*. Cormac McCarthy Society, 2014, 78–86.
Welty, Eudora. "Where Is the Voice Coming From?." *New Yorker*, June 28, 1963.
Whitman, Walt. *Leaves of Grass*. Edited by Malcolm Cowley. Penguin Classics, 1986.
Wofford, Susanne. *The Choice of Achilles: The Ideology of Figure in the Epic*. Stanford University Press, 1992.
Woodward, Richard. "Cormac McCarthy's Venomous Fiction." *New York Times Magazine*, April 19, 1992, Section 6: 28. https://www.nytimes.com/1992/04/19/magazine/cormac-mccarthy-s-venomous-fiction.html.
Yarborough, Scott. "The Intertextual 'Suttree': Walker Percy, Cummings and Community." *Southern Literary Journal* 45, no. 2 (Spring 2013): 103–20.
Yasayan, Vahit. "Enforcing Masculinities at the Border: An Ecomasculist Reading of Cormac McCarthy's *The Crossing*." *Critique: Studies in Contemporary Fiction* 64, no. 1 (2023): 111–31.

Index

actor-network theory, Latour, 9
Adorno, Theodore, 181
The Aeneid (Virgil), 68, 70
age before history, Frye, 76–78
Agee, James, 80–85, 183–86
Alderman, Derek, 133, 138
Alighieri, Dante, 71–72, 85–86
All the Pretty Horses, 41, 46, 52, 95, 105, 169
allusions, 69–70, 72–74, 83–86
Alter, Robert, 46–47, 49
ambiguity, 60–62
American city novels, 72–73, 85
"and" clauses, 90
Anthropocene, 143–46
anxiety of influence, Bloom, 69–70, 84
Anzaldúa, Gloria, 98–100
apastoral mood, 127–33; Appalachian literature, 127–31; in *Child of God*, 131–33; in *Suttree*, 133–40
Appalachia, 51, 113, 116, 185–87
Appalachian literature, 118, 127–31
archeological narrative position, Bartlett, 15, 31, 132
As I Lay Dying (Faulkner), 49
atomic age, 143–46, 168–82
attachment theory, Felski, 9
Aubry, Timothy, 7, 16

Bakhtin, Mikhail, 69
Bartlett, Andrew, 15, 31, 132
Bartram, William, 113, 116
beauty, 4, 12–13, 40, 42–45, 87–88, 90, 127, 136–37, 179
Bell, Vareen, 30–31
Bellini, Federico, 41

Beloved (Morrison), 33
Best, Stephen, 6–8
biblical mode, 45–51
blind narrative position, Bartlett, 15, 31
Blood Meridian: biblical mode, 46; character development, 1–2; craft/craftmanship, 41, 43–44; dialogue, 52; environmental precarity, 142; epic mode, 68, 86–94; erased history, 78; heroic quest, 90–94; incommensurability, 14; italicized epilogue, 94; literary references, 69; "misbehaving" images, 37; optical democracy, 87, 104; pastoralism, 131; repetitive and redundant actions, 86–87; stylistic restraint, 103; taxonomic mood, 125–27; tender mode, 39
Bloom, Harold, 69–70, 84
Books Are Made Out of Books (Crews), 69–70
Booth, Wayne, 11
borderlands, 86, 98–99, 103, 105
Borderlands/La Frontera (Anzaldúa), 98–99
Border Trilogy, 98–99, 131. See also *All the Pretty Horses*; *Cities of the Plain*; *The Crossing*
Brinkmeyer, Robert, 41–43
brook trout, 148

calutron girls, 144, 170, 173–75
Cant, John, 52
Catholic iconography, 40–41
Ceremony (Silko), 140
character development, 1–5, 61–62, 90–93, 157
chautauquas, 54–56, 165–66
Child of God: ancestry in, 76; apastoral

Child of God (continued)
    mood, 127, 131–33; Bartlett on narrative modes, 15; biblical mode, 45–46; calling together of a life's work, 188; character development, 2–3; craft/craftmanship, 41, 43; dialogue, 52; disturbed graves, 186; environmental precarity, 145; Greek chorus, 55; literary references, 69; macabre elements, 110; narrative mischievousness and shifting narrative perspectives, 30–32; sermonic mode, 48; tender mode, 34–37; voyeuristic feel, 124; weeds metaphor, 138
Child of God (film), 3
Cities of the Plain, 27, 95, 169
City Behind a Fence (Johnson and Jackson), 178
classification, 112–14, 118, 122, 143–44. See also taxonomic mood
Coen, Ethan and Joel, 123
Coleman, Dawn, 47–48
complexity theories, 151–52
conscious and unconscious mind, 151–54
conspiracies, 158–64
contingency of meaning, 77–80, 89
Cooper, Lydia, 14–15, 41, 46
Cormac McCarthy Society, 152
Cormac Visits Oprah (Murphy), 32–33
corridos (folk ballads), 100–103
Covino, William, 62
Cowley, Malcolm, 6
craft/craftmanship, 41–45, 127, 179
Crews, Michael Lynn, 69–70
The Crossing: biblical mode, 46; cross-cultural exchange, 97–104; epic mode, 68, 95–104; knowledge, passed-down, 120, 122; photo album, 105; stylistic restraint, 103; wolf trapping scene, 96–97
cummings, e. e., 73

A Death in the Family (Agee), 80–86
DeCoste, Marcel, 46
deforestation, 146
desert landscapes, 86–88, 123–27
dialogue/dialogic novels, 52–53, 59–65

dispossession in East Tennessee, 168–88
Divine Comedy (Dante), 71–72, 85–86
dramatic mode, 52–59
"Dream Sequence" (Agee), 82–83
"A Drowning Incident," 114–17

Eclogues (Virgil), 128
ecocritical readings, 142–47
Elements of Taste (Errett), 8–9
Eliot, T. S., 71, 76
Ellis, Jay, 41
Ellison, Ralph, 67
Ellsberg, Daniel, 159
environmental precarity, 142–49
epic mode, 68–105; in *Blood Meridian*, 68, 86–94; in *The Crossing*, 68, 95–104; literary references, 69–70; overview, 68–70; restraints of genre, 69; in *Suttree*, 68, 70–80; and violence, 90–94
erased history, 78
Errett, Benjamin, 8–9
Erskine, Albert, 6, 67
Erwin, Doug, 146–47
extinctions, 145–47

fathers, 7, 84–85, 114, 178
Faulkner, William, 6, 11–12, 49, 64, 67, 75
Felski, Rita, 8–10, 12
flowers, 36–39, 136–37
Fortune, 183, 185
Franco, James, 3
Frye, Steven, 19, 46, 76–78

Gauss, Carl Friedrich, 54
Genette, Gérard, 11
Giemza, Bryan, 151–52
Gifford, Terry, 128–29, 131
Ginsberg, Allen, 136–37
The Girls of Atomic City (Kiernan), 174–75
Goodman, Gary, 191–92
Gospel of Matthew, 51
governmental conspiracy, 159–64
government planning, 171–72, 183–87
Grammer, John, 75
graves, relocation of, 185–86

The Guardian, 123
Guillemin, Georg, 75, 130–31, 133
Guilty Aesthetic Pleasures (Aubry), 7, 16
Guinn, Matthew, 76

Hale, Dorothy, 12
Hale, Mike, 57–59
Hamlet (Shakespeare), 73–74
Hawbaker, S. Stanley, 119–21
Hemingway, Ernest, 62, 129
herida abierta, Anzaldúa, 98
heroic quest, 90–94
high narrative voice in epics, 68
Hiroshima, Japan, 143–44, 172–73
Hoberek, Andrew, 13–14
Honebana, Tokushige's, 37–39
Hooked (Felski), 9
humor, 190–92
Hurston, Zora Neale, 188

iceberg theory of literary minimalism, Hemingway, 62
immigrant voices, 73
"In a Station of the Metro" (Pound), 37
incest taboo, 63–64
incommensurability, 14, 34
indeterminacy, 105, 151–52, 157, 187
influences, 69–70
"[In Just-]" (cummings), 73
In the Tennessee Mountains (Murfree), 128–29
Irons, Ellie, 134–39
ivory-billed woodpecker, 146

Jackson, Charles O., 178
Jacobs, Alan, 12–13
James, David, 13–14, 36–37
James, Henry, 69, 70, 73, 95
JFK assassination, 158–63, 167
Johnson, Charles W., 178
Jones, Gavin, 72–73
Josyph, Peter, 52
Joyce, James, 85

"The Kekulé Problem," 152–54
Kiernan, Denise, 174–75

King James Bible, 46–51
knowledge, passed-down, 119–22
Knoxville, TN, 80–85, 133–42, 169–70, 188
"Knoxville: Summer of 1915" (Agee), 82–85
Komunyakaa, Yosef, 159–61
Krakauer, David, 151

language, 3–5; biblical mode, 45–51; craft/craftmanship, 41–45; defining attribute, 5–8; dramatic mode, 57–59; epic mode, 89–90; incommensurability, 14, 34; "The Kekulé Problem," 152–54; lyrical style, 13; narrative mischievousness and shifting narrative perspectives, 28–32; preciousness, 36, 42–44, 127; Spanish passages, 99–100
Lask, Thomas, 50–51
Latour, Bruno, 9
Lawrence, Anna, 135, 138
Lawrence, Ernest O., 175–76
Levinson, Marjorie, 7
Lilienthal, David, 183
Lilley, James, 169
The Limits of Critique (Felski), 8–9
linguistic degeneration, 73
literary references, 69–70
Lofaro, Michael, 82–83
long novels, James, 69, 95
"The Lovesong of J. Alfred Prufrock" (Eliot), 71
Luce, Dianne, 189

Manhattan Project, 168–82
Marcus, Sharon, 6–8
masonry, 55–56
McCarthy, Charles, 184–86
McDowell, David, 82
McNamara, Robert, 159
Melton Hill Dam, 180–81
Melville, Herman, 5, 140
memento mori, 37–39
Mendelsund, Peter, 4–5, 12, 23, 66, 91–92
Mere Reading (Mitchell), 5, 10
Mitchell, Lee Clark, 5, 10
Moby Dick (Melville), 5, 140

Monod, David, 165
monologues, 54–56
morality, 46, 55–56, 92–94, 130, 132–33
Morgan, Wes, 75
Morrison, Toni, 33
multiple realities, 167
Murfree, Mary Noailles, 128–31, 140
Murphy, Palmer, 32–33
musical modes and moods, 16–21, 153–54
mystery, 148

Nabokov, Vladimir, 13, 15
narrative distance, 31–32
narrative fragmentation, 30–32, 154–55, 163–64
narrative modes, 27–66; and Bartlett, 15, 31; biblical mode, 45–51; dramatic mode, 52–59; epic mode, 68–105; narrative mischievousness and shifting narrative perspectives, 28–32; sermonic mode, 47–48; tender mode, 32–45
narrative shifting, 31, 156, 173
natural world, 109–48; Appalachian literature, 127–31; in *Blood Meridian*, 125–27; classification, 112–14; environmental precarity, 142–49; knowledge, passed-down, 119–22; in *No Country for Old Men*, 123–25; and pastoralism, 127–33; in *Suttree*, 133–42; thick descriptions, 115–17; trapping, 118–22; in "A Wake for Susan," 114, 141; weeds metaphor, 133–40. *See also* taxonomic mood
Nautilus (journal), 152
New Formalism, 7
New York Times (newspaper), 50, 57
Nichols, John, 127
nihilism, 46, 59
Noble, Alan, 46
No Country for Old Men, 44–45, 53, 123–25, 179, 188
Nolan, Christopher, 144, 168
No More Heroes (Cooper), 14–15
Norris Dam, 182–84
nostalgia, 167

noun phrases, 47
"The Novel of Dialect" (James), 73
"Nude Interrogation" (Komunyakaa), 159–60

Oak Ridge, TN, 168–82
oblivious narrative position, Bartlett, 15, 31
O'Connor, Flannery, 45
Oppenheimer (film), 144, 168, 175, 178
Oppenheimer, Robert J., 176–78
optical democracy, 104
The Orchard Keeper: calling together of a life's work, 187–88; Ellison blurb, 67; environmental precarity, 142; knowledge, passed-down, 122; literary references, 69; overreach of governmental policy, 179, 181, 185–86; pastoralism, 131; precarious mood, 181; thick descriptions, 116–19
Outer Dark, 33, 38–39, 48–51, 69, 131

Palmer III, Louis, 84–85
paranoid mood, 158–64, 176
paratactic terseness, Alter, 46–47
Partisan Review, 82
The Passenger: atomic age, 169–70, 171–73, 176–82; biblical mode, 46; calling together of a life's work, 187, 188; calutron girls, 173; childhood interest in the outdoors, 111–12; conspiracy theories, 158–64; construction of the past, 105; craft/craftmanship, 44; and displacement, 171–87; dispossession in East Tennessee, 178–82; environmental precarity, 143–47; epic mode, 68; italicized preface, 39–40; overreach of governmental policy, 118, 171–82; personal and familial stories, 179–82; precarious mood, 150–52, 154–58, 171–87; prewar forms of entertainment, 164–68; sermonic mode, 48; taxonomic mood, 117; tender mode, 39–40; Thalidomide Kid character, 154–58, 164–68; Vietnam engagement, 158–61

pastoralism, 127–33, 140
The Pastoral Vision of Cormac McCarthy (Guillemin), 130–31
Peebles, Stacey, 32, 52
The Pentagon Papers, 159–61
"perhaps," 49
Phelan, James, 11–12
The Phoenix, 114
postsecular studies, 53
Pound, Ezra, 37
precarious mood, 149–88; atomic age, 168–82; and displacement, 171–87; in *The Passenger*, 150–52, 154–58, 171–87; in *Stella Maris*, 150, 152–53, 154–55; Thalidomide Kid character, 154–58, 164–68
profile in *The Gold and Blue*, 110–12
Purcell, Aaron, 187

Quint, David, 68–69

real-life characters, 190–91
restraints of genre, 69
rhetorical communication model, Phelan, 11–12
Rivera, Tomás, 99
River of Earth (Still), 129–30
The Road: biblical mode, 46–47, 50; craft/craftmanship, 42, 44–45, 179; dialogue, 53; environmental precarity, 142–45, 147–48; erased history, 78; incommensurability, 14; language, 4; lyrical style, 13; "misbehaving" images, 36–37; narrative mischievousness and shifting narrative perspectives, 28–30; sermonic mode, 48; taxonomic mood, 147–48; tender mode, 34–35
Rockwell, Theodore, 174
Roosevelt, Franklin D., 183–84
Ross, Jordon, 148
Ryan, John Fergus, 191–92

"The Sanctuary for Weediness" (Irons), 134–35
Santa Fe Institute, 146–47, 151–52, 176

science, 111–12, 127, 151–52, 157–58
Science and Literature in Cormac McCarthy's Expanding Worlds (Giemza), 151–52
sermonic mode, 47–48
Shakespeare, William, 58, 73–74, 84
Sheddan, John, 190–91
Silko, Leslie Marmon, 140
Smith, Ray, 170, 173, 177–78, 180
"Song of Myself" (Whitman), 88–89, 90
The Sound and the Fury (Faulkner), 11, 12, 64
Spanish passages, 99–100
spatial constraints, 125, 127
stage directions, 53–54, 59–60
Steinberg, Theodore, 73
Stella Maris: atomic age, 169, 176; calling together of a life's work, 187, 188; calutron girls, 173; childhood interest in the outdoors, 111–12; craft/craftmanship, 44–45; dialogic novels, 59–65; dispossession in East Tennessee, 178–82; dramatic mode, 53, 57–59; environmental precarity, 143; personal and familial stories, 179–82; precarious mood, 150, 152–53, 154–55; tender mode, 39; women in, 52
Still, James, 129–31, 140
The Stonemason, 41, 52, 53–56, 59–62, 120–21
storytelling, 27, 95, 101–4, 151
style, 5–15
subject-verb object constructions, 44, 87
subsidence, 187, 188
"Sunflower Sutra" (Ginsberg), 136–37
The Sunset Limited, 52, 56–57, 60–65, 166
The Sunset Limited (film), 57
surface reading, 6–8, 12
surveillance, 7, 139, 142, 154, 158, 161–62
suspicious reading, Felski, 8
Suttree: allusion in, 72–74; apastoral mood, 127, 133–40; biblical mode, 46, 49; calling together of a life's work, 188; circular plot, 85; dialogue, 52; epic mode, 68, 70–80; as existential epic, 70–74; italicized prologue, 71, 73–74, 76, 78–85; literary references, 69; mansion scene, 74–80; medieval images in, 74–80;

INDEX

Suttree (continued)
  photo album, 104–5, 167–68; regional context, 67–68; repetitive and redundant actions, 75; sermonic mode, 48; urban setting, 72–73, 133–42; vanity, 77

taste, 8–10, 15
taxidermy, 110–11, 122
taxonomic mood, 110–48; and Bartram, 113; in *Blood Meridian*, 125–27; in "A Drowning Incident," 114–17; in *No Country for Old Men*, 123–25; in *The Passenger*, 117; in *The Road*, 147–48; in "A Wake for Susan," 114
technology, 157–58, 169, 171–82. *See also* atomic age
tender mode, 32–45; in *Child of God*, 34–37; overview, 27–28; in *The Passenger*, 39–41; refuge of language, 42–45; in *The Road*, 34–35, 42–43, 45; and violence, 32–39
Tennessee period, 48–51, 67–68, 118, 128–31, 168–70. *See also Child of God; The Orchard Keeper; Outer Dark; Suttree*
Texas Quarterly, 83
Thalidomide tragedy, 157–58
Their Eyes Were Watching God (Hurston), 188
theoretical mathematics, 151–54, 167, 170, 181
thick descriptions, 115–17, 124
Thoreau, Henry David, 121–22, 140, 142
Tokushige, Hideki, 37–39
trans characters, 188
trapping, 96–97, 99–100, 118–22, 140
Trapping North American Furbearers (Hawbaker), 119–20

"TVA and the Tennessee Valley" (McCarthy), 184
TVA projects, 171–72, 178–86

urban spaces, 72–73, 133–40. *See also* environmental precarity

vaudeville, 164–67
Virgil, 68, 70, 85, 128
Virgin Mary, 40–41
voyeuristic/voyeurism, 15, 31, 92, 124, 160

"A Wake for Susan," 114, 141
Wallach, Rich, 83–84
Wall Street Journal (newspaper), 85
Walsh, Richard, 46
weeds metaphor, 133–40
Welty, Eudora, 139
Westcott, Ed, 174–75
westward expansion, 91–94
"What Is New Formalism?" (Levinson), 7
What We See When We Read (Mendelsund), 4–5, 12, 23, 66, 91–92
whim, 2, 12–13
Whitman, Walt, 88, 90, 103
wild spaces, 94, 113, 125–26, 142. *See also* natural world; taxonomic mood
Winfrey, Oprah, 32–34, 52
women, 52, 152, 173–75
Woodward, Richard, 70
World War II, 171–82

…y no se lo tragó la tierra (Rivera), 99

www.ingramcontent.com/pod-product-compliance
Lightning Source LLC
Chambersburg PA
CBHW032135250426
43661CB00077B/2089